Theodore Roosevelt

Wilderness

Vol. 1: Journalism 1886 - 1901

The Archive of American Journalism

Lincoln Steffens

Henry Stanley

Theodore Roosevelt

Richard Harding Davis

Ida Tarbell

Ray Stannard Baker

Nellie Bly

H.L. Mencken

Ambrose Bierce

Stephen Crane

Jack London

Mark Twain

Ernest Hemingway

Horace Greeley

Theodore Roosevelt

Wilderness

Vol. 1: Journalism 1886-1901

The Archive ▲ *St. Paul, Minnesota*

Note on Sources

All articles are complete and unabridged, with headlines, subheads and formatting that match those of the original publication. Note that minor edits have been made to correct obsolete spelling and punctuation. Students and researchers: these are "public domain" texts that can be freely copied, reproduced and distributed without permission or cost. Please credit The Archive of American Journalism as your source.

The Archive LLC, 9269 Troon Court, Woodbury, MN 55125.

Article selection and original Introduction Copyright ©2014 by Tom Streissguth

Cover Image: George Grantham Bain, Theodore Roosevelt in Buckskin, 1885. From the Library of Congress, Bain Collection.
Facing Page One: North Room, Sagamore Hill. From the Library of Congress Prints and Photographs Division.

Library of Congress Control Number: 2014949765
ISBN: 978-0-9907137-1-5
Printed in the United States of America

Acknowledgments

For their encouragement and suggestions, sincere thanks to Mark Lerner, Gordon Hagert, Pier Gustafson, Phil Gapp, Jonathan Peacock, John Hatch, Marian Streissguth and our original founding supporters:

William F. Zeman
Phil Gapp
Walter Crowley
Adele Streissguth
Richard Prosser
Abhilash Sarhadi
James McGrath Morris

Contents

Introduction
viii

The Ranch
Outing/March, 1886
1

Antelope Shooting on the Cattle Trail
Outing/April, 1886
6

Shooting Near the Ranch-House--The White-Tail Deer
Outing/May, 1886
12

The Deer of the Upland and the Broken Ground
Outing/June, 1886
19

The Last of the Elk
Outing/July, 1886
24

Water Fowl and Prairie Fowl
Outlook/August, 1886
29

Big Game in Dakota
Forest and Stream/December 15, 1887
34

In the Cattle Country
Century Magazine/February, 1888
35

The Home Ranch
Century Magazine/March, 1888
57

The Round-Up
Century Magazine/April, 1888
77

Sheriff's Work on a Ranch
Century Magazine/May, 1888
104

Letter to the Editor
Forest and Stream/April 11, 1889
124

Buffalo Hunting
St. Nicholas/December, 1889
125

An Elk Hunt at Two-Ocean Pass
Century Magazine/September, 1892
136

A Shot at a Bull Elk
Liber Scriptorum/January, 1893
153

In Cowboy-Land
Century Magazine/June, 1893
157

Wolfish Marauders
Youth's Companion/June 22, 1893
175

A Man-Killing Bear
Youth's Companion/July 13, 1893
181

Big Game Disappearing in the West
Forum/August, 1893
186

A Mysterious Enemy
Youth's Companion/August, 1893
195

Hunting in the Cattle Country
Travel/January, 1895
200

A Plan to Save the Forests
Century Magazine/February, 1895
207

Among the High Hills
The Outlook/June 3, 1899
209

With the Cougar Hounds: First Paper
Scribner's/October, 1901
215

With the Cougar Hounds: Second Paper
Scribner's/November, 1901
237

Sources

For Further Reading

Online Resources

Introduction

For the young Theodore Roosevelt, the wilderness was not an escape from civilization, a final frontier, or a Garden of Eden. It was a testing ground where he could prove himself physically worthy. At the end of the line, a sickly child of New York privilege could be someone else: a man of vigor and strength, a hardy, red-blooded and self-reliant American. In TR's view, it was just sheer fun to ride, shoot and bear the elements with the cowboys and hunters who knew their business better than any upper-crust eastern dude ever could.

As for hunting, Roosevelt found in it every physical and mental challenge a man could handle. Patiently tracking game through canyons and forests, enduring severe cold or blistering heat without complaint, and outsmarting a canny prey in its own element: these were the test of a capable hunter, and their own simple and satisfying rewards.

Roosevelt's first wilderness journeys took place in backwoods Maine. The green, citified Harvard student braved 30-mile treks through the backwoods with an experienced guide, Bill Sewall, and tested his skill, without much success, as a game hunter. In September 1883, Roosevelt took his first train west to the Dakota Territory and the town of Little Missouri River, near the border between Dakota and Wyoming. The decimation of the buffalo herds throughout the northern Great Plains had allowed the local ranchers plenty of room to graze cattle for the beef market, now readily accessible via the Northern Pacific railroad.

In search of a buffalo guide, Roosevelt met up with local cowboy Joe Ferris. The easterner's expensive clothes, dandyish spectacles and high-pitched voice made a bad impression on Ferris and other hands, but in a short time his energy and sheer enthusiasm won them over. The harsh conditions and lack of game only seemed to push this odd easterner to greater efforts and bring him a perplexing enjoyment. TR rode, tracked and marched relentlessly from sunup and throughout the day, exhausting Ferris and everyone else who accompanied him. At night, he took a sybaritic pleasure in the awesome silences, the clear black skies and the dying campfires, as described in one of his earliest pieces for *Outing* magazine:

> *The tired horses grazed on the luscious grass almost within the circle of the flickering fire light, while we sat before the roaring logs, as the venison steak simmered over the hot coals that had been raked out to one side. Men living all the time in the open air are willing enough to go to bed early, and soon after supper we crept in under the heavy blankets, which the chill fall night already rendered so comfortable. But long after going to bed I lay awake, looking up at the myriads of stars that were shining overhead, with that peculiar and intense brilliancy so well known to the wanderer over the lonely western plains.*

During this journey Roosevelt conceived the idea of buying a working cattle ranch. He had ready inherited money to invest, and while hiking through the Dakota Badlands on a foray for game, he abruptly proposed a partnership with Sylvane Ferris, the brother of his guide, and Bill Merrifield. He then sweetened the offer by making out a bank draft in the amount of $14,000, with which Ferris and Merrifield would buy the starter herd and meet other expenses. To Roosevelt's way of thinking, no negotiations or written contract would be necessary. He simply trusted the men, and the deal to establish the Chimney Butte Ranch was struck. A few days later, the nearsighted but persistent easterner proudly bagged his first buffalo.

Returning in the spring of 1884, and now calling himself a professional rancher, Roosevelt accompanied Bill Merrifield on a trip to Wyoming's Bighorn Mountains. Intending to hone his hunting ability in a fast-disappearing wildernes, Roosevelt bagged antelope, deer, and his first brown bear, shot at close range and right between the eyes. Convinced that he could run an even bigger cattle operation, he bought the Elkhorn Ranch some

40 miles north of Chimney Butte, and brought west two Maine outdoorsmen, Bill Sewall and Wilmot Dow, to manage it.

Despite his well-appointed cabin and his expensively tailored cowboy wardrobe, Roosevelt earned the respect of his ranch hands and far-flung Dakota Territory neighbors. Simply to go quietly as a high plains rancher was not enough, however; TR had to write about it, and bring the natural world to the public in his book *Hunting Trips of a Ranchman* and dozens of articles written for popular magazines. In these accounts, including *The Wilderness Hunter*, a crucial theme recurs: the challenge of survival in the wilderness stands for the challenge to an entire nation's soul and its aptitude for greatness.

> *In hunting, the finding and killing of the game is after all but a part of the whole. The free, self-reliant, adventurous life, with its rugged and stalwart democracy; the wild surroundings, the grand beauty of the scenery, the chance to study the ways and habits of the woodland creatures—all these unite to give to the career of the wilderness hunter its peculiar charm. The chase is among the best of all national pastimes; it cultivates that vigorous manliness for the lack of which in a nation, as in an individual, the possession of no other qualities can possibly atone.*

But as Roosevelt's ranch flourished, and his political career advanced, the American wilderness retreated. Bison and other once-plentiful species vanished from the Plains; overgrazing by cattle and sheep destroyed habitat and drove fauna further west, into the mountains. Roosevelt noticed; poor hunting was the first sign that civilization was beginning to overtake the natural environment, as he had already noted in the very first words he set down as a journalist:

> *To see the rapidity with which the larger kinds of game animals are being exterminated throughout the United States is really melancholy . . . The buffalo are already gone; a few straggling individuals, and perhaps here and there a herd so small that it can hardly be called more than a squad, are all that remain . . . There are but few places left now where it is profit-*

able for a man to take to hunting as a profession; the brutal skinhunters and meat-butchers of the woods and prairies have done their work; and these buckskin-clad and greasy Nimrods are now themselves sharing the fate of the game that has disappeared from before their rifles.

Overgrazing by the multiplying cattle herds in western Dakota also drew his attention; Roosevelt arrived at the solution of a natural yet pragmatic politician. Forming the first stockman's association among the Dakota ranchers along the Little Missouri, he presided over regular meetings in the makeshift town of Medora and drafted a founding constitution for the group. To publicize the effort, he wrote various hunting articles and then organized several of them into a book, *Hunting Trips of a Ranchman*. All members were then invited to join the newly formed Boone & Crockett Club, to advance the conservation of large game animals in the west.

Roosevelt came to understand why a skilled and worthy hunter conserves the resources that sustain him. The long stream of articles he wrote for *Century, Outing, The Outlook*, and other journals reveal a worsening antipathy for those who kill for the sake of killing; he found Native Americans especially wasteful and inefficient hunters, and he didn't much care for the eastern dilettantes—a class to which he once belonged—who came to the mountains for a few days of comfortable quarters and easy shooting. As president, he was the first to make the preservation of wilderness a priority, and made pronouncements that, if heard a century later, would be mistaken for the ravings of a loopy, tree-hugging environmentalist.

It is also vandalism wantonly to destroy or to permit the destruction of what is beautiful in nature, whether it be a cliff, a forest, or a species of mammal or bird. Here in the United States we turn our rivers and streams into sewers and dumping-grounds, we pollute the air, we destroy forests, and exterminate fishes, birds and mammals -- not to speak of vulgarizing charming landscapes with hideous advertisements. But at last it looks as if our people were awakening.

After reaching the White House, Roosevelt -- with the cooperation of the US Congress -- established four national game preserves, 150 national forests, five national parks, 18 national monuments and the US Forest Service. During his two terms in office, 230 million acres of land passed under federal control. When Roosevelt's second term ended in 1909, he regretfully kept the promise made long before, when William McKinley's assassination brought him to the White House, not to seek a third term. By this time, escape from the press of public business and public adulation was his goal, but there was no president in history more poorly suited to a quiet retirement. Sponsored by the Smithsonian Institution, he set out on a safari to Sudan and East Africa that spanned 11 months and 2,500 miles. Roosevelt's party joyfully tracked, cornered and shot rhinoceros, hippopotamus, and elephants, and collected thousands of intriguing, rare specimens for the Smithsonian's dusty museum shelves back home.

On his return, Roosevelt discovered several things strangely amiss in Washington. President William Taft's dismissal of Gifford Pinchot, Roosevelt's pick as head of the Forest Service, revealed the new president as a compliant corporation man, one who held little regard for Roosevelt's progressive agenda. The Taft administration had also reneged on the preservation of wetlands and forest; the National Conservation Commission was rendered powerless; Secretary of the Interior Richard Ballinger had cleared away federal regulations on coal companies and allowed hydropower projects on "protected" Alaskan waterways.

The rift between Ballinger and Pinchot, Taft and Roosevelt drove a wedge between the two wings of the Republican party--the Progressives, represented by the still-vigorous figure of Roosevelt, and the pro-business right wing that, in Roosevelt's own opinion, was tearing down his legacy of conservation. Seeing his good work repealed or ignored by the Taft administration, Roosevelt let fly with a rousing denunciation of recent events at Osawatomie, Kansas in 1910.

The Constitution guarantees protections to property, and

we must make that promise good. But it does not give the right of suffrage to any corporation. The true friend of property, the true conservative, is he who insists that property shall be the servant and not the master of the commonwealth.

In any comparison between himself and William Taft, Roosevelt was bound to find himself the better man, and the better candidate. There was no limit to his self-regard or to his energy; he could spend weeks rousing the crowds from the back of a train, or an entire presidential term greeting a flood of visitors to the White House while commandeering legislation and writing magazine articles by the hundreds. Encouraged by the enthusiasm of the crowds and sympathetic journalists, Roosevelt ran again for president in 1912 on a Progressive party ticket. This time, his ambition had unfortunate results: the campaign split the Republicans and gave the victory to Woodrow Wilson.

Although Roosevelt had met and overcome all challenges as a politician, he could still be reached by the call of the wilderness. Not the man to shrink from a physical challenge, TR agreed to lead a scientific expedition in late 1913 to one of the most remote and dangerous sections of the Amazon wilderness in western Brazil. Accompanying him were the legendary Brazilian explorer Candido Rondon, American naturalist George Cherrie, a Brazilian doctor and officer, more than a dozen porters, and his son Kermit. Tracing the mysterious Rio da Duvida, or River of Doubt, Roosevelt followed the uncharted stream more than 400 miles north to its mouth on the Madeira River, a tributary of the Amazon.

When he returned, Roosevelt was 50 pounds lighter and permanently weakened by lingering malaria and a severe bacterial infection that resulted from an open leg wound. The infection never quite healed; it continued to affect Roosevelt's declining health until his sudden death from a blood clot in 1919. Instead of enhancing his vigor, the wilderness, this time, had cut his astounding life short.

--Tom Streissguth.
December, 2014

Theodore Roosevelt

Wilderness

Vol. 1: Journalism 1886-1901

Outing
March, 1886

Ranch-Life and Game-Shooting in the West

I. The Ranch

To see the rapidity with which the larger kinds of game animals are being exterminated throughout the United States is really melancholy. Twenty-five years ago, the Western plains and mountains were in places fairly thronged with deer, elk, antelope, and buffalo; indeed there was then no other part of the world save South Africa where the number of individuals of large game animals was so large. All this has now been changed, or else is being changed at a really remarkable rate of speed. The buffalo are already gone; a few straggling individuals, and perhaps here and there a herd so small that it can hardly be called more than a squad, are all that remain. Over four-fifths of their former range the same fate has befallen the elk; and their number, even among the mountainous haunts, which still afford them a refuge is greatly decreased. The shrinkage among deer and antelope has been relatively nearly as serious. There are but few places left now where it is profitable for a man to take to hunting as a profession; the brutal skin-hunters and meat-butchers of the woods and prairies have done their work; and these buckskin-clad and greasy Nimrods are now themselves sharing the fate of the game that has disappeared from before their rifles.

Still, however, there is plenty of sport to be had by men who are of a more or less adventurous turn of mind, and sufficiently hardy and resolute to be willing to stand rough work and scant fare; and of course, excepting men who go out to spend some months in traveling solely for purposes of sport, no class has as much chance to get it as is the case with the ranchmen, whose herds now cover the great plains of the West, and even range well up on the foothills of the mighty central chain of the Rocky Mountains. All of my own hunting has been done simply in the intervals of the numerous duties of ranch life; and in order to understand the way we set out on a trip after game it is necessary also to understand a little about the nature of our homes and surroundings.

Many of the ranches are mere mud-hovels or log shanties, stuck down in any raw, treeless spot where there happen to be water and grass; but many others are really beautifully situated, and though very rude in construction, are still large enough and solid enough to yield ample comfort to the inmates. One such, now in my mind, which is placed in a bend of the Heart River, could not possibly be surpassed as regards the romantic beauty of its surroundings. My own house stands on a bottom of the Little Missouri nearly two miles in length, and perhaps half a mile or over in width, from the brink of the current to the line of steep and jagged buttes that rise sharply up to bound it on the side farthest from the river. Part of this bottom is open, covered only with rank grass I and sprawling sage-brush; but there are patches of dense woodland, where the brittle cottonwood trees grow close together and stretch their heads high in the air. The house itself, made out of hewn logs, is in a large open glade many acres in extent. It fronts the river with its length of sixty feet, and along the front runs a broad veranda, where we sit in our rocking-chairs in the summer time when the day's work is done. Within it is divided into several rooms; one of these is where we spend the winter evenings at the time when the cold has set in with a bitter intensity hardly known in any other part of the United States. A huge fireplace contains the great logs of cedar and cottonwood; skins of elk and deer cover the floor, while wolf and fox furs hang from the walls; antlers and horns are thrust into the rafters to serve as pegs on which to hang coats and caps.

In the glade, besides the house, there are several other buildings,— a stable, a smithy, and two or three sheds and outhouses, besides a high, circular horse-corral, with a snubbing-post in the center, and a fenced-in patch of garden land. The river itself is usually a shallow, rapid stream that a man can wade across, but that cannot carry the lightest boat; but when the snows melt, or after heavy rains, it is changed into a boiling, muddy torrent that cannot be crossed by man or beast, and that will bear huge rafts. It is at all times dangerous to cross on account of the quicksands; but after a series of freshets the whole river can be described as simply four or five feet of turbulent water running down over a moving mass of quicksand three feet in depth, that fills the entire bed of the stream. In ordinary floods there will remain certain fords and rapids that can be crossed; but at times any horse that dared to attempt a passage, no matter where, would be almost certainly lost.

Back from the river for several miles extends a stretch of broken and intensely rugged country, known in plains parlance as "bad lands." It consists of chains of steep buttes or hills, often spreading out into table-lands, and separated by a network of deep ravines and winding valleys, which branch out in every direction. When we pass these bad lands we come to the open prairie, which stretches out on every side in level or undulating expanse as far as the eye can reach. In a few of the gorges in the bad lands there are groves of wind-beaten pines, or dwarfed cedars, favorite haunts of the black-tail deer.

A hunting expedition from the ranch needs but scant preparation, because all of our business is carried on in the open air, and our whole outfit is such as is best suited for an out-door life. After cattle the most conspicuous adjuncts of a cow-ranch are horses. Everything is done, and almost all of each day is spent, in the saddle. The horses run free in a bond, which is driven to the corral every day or two, when the animals needed at the moment are roped (no plains-man, by the way, ever on any occasion uses the word lasso; in its place he uses the verb to rope; it is sure sign of being a "tenderfoot" to use the former), and the rest of the band again turned loose. Every day some rider goes out among the neighboring cattle; and from May to November most of the hands are away from the ranch-house on the different round-ups. For a short expedition only three or four men may go, taking a pack outfit; that is, each man taking a spare horse, on which his bedding, food, and the indispensable branding-irons are packed. On a longer trip a wagon is needed. The regular plains-wagon is perforce a stout, rather heavy affair, or it would not stand the rough usage to which it is exposed. It needs a team of at least four horses to handle it properly, can carry a very large load, and with its hooped canvas top offers a good shelter to a small number of men in the event of a sudden night storm of rain. This is the wagon we take when going on a trip of any duration ; but for quick, light work we use the buckboard. This will carry a couple of men and their traps in good style, can go almost everywhere, and moreover can travel nearly as fast as can a man on horseback. A pair can drag a buckboard perfectly, although if merely going up to a neighboring ranch or to some definite point we often put in a team of four, who bowl us along over the prairie at a great rate, trotting or galloping. The stock-saddles used throughout the cow-country are admirably suited for a hunting-trip, as they have pockets in which various articles can be stowed, and things can be tied on them almost everywhere, thanks to the raw-hide strings with which they are plentifully provided. Thus a couple of antelope, or a brace of young deer, or a big buck can be carried behind the saddle with perfect ease. Both ranch-men and cow-boys habitually spend their days in the very costume in which they hunt,—broad hat, flannel shirt, trousers tucked into top-boots. In winter the biting gales render it necessary to take to fur caps and coats, great mittens, and the warmest wool-lined shoes. Leathern overalls or "chaps" (the cowboy abbreviation for the Spanish word chaparajos) are very useful when riding through thorns or to keep out the wet. The same blankets and bedding that are taken on a round-up of course do for a hunting-expedition. Though we have a tent we do not often use it, shielding ourselves from wet weather by sleeping under the canvas wagon sheet. The cooking utensils need not be very numerous; a kettle and a frying-pan, a "Dutch-oven," merely of short trips made from the ranch. If we make longer ones, such as an expedition after bear and elk to the Big Horn Mountains, which would take a couple of months, we would need to make much more ample preparations.

   Almost every cow-boy carries on his hip a heavy Colt or Smith & Wesson revolver but this is of very little use for game. The regular hunters use rifles, for the most part Winchesters, although many of them still carry the ponderous Sharps, of .40 or .45 caliber, carrying a long, narrow, heavy ball, an ounce or so in weight; weapons which are relics of the days when a war of extermination was waged on the herds of the buffalo, and than which no hunting-rifles in the world possess greater accuracy, range, and penetration. They are, however, very cumbersome, have but one shot, and, now that the larger kinds of game have so grown scarce, are giving way to the handier Winchester. A ranchman, however, with whom hunting is of secondary importance, and who cannot be bothered by carrying a long rifle always round with him on horseback, but who, nevertheless, wishes to have some weapon with which he can kill what game he runs across, usually adopts a short, light saddle-gun, a carbine, weighing but five or six pounds, and of such convenient shape that it can be hung under his thigh alongside the saddle. A 40-60 Winchester is perhaps the best for such a purpose, as it carries far and straight, and hits hard, and is a first-rate weapon for deer and antelope, and can also be used with effect against sheep, elk, and even bear, although for these last a heavier weapon is of course preferable.

There is thus very little need of preparation indeed when one starts off to hunt from his own ranch: horse, dress, outfit and weapon are already all there. Our supply of fresh meat depends entirely upon what we ourselves kill; and even now we can generally get a deer in an afternoon's walk from the house, without having to make a regular trip; but, to insure the capture of anything else, it is now necessary to go prepared to spend a night or two out on the hunting-grounds.

Outing
April, 1886

Ranch Life and Game Shooting in the West

Part II. Antelope Shooting on the Cattle Trail

EARLY last May I had to take a thousand head of young cattle, mostly of Eastern origin, from the railroad down to my range. Ordinarily we drive cattle down along the river bottom, but at that time there had been a series of freshets which had turned the stream itself into a raging torrent and its bed into a mass of treacherous quicksands, and as the cattle were for the most part young, and as is always the case in the spring, weak, we did not dare to trust them at the crossings, and indeed, had we done so, we would have run serious risk of losing the greater number. Accordingly we drove down along the great divide between the Little Missouri and the Beaver, making a six days' trail.

Owing to a variety of causes, our preparations had been very inadequate. The ranch wagon with a team of four accompanied us to carry our food and bedding. To work the cattle there were five men and myself, each with two horses, none of the latter being very well broken by the way. All of the five men were originally Easterners, backwoods men, stout, hardy fellows, but with only one cowboy in the lot, the others being raw hands at the cattle business. I had intended said cowboy to assume control of the whole outfit on the trail, but though a first-rate cow hand, he very shortly proved himself to be wholly incapable of acting as head, and after the first morning's work, during the course of which we got into inexplicable confusion, I was forced to take direct charge myself.

Our course lay for the most part through the bad lands, which enormously increased the difficulty of driving the cattle. A herd of cattle always travels strung out in lines, so that a thousand head, thus going almost in single file, stretch out to be a very great distance. The strong, speedy animals occupy the front, while the weak and sluggish fall naturally to the rear. On the march, I put two of the men at the head, a couple more to ride along the flanks, and the other two to hurry up the phalanx of reluctant beasts that hopelessly plodded along in the rear. In traveling through a tangled mass of rugged hills and winding defiles, it can readily be imagined that it was no easy task for six men to keep the cattle from breaking off in many different directions and to prevent the stronger beasts that formed the vanguard from entirely outstripping and leaving behind their weaker brethren. In addition, one of our numbers had always to keep an eye upon the band of our spare saddled ponies, which ran loose.

Driving cattle is at all times most tediously-irritating work. To get the animals to string out and to begin walking is often a task of no mean difficulty, and when it is once done, it becomes almost as hard to keep the wedge-shaped bunch that always forms in the rear from dropping altogether out of connection with the front animals. The horses have to be perpetually ridden to and fro and hither and thither, to head off a refractory steer, to keep the line from making a break down into a valley, to hurry up the loiterers, or to prevent the thirsty brutes from making a rush towards some quaking quagmire. The progress of a herd, such as this was, is always slow, and we could make but a few miles a day, generally dividing the distance into a morning and an afternoon march, so as to give the cattle feed and rest at midday, when we ourselves would drive the spare change.

The weather during the course of the trip went through a gamut of changes with that extraordinary and inconsequential rapidity that characterizes atmospheric variations on the plains. The second day out there was a light snow falling all day, the wind blew so furiously that early in the afternoon we were obliged to drive the cattle down into a sheltered valley to keep them over night, and the cold was so intense that even in the sun the water froze at noon. Forty-eight hours afterwards we really suffered from extreme heat.

Owing to the slowness with which the cattle traveled, we were obliged to make one dry night camp. This was on the night of the third day. After watering the cattle, at noon, we had driven them along the very-backbone of the divide through a grimly barren and forbidding country across which ran lines of buttes wrought into the most fantastic shapes of the peculiar bad lands formation. Night came on while we were still many miles from the string of deep spring pools which held the nearest water. The fagged-out condition of the cattle forced us to go into camp even before the sun set. The animals were already very thirsty, and it was evident that we would have hard work to keep them closed up during the hours of darkness.

Our usual course at night had been for all hands, about six o'clock, or shortly after, to bed the cattle down; that is, by keeping the bunch close together and by continuously riding round and round it to finally persuade the animals to lie down in a comparatively small space. Most of them being pretty tired, the odds were that they would not try to break out until morning, and the night hours were divided into four watches of two hours each, two of the six men taking each watch; thus every man had two watches one night and one the next.

On the night in question, however, it was evident that no two men would be able to hold the cattle, and practically, all six of us were up all night long, part of the time lying or sitting on the grass by our horses, watching the slumbering beasts, but for almost as much of it galloping furiously around the cattle in the darkness, every rider receiving one or more severe falls before morning, while heading back the strings of thirsty animals that continually tried to break out first from one side and then from the other of the bedding ground. Of course, had they once succeeded in breaking out in such stretch of rough country as we were in, it would have been an impossibility to have gotten them together again.

The next morning we made a very early start, as soon as the cattle began to again grow restive, for it is much easier to drive restive beasts than to keep them together while stationary, and after a long and very tiresome journey, during the course of which the herd spread out to an even greater extent than ordinary, the thirst making the stronger animals travel faster than usual, while the weaker ones, becoming exhausted, could hardly be moved along at all, we finally reached, in the middle of the afternoon, the line of spring pools spoken of. Our own fare had so far been very rough. We had slept under our blankets in the open with our oil skin slickers to at least partially shelter us from rain and snow, and our food had consisted simply of coffee, pork, and rather soggy biscuits.

Both the horses and cattle were so exhausted that I thought we had better make a thirty-six hours' halt where we were, especially as there was excellent water, very good feed, and as the country was admirably adapted for keeping a guard over the herd with little trouble to the men or exhaustion to the ponies. All our work had not ended yet, however, for at least a score of the steers and cows managed to get firmly stuck in the mud holes along the edges of the pool, and we spent until well on into the evening drawing them out.

The land here was a rolling prairie with a few rounded hills. We camped in the bottom of a winding valley whose sides sloped steeply down, their lower portions covered here and there with groves of tall cottonwood trees. Near one of these groves, we drew up the wagon, a deep pool of icy water being but a few yards distant. A more beautiful place for a camp cannot be imagined, and we were ourselves almost as glad to be free from the worry and labor of the drive as was the unfortunate herd. But one drawback to our complete happiness still existed in the fact that we did not have, and had not for some time had, any fresh meat, and it is wonderful how men leading an active out-of-door life get to feel their carnivorous tastes develop. Next day, accordingly, I determined to devote to going after antelope, one or two bands of which we had seen near the trail. The cattle were more than content to feed quietly on the thick bunch grass and, from the nature of the ground, two men at a time were amply able to watch them and to head off any bunch which seemed inclined to wander far away.

I started soon after breakfast, for antelope are the only game which can be hunted as well in the middle of the day as early or late. I was riding a well-trained hunting pony, and had with me the little forty-sixty Winchester saddle gun. Before I had left the wagon camp a mile behind me, I came across a little band of pronghorns, catching a glimpse of them as they lay sunning themselves on the side of a hill, a very long distance off. Tying my pony to a sage bush, I executed a most careful stalk up a shallow dry-water course to a point from which I deemed I could get a shot, only to find to my chagrin that the band had left the place. I suppose they had seen me in the distance and had promptly run off the instant that I began the approach — a favorite trick with antelopes.

I made one other unsuccessful stalk in the morning, and spent nearly half an hour in trying to flag an old buck up to me, lying behind a ridge and waving a handkerchief fixed to the end of a rifle to and fro over its top. Curiosity is with antelope a perfect disease, and they will often be unable to resist the temptation to find out what an unknown object, or one going through singular motions, means, even if the price of gratifying their mania for information has to be paid with their lives. This particular old buck, however, although greatly interested and excited by the motions of the handkerchief, could not make up his mind to approach close enough to give me a fair shot, and after cantering to and fro, snorting and stamping his feet, advancing a few yards towards me, suddenly bolting back as many, and then returning, he eventually evidently came to the conclusion that there was something uncanny about the whole affair, and took to his heels for good.

I went back to the pony and rode on several miles further to where the country became less prairie-like in character, the valleys being somewhat deeper and the ridges closer together, when I again dismounted and began to hunt over the ground on foot; and this time my perseverance was rewarded. As I was topping one ridge, I saw a little band of five bucks slowly walking over the crest of the one directly across. I had come up very cautiously, and felt certain that I had not been seen. The instant that the last of the animals disappeared I raced forward at a sharp gait, pulling up as I breasted the hillside opposite, so that I should not be blown when I came to shoot. The antelope had been proceeding in a very leisurely manner, stopping to indulge in mock combats with each other, or to nibble a mouthful of grass now and then; and when I came to the top of the ridge, they had halted for good, perhaps 150 yards off.

I was out for meat, not for trophies, and so I took the one that offered me the fairest shot, a young buck which stood broadside to me; he was fat and in good condition for an antelope, but with small horns. The bullet went fairly in behind the shoulder, and though he galloped off with the rest of the band for a couple of hundred yards, his pace gradually slackened, he came to a halt, then walked backwards in a curious manner for a few feet, fell over, and was dead when I came to him.

After dressing him, and I may remark parenthetically that this work of butchering, especially when far from water is one of the disagreeable sides of a hunter's life, I got him on the pony (it was a quiet little beast, used to packing all sorts of strange things behind its rider) and started towards the camp. The shadows had begun to lengthen out well before I got there, to receive a very real and cordial welcome from my hungry associates. Before long the venison steaks were frying or broiling over the mass of glowing coals raked out from beneath the roaring and crackling cotton wood logs, and I should be almost afraid to state how much we ate. Suffice it to say that there was very little indeed left of that antelope after next morning's breakfast.

The following day we took the somewhat refreshed cattle away from our resting ground, and after two rather long and irksome drives, were able to head them out upon the great river bottom where the ranch house stands.

Outing
May, 1886

Ranch Life and Game Shooting in the West

III. Shooting Near the Ranch-House--
The White-Tail Deer

But a few years ago any ranchman in the wilder portions of the great western plains country was able to get a large variety of game without having to travel very far from the immediate neighborhood of his own ranch house. When my cattle first came to the Little Missouri almost every kind of plains game was to be found along the river; but circumstances have widely changed now. Antelope, mountain sheep, and two species of deer are still to be found in greater or less numbers scattered through the country over which my cattle ranch, and occasionally not so very far from the house; thus, last winter one of my foremen shot a mountain ram on a ragged bluff-crest but half a mile away; and I have myself killed antelope on the bottom directly across the river, while, but a year or two ago, the black-tail deer were more plentiful in my immediate neighborhood than were all the other kinds of game put together, and even last fall I more than once shot them but a mile or so from the house. These are now, however, but exceptional instances, and if we have time to go off for but two or three hours with the rifle we cannot reckon with any certainty upon the chance of a shot at any game, excepting the white-tailed deer. Of some forty odd deer killed last season (for meat, not sport, and not while on any regular wagon trip) at least nine out of ten belonged to this species. The white-tail, partly from its superior cunning, from a kind of shrewd, common sense with which it is gifted to a preeminent degree, and partly from the nature of its haunts, survives in a locality long after all other of the larger game animals have been driven out by the hunters. It is preeminently the deer of the river bottoms, dwelling among the dense, swampy thickets, that form in the bends of the streams and in the larger patches of woodlands. It is mainly nocturnal in its habits, spending the day in impenetrable depths and tangled recesses, where it is practically entirely secure from the approach of the hunter. Its chase is thus very tedious, as in the localities where it is found it is almost impossible for a man to walk at all, and even with the most painstaking caution, he will hardly be able to avoid making a noise. The white-tail relies alike on ears, nose, and eyes to warn it of danger; and, indeed, it is almost impossible to successfully still-hunt it while lying or feeding in an extensive belt of woodland, and usually the only way to get an animal living in such a locality is to catch it on the outskirts in the very early morning or late evening. Such a meeting is more or less accidental.

    At times, however, the deer will be found in the smaller, though still moderately extensive, patches of brushwood and dwarf trees that stud the winding bottoms of the larger creeks for miles up their courses, away from the river. In these localities a man runs a much better chance of getting his game, both because he can frequently "jump" it, getting a close, running shot; and also because if out still-hunting at eventide or in early morning he is almost certain of having a chance to see the deer feeding along the edges of the brush. I have hardly ever been successful in single-handed still-hunting and killing the white-tail among the timber of the river bottoms, and though I have tried often enough, most of my shots have been taken when it was so dark that it was impossible to fire with any accuracy. When there is snow on the ground, however, we can often kill them along the river bottom, by dividing forces and sending one or two men to beat down through a good locality, while the others watch the probable places for the deer to pass.

    As is the case with some other kinds of game, a man is not unapt to run across a deer by accident while riding about among the cattle, or while on one of the 100 errands that keep a ranchman perpetually on horseback. Accordingly, it is very rare for me to go off for any distance from the ranch-house without carrying the little saddle-gun with me. Once, early last September, when we had been out of meat for nearly a week, owing to the stress of work having been so severe as not to give any of us time from our duties in which to go hunting, this custom of mine procured us a welcome addition to our exceedingly monotonous and scanty bill of fare. A small band of horses had strayed away from the rest, and I had ridden out with one of the cowboys to look for them. A ranchman's horses are, as might be expected, perpetually astray, and one of the most necessary, and at the same time one of the most irksome, parts of his business is to look them up. They may wander one or more hundred miles if not found, and as to have plenty of good horses is the condition precedent for the successful carrying on of the cattle industry, it may be readily imagined that a plainsman takes peculiar care of his saddle band. Often all the horses will keep well together, but frequently they will show a tendency to split into little groups, whose individuals are never found far from each other; and at times there will be some one horse that shows a marked inclination to wander off by himself. If one of these individuals or little groups is absent when the bunch is rounded up and driven into the corral, which happens every day or two, some man has to immediately start out and look it up.

  This seems at first a good deal like looking for a needle in a hay stack; and indeed, at times it does possess a most painful similarity to such a feat; but if a man knows the country as well as the habits of the horse he is looking for, his work is greatly simplified. Time and again horses have been absent from my ranch for an amount of time varying from a week to six months, but with only two exceptions I have always hitherto recovered them in the end. As already said, it is particularly dreary and tiresome work to look after them, as one has to ride along at a slow jog, continually straining one's eyes in every direction and minutely examining every patch of broken ground or timber that could contain the missing animals. After a rain it is much easier, as then their tracks can be followed pretty readily, while on hard dry ground they leave no trace; an immense amount of land has to be covered each day, and the probability is, that several days' fruitless search will have to be gone through before the animals are really found. One gets gradually to have a certain hopeless and irritated feeling that makes this kind of duty rank as one of the least attractive of a ranchman's life.

Shooting Near the Ranch House--The White Tail Deer / 15

On the particular day in question, which was the second one of our search, I and my companion were riding along about noon in the somewhat sullen silence that comes to be one's natural mood after a long course of monotonous exercise in a land whose general aspect is as same as it is barren. We traveled mostly along the higher ridges, whence we could survey the landscape far and near, but finally we came to a place where a creek headed up, and where the ravines twisted to and fro, their beds being filled with underbrush and young trees, and where, in consequence, horses might easily remain hidden in the thickets or in the clefts in the side of the hill without our observing them from the distance. Accordingly we descended to hunt them through more carefully; coming down into a smooth open valley, through whose bottom extended a dry watercourse, filled up with a dense growth of wild plums, ash and chunk cherries, with a few trees of larger growth. We started to ride down along the side of, and some little distance from, this thicket, which was several hundred yards in length and only thirty or forty in breadth; as the thicket lay in the bottom of the valley, while we were on considerably higher ground, we could look down into it. While the horses were jogging along with their heads down, I was suddenly aroused from my condition of listless apathy by the sudden mashing of dead branches among the underbrush but a rod or two from where I was passing. My blood tingled with that thrill of excitement known only to the man who has a genuine and intense fondness for the nobler kinds of field sports. I was off my horse in a second, running down with the rifle to where the valley sloped abruptly downwards to its brush-covered bottom. After the first plunge a deer will often run almost noiselessly through places where it seems marvelous that animals should go at all and I could not tell for a minute which way the game had gone; hearing, however, a twig snap farther down, I raced along to where the valley turned round a shoulder of the bluff and then again peered over into the dry water course. For a second I then experienced a keen disappointment, for a long distance off I saw a yearling white-tail break out of the brush and canter off out of sight round a bend of the valley. I concluded that I had run down the wrong way from that in which the game had been going,

but staying still for a second, I again heard a twig break beneath me, and in another minute a white-tail stole out and stood in a little opening in the brush; it was evidently, from its size, a this year's fawn, just out of the spotted coat, and I gathered at once that there must be a third deer somewhere near, it being not at all an uncommon thing for a doe, a yearling fawn, and a this year's fawn to be together. As we were in need of fresh meat, 1 leveled on the fawn, which stood facing me, offering a beautiful mark; at the report it plunged wildly forward a few feet and turned a somersault over a small bank. Immediately afterwards the doe, which I had not previously seen, broke out within twenty yards of me. I fired three shots at her with the repeater, and with the last one hit her very far back, injuring her hips and causing her to turn round and run back into the brush. It seems a curious thing, doubtless, to those who have not tried, that a man should, at twenty yards, need three shots to disable, and even then not to kill, a deer; but unless one is a real expert with the rifle, he soon finds that he makes an unusually large percentage of misses on running shots, even when close up, and it is peculiarly difficult to remember to hold far enough ahead. The doe was evidently badly hurt; and by running on rapidly down the creek and taking up my station at a point where the water course was narrow, I headed her off; then the cowboy rode down through the bottom, and, when frightened by his approach, she tried to break by me, I killed her. Each of us took one of the deer behind his saddle and, abandoning for that day our search for the strayed horses, we rode back to the ranch house.
    Although these deer were killed while on horseback, yet as a rule we hunt white-tail on foot and this is especially the case if we go out merely for an afternoon or morning's work near the ranch. As a sample of such work, may be mentioned a hunt I made a week or so after the above mentioned incident.
    About three o'clock in the afternoon I shouldered my rifle and walked away from the ranch, intending to strike back over the hills to a part of the divide some eight miles distant and from thence to hunt slowly back against the wind through a stretch of broken country, where toward evening one would be not unlikely to find deer. When I had reached the divide and

started homewards the shadows had already begun to lengthen out, the heat of the day was well over, and the fall air was already cool enough to make walking pleasant. The country consisted of little else than a series of chains of steep, rounded hills, separated from each other by narrow valleys that split up and wound around in every direction. For the purpose of commanding as extensive a view as possible, I kept near the summits of the hills, avoiding, however, walking on the very crest, as that would throw my body out so sharply in relief against the sky as to almost of necessity attract the attention of any animal within the ken of whose vision I might be. The walking was very rough, the grassy hill tops and hill sides being exceedingly steep and slippery, nor did I at first see anything. But at last, when the sun was so near setting that the bottoms of the valleys had already almost begun to be in shadow, I crept out on the face of a great cliff shoulder that jutted over the broad bed of a long ravine, and my eye was at once caught by five or six objects below me in the valley, and probably nearly half a mile off. A second glance convinced me they were deer, and I drew back to make a rapid calculation as to the best means of getting near them, for I had to be quick about it if I wished to get a shot before the light failed. Running back at speed nearly half a mile, I crossed the ridge on which I was and slid down into a little washout that opened into a small ravine, whose mouth I had seen, joined the larger valley not very far from where the deer were. This ravine was entirely bare of underbrush, and I had to clamber along one of its sides in spite of the steepness of the ground, as I did not dare to run the risk of an outlying deer catching a glimpse of me if I came openly down the bottom. Nor was my caution thrown away. I found that the animals I was after, having grazed slowly down the main valley, had come directly opposite the mouth of the cleft in which I was. Wriggling along, however, flat on my face, and taking advantage of every boulder or patch of sage brush, I managed to get down near the very mouth. The wind was perfectly favorable, and after a few minutes' patient and motionless watching I saw four or five deer slowly moving along past the other side of a thicket but a couple of hundred yards away, and leaving between me and them a kind of natural embankment, just on the other side of which they halted. I was now able to walk rapidly and quietly up without danger of detection; throwing off my cap, I peered over the edge of the bank to see them feeding in perfect unsuspicion, forty or fifty yards away. They were all does or yearling bucks; one of the latter, a fine fat young fellow, stood broadside to me. There was still plenty of light to shoot, and I was able to put the bullet within a hair's breadth of the right place behind the shoulder. Taking off the saddle, hams, and forequarters, and cutting thongs out of his hide to tie them with, I slung them over my back and started off at a rapid rate for home, which I did not reach until long after the moon was well up above the horizon; for even if one knows the country fairly well, he soon finds that he makes but slow progress at night time over broken, difficult ground.

Outing
June, 1886

Ranch Life and Game Shooting in the West

IV. The Deer of the Upland and the Broken Ground

TILL very recently the black-tail deer was the most plentiful of all plains game, and it is still common in many localities; but after the extermination of the buffalo and the elk, it became itself the chief object of the chase with the professional hunters and their ceaseless persecution has in many places totally destroyed it, and elsewhere has terribly thinned its ranks. It differs widely in haunts, habits, and gait from its white-tailed relative, which in form and size it so closely resembles, although rather larger. It is fond of very rough, open ground, and although in many places, as, for example, in the great chains of the Rockies, it is found in dense timber, yet it is also frequently found where there are hardly any trees, or else where they are so sparse and scattered as to afford but the scantiest cover.

It is, with us, the rarest thing in the world to find black-tail on the timbered river bottoms, and it never penetrates into the tangled swamps in which the white-tail delights. The brushy coulees and the heads of the ravines are its favorite resorts, and it also ranges into the most sterile and desolate portions of the bad lands, intruding upon the domains of the mountain sheep. The cover in which it is found is almost always too scanty to, of itself, afford the deer adequate protection; it cannot, therefore, as is the case with its white-tailed relative, often escape by hiding and remaining motionless and unobserved while the hunter passes through the locality where it is found; nor can it, like its more fortunate cousin, skulk around without breaking cover and thus bid defiance to its pursuers. White-tailed deer may abound in a locality, and yet a man may never so much as catch a glimpse of them; but if black-tail exist they are far more commonly seen. The nature of their haunts, too, renders them much more easily approached. Out in the open country the hunter can advance far more noiselessly than in the woods, can take advantage of inequalities of ground for cover much more readily, and can also shoot at a longer distance; then, again, the black-tail, although with fully as keen senses as the white-tail, is put at a disadvantage in the struggle for life by his much greater curiosity. He has a habit, when alarmed, of almost invariably stopping, after having galloped a hundred yards or so, to stand still and look round at an object that has frightened him, and this pause gives the hunter time to make a successful shot. A black-tail is, on the other hand, more difficult to hit while running than is the case with the white-tail. The latter runs more as a horse does, with a succession of long bounds, going at a rolling or almost even pace, while a black-tail progresses by a series of stiff-legged buck jumps, all four feet seeming as if they left the ground together. This gives him a most irregular and awkward-looking gait, but yet one which carries him along, for a short time, at a great speed, and which enables him to get over broken, craggy country in a manner that can only surpassed by the astounding feats of the mountain sheep in similar localities.

    Most of my plain shooting has been done after black-tail, and, indeed, I have killed nearly as many of them as of all other large game put together; but they are now pretty well thinned out from round the immediate neighborhood of my ranch, and if I wish to get them I generally have to take a wagon and make a general trip of two or three days' duration. There is no locality nearer than ten or twelve miles where they can really be considered at all plenty, and as the best time for hunting them is in the early morning or late evening, one should be able to camp out directly on or by the ground he intends to hunt over, if he wishes to be even moderately certain of success. At times, however, when the black-tail have gathered in bands of eight or ten or more individuals, they will wander away from their usual haunts, and then maybe put up in rather unexpected places. On one occasion, last fall, when I had walked eight or ten miles away from the ranch, preparatory to beginning an afternoon's hunt after white-tail, I unexpectedly came across such a small band. I had struck the trail that we follow with our wagon in going in toward the settlement when the river is too high to permit us to travel along the river bottom, and was walking quietly along it, following the faint scrapes made in the dry ground by the wagon wheels (for the trail is a blind one at best), when, as I came over the crest of a little hill, I saw a deer jump up out of a thicket, about two hundred yards off to one side of the trail, take two or three of the jumps so characteristic of the black-tail, and then turn around to look at me with his great ears thrown forward. In another second a dozen others also rose up and stood in a clump around him. I fired at them as they thus stood clustered together, and more by good luck than by anything else my bullet broke the back of a fine fat young doe.

Only twice last fall did I make a regular trip after black-tail; in each case taking one of my men, himself a very good hunter, with me, and camping out all night right by the ground through which we intended to search. On the first of these occasions I killed a young buck by the side of a shallow pool in a deep gorge, almost as afterwards my companion and I killed a doe and one well-grown fawn, as the result of an immense expenditure of cartridges. The doe and fawn were down in the bottom of a valley; we saw them as we were riding along the ridge above. They were in ground where it would have been almost impossible to have gotten near them, as almost the only piece of brush was that in which the two were standing; and as they both offered fair broadside marks, although at least four hundred yards off, we opened fire on them, I with a Winchester, my companion with a 40-90 Sharp's rifle. The deer, not seeing us, seemed to be perfectly confused by the firing and the echoes, and after each shot merely jumped a few paces and again stood still. I fired much more often than my companion, but without any success, and just as I had emptied my magazine he brought down the doe. The fawn then ran down the valley half a mile or so and entered a deep thicket, in which, after a somewhat careful stalk, I killed it. My companion was a really good shot, and he had killed the doe fairly at about four hundred yards; but even for him to kill at such a distance as this is an exceptional feat, and almost invariably represents the expenditure of a large number of cartridges.

On our next hunt, however, he made one shot that was even better. We had, as before, camped out all night, and started off early in the morning through as rugged and precipitous a tract of country as could be found anywhere, the sheer cliffs, deep gorges, and towering ragged hills rendering the walking very difficult, and in some places even dangerous. Game was plenty, however, and during the course of the morning we killed five black-tail deer, three bucks and two does. One of these, a very fine buck with unusually large antlers and as fat as a prize sheep, I shot in a rather unusual locality. We had been following up three mountain sheep, which, however, having caught a glimpse of us, went off for good and were seen no more. The course led over and across a succession of knife-like ridges of rock and sandstone, separated by sheer narrow gorges of great depth, and with their sides almost overhanging. On coming to the edge of one of these, and, as usual, peering cautiously over, I was astonished to see a great buck lying out on a narrow ledge along the face of the cliff wall opposite; the gorge must have been at least a couple of hundred feet deep and less than one-half as much across. He was lying below, diagonally across from me, with his legs spread out and his head turned round so as to give me a fair shot for the center of his forehead, and as in the position where I was I could not be sure of killing him instantly with a bullet elsewhere, I fired between his eyes, and, beyond a convulsive motion of one of his hind legs, he did not move an inch out of the place where he was lying. So steep was the cliff, and so narrow the ledge where he had made his bed, that it was a long and really difficult climb before we could get to him, and it was then no mean labor to get him out unharmed to where we could dress him. The time when he was shot was near midday, and he had evidently chosen the cliff for the purpose of getting a regular sun-bath. It is a rare thing even for this bold and rock-loving species, however, to take its noonday siesta in such an exceedingly open place. The locality had probably not before been visited by hunters that season, and the deer had gotten very bold, as the result of being unmolested. Three of the other deer that were killed on this day were shot without any special or unusual incident attending their death; but the fifth represented another piece of good marksmanship on the part of my companion, whose name, by the way, was Will Dow. We were going back to camp, not intending to shoot anything more, but to fetch out the ponies in order to pack back to camp the game we had already gotten. While walking along a line of hills, bounding one side of a broad valley, we saw on the face of the steep bluff-side opposite two deer standing near a patch of cedars; owing to the difficulty of the intervening ground I was unable afterwards to pace off accurately the distance, a thing I usually do in the case of an unusually long shot; but it must certainly have been close upon 500 yards. We sat down and began to fire at them. With his fourth shot Dow apparently touched one, and both went off up the hill; immediately afterwards, however, another rose up from a thicket by which they went and stood looking around. We transferred our attention to this one; again I missed three or four times, and again my companion (thanks doubtless in part to his own superior skill, and in part also to the superior efficacy of his weapon for long-range shooting), after having wasted two or three bullets, sent one ball home, breaking a hind leg, and. after a rather long and tedious chase, we succeeded in overtaking and kill¬ing the animal. As a rule, I may explain, I do not shoot at anything but bucks; but during the past season, when game had become so scarce, and when our entire supply of fresh meal depended upon our prowess with the rifle, it was no longer possible to choose what we would kill, and, after the first of September, when we could keep deer hanging up for a long time, we did not spare either buck or doe if we were able to get one within range of our rifles.

Outing
July, 1886

Ranch Life and Game Shooting in the West

V. The Last of the Elk

FROM that portion of the plains country, over which my cattle range, the elk have disappeared almost as completely as the buffalo; but in the more remote and inaccessible fastnesses one or two scattered individuals still linger. A year ago a couple of cowboys, while on the round up, killed an elk near the head of a very long and almost dry creek, up which they had gone in search of a small bunch of cattle; and the last individual of the species seen on the Little Missouri was shot by myself last September.

 An old hunter, who had been under some obligations to me, brought me word, shortly before the fall round up began, that he had come across unmistakable fresh elk sign in a piece of wild broken land, some thirty miles from my ranch house. My informant was perfectly trustworthy, and was able to describe to me the position of the probable haunt of the game with great accuracy, and as the chance was too rare a one to be lightly thrown aside, I at once prepared to start the following morning in search of the doomed deer, it being more than doubtful whether we would be able to strike the trail of the beast for a day or two. I took along the ranch wagon, drawn by four shaggy horses, and driven by a weather-beaten old plainsman, who had been teaming for me during the summer; while I and one of my men, Will Dow, rode our hunting horses, I taking old Manitou, who for speed, strength, good-tempered courage, and downright common sense, surpasses any horse I have ever been on. There was, of course, no wagon trail for us to follow, and as the country was very wild and broken, one of the horsemen had continually to be riding ahead of the wagon, to choose the easiest and most practicable routes. Even thus, it seemed incredible that the wagon should be able to go through and over the incredibly rough places that we had to pass, and no man less expert than the old California stage driver, who was guiding it, could have carried a four-horse team, or indeed, any wheeled vehicle whatsoever, through such a country. The day's march had its monotony, varied by the usual incidents and accidents attendant upon plains travel. Across some of the steep canon-like gullies, the wagon had to be brought by the help of the saddle horses; all the team pulling together; often the ground being so steep as to render it necessary to unharness the hauling horses, and slip a rope from the end of the pole to the high ground upon which the animals could get good footing. There was little water, and when we finally struck an alkali pool, my own horse got mired in trying to reach it to drink.

We had started very early in the morning, and had pushed on at as fast a pace as possible, but it was well towards sunset before we reached the curious cluster of conical red Scoria Buttes, which the old hunter had told us to take as a landmark; and not far from their foot, in a winding valley, closed in by low hills, with steep sloping sides, we found, as we had expected, the three essentials for a camp in the plains country—wood, water and grass. There were two or three deep spring pools of cool clear water; clumps of small scattered cottonwood trees grew along here and there through the valley, whose bottom was covered with rich grass. A better spot for a camp could not have been imagined, and that its beauties had been appreciated by others before us was shown by the presence of the remains of half a dozen old Indian tepees. We had taken no tent with us, making our beds under the protection of the canvas wagon sheet. Soon after reaching camp the sun went down, and by the time supper was ready, darkness had fallen. The tired horses grazed on the luscious grass almost within the circle of the flickering fire light, while we sat before the roaring logs, as the venison steak simmered over the hot coals that had been raked out to one side. Men living all the time in the open air are willing enough to go to bed early, and soon after supper we crept in under the heavy blankets, which the chill fall night already rendered so comfortable. But long after going to bed I lay awake, looking up at the myriads of stars that were shining overhead, with that peculiar and intense brilliancy so well known to the wanderer over the lonely western plains.

We were up by the first streak of dawn, and were ready to start after the shortest preparation. It was a beautiful hunting morning—the sun-dogs hung in the red dawn, the wind moved gently over the crisp brown grass, and the weather had that peculiar smoky hazy look so often seen about the time of the Indian Summer. We moved off along toward the edge of a great plateau, and by the time the sun was well up had reached the hunting grounds. From the jutting shoulder on which we stood we looked off far and wide over a great stretch of barren brown country, broken into countless valleys and ravines, which were separated by ridges of low, round hills. Although it was early fall, the touch of the frost had already changed the leaves of the trees, and the sameness of the landscape was relieved by the patches of vivid color that marked where the thickets of ash, cherries and wild plums were scattered along the hillsides, or where the tall cottonwood trees grew in the bottoms of the larger valleys.

Before long, we, ourselves, came upon the fresh sign of large game, finding a small muddy pool, at which one or more elk had evidently drunk but a day or two previous. After this we proceeded- with great caution, hunting silently and stealthily through every locality where we deemed it possible that the animals we were in search of might be found. An elk, from his greater size, needs, of course, much more cover than does a deer, and we expected to find our quarry in one of the heavy timber coulies. A "coulie," I may explain, is a plains word, derived from the old-time French trappers and hunters, who traversed the basins of the upper Missouri and Saskatchewan before the men of the Anglo-Saxon race had penetrated even to their borders. The term is used to denote any small ravine or side valley, usually up near the head of a creek or water system, through which the snow or rain runs at certain seasons, but which does not contain a regular water course.

Near the base of the great plateau in whose neighborhood we were hunting, the creeks forked and branched again and again, and finally resolved themselves into a multitude of deep narrow coulies, in many of whose bottoms grew groves of cottonwood trees, which, favored by the shelter and moisture, reached a height that they rarely attain in the barren plains country. The look of the land, and our knowledge of the habits of the elk, led us to suppose that if we found one of the latter at all, we would be most apt to find it in one of these timber coulies, nor were we disappointed. After some hours of patient and fruitless search, mostly conducted on foot, I rode Manitou up to the edge of a deep and narrow defile, in whose bottom grew a band or grove of tall trees. As I peered over the edge, there was a crash and a scramble in the woods beneath me, and immediately afterwards 1 saw dimly through the scanty tree tops the glistening, light-colored hide of a great bull elk as he gallantly breasted the steep hillside opposite. I was off the horse in a minute, and, kneeling on one knee, waited for him to come above the tree tops into plain sight. In another moment he stood out on the bare hillside over against me, and turning round, half faced us, throwing his head up into the air. Although less than a hundred yards off, and offering a splendid side shot, I yet, for some cause or other, pulled too far back on him. Nevertheless, the bullet inflicted a fatal wound; for the moment, however, he hardly seemed as if he were hurt, but breaking from the long ground-covering trot, which is so characteristic a gait for this species, and at which he had been going, he went off over the hill crest at a wild plunging gallop. Mounting old Manitou, I scrambled down into the ravine at a break-neck pace, then strained up the other side, the old fellow going over the rough ground at a speed that would be impossible for any horse not well accustomed to such country. On reaching the top of the crest, the elk was not in sight, and I feared I had lost him; with much labor, however, we followed his footprints, marked by an occasional drop of blood, for a half mile or so, till we came to a broader, shallower valley, with brushwood thick in its bottom. With increasing difficulty, we followed the trail that was ever growing fainter, and finally found where the great beast, changing his pace to a trot, had entered the thicket; and but a few rods within it, close to the opposite side, we found the elk himself already stone dead. He was a fine-large one, in excellent condition, but his antlers were small with few points.

This was an unexpectedly early and successful termination to our hunt, for although, from the sign, there must have been one or two other elk about, yet the latter were evidently much smaller, probably cows, and I did not wish to molest them, especially as the one we had killed furnished us with all the meat that we then needed. Accordingly the animal was skinned and cut up, and carried back on our horses to the wagon, by which time it was already late in the afternoon; and early next morning we broke camp and started home to the ranch. It is possible that other elk may be killed in our neighborhood hereafter, but I doubt this myself; and unless I am mistaken, the bull I shot will be the last of his kind to be shot in the immediate vicinity of the ground over which our cattle range.

Outlook
August, 1886

Water Fowl and Prairie Fowl

Ordinarily the Little Missouri is not navigable for the lightest craft, but in the season of the floods it will bear an even large boat; and as these floods come at the times when there are apt to be many wild duck and a few geese on the river, I keep at the ranch house a small light boat especially for use in shooting water fowl; my usual course being to send it up the river to a convenient point sometime when the wagon happens to be going empty toward the settlement, and then coming down stream in it when the water is high enough. The current is altogether too swift to make it possible to paddle against it and it would be most slow and tedious work to pole up stream over such a bad bottom as that of the Little Missouri. Accordingly, whatever shooting I get, must be done while drifting down the river. The course of the latter is very winding, and in coming round the points one can often get close up to a flock of ducks or a couple of geese without being observed.

It is pretty good fun to go down the stream, even apart from the shooting. The scenery in the Bad Lands having for me a great attraction from its strange, bizarre wildness; although I suppose it could hardly be called really beautiful. In many places the river has cut its way through lines of hills, making sheer bluffs, that rise straight out of the water, and whose faces show the lines of parallel strata, of which they are composed, with most abrupt clearness. These strata are composed of lignites, marls, chalks and clays, and exposure to the weather causes them to turn most extraordinary colors; and the face of the cliff is thus often marked by broad horizontal bands of black, red, purple, brown and yellow. Floating down stream one will thus first be passing between banks overgrown with tall cottonwood trees, then going through a region of barren sage plains, then again winding and twisting through bluffs and hills that are as fantastic in color as they are in shape.

The shooting itself is never as good for water fowl, on the Little Missouri or elsewhere throughout the cattle country, as it is in the more fertile farmland prairies to the eastward. Still, occasionally, we can make fair bags. The little teal are the commonest, and least shy of the water fowl. As they sit out on a sandbar, they often let a boat drift close up to them, and it is quite easy also to creep within gunshot from the bank. I have killed eleven of them with a single barrel. The mallard duck, shoveler duck, and broad bill are also common, annd afford excellent sport. These, however, are shyer, and will rarely let a boat drift down upon them, unless one is able to take advantage of some cover, or come quickly round the point. Geese are more wary still. Quite a number of these breed with us sometimes in the river, sometimes in the reedy slews or pools far up in the creeks, out in the Bad Lands, or on the prairie. When they are moulting, it is not difficult to get them if one cares to; and on such occasions, although there cannot be said to be any sport to be obtained from them, yet I have shot the young birds for the table for there can be no better eating than a fat, three-parts grown young goose. When their feathers are grown, however, the geese show themselves most amply fit for self-protection, and it needs then very careful stalking, indeed, before one can come up to them.

In addition to the waterfowl proper, to be obtained while drifting or paddling down the river, there are also, at times, flocks of waders at which one can get a shot. Avocets, Stilts, Yelper, Marlin and Yellow Legs are all occasionally found, although not plenty. They are not apt to be very shy, and if a shot is taken just as they rise or as they wheel, the expenditure of a single cartridge loaded with a small shot, will often suffice to bring down a dozen birds, which may prove a pleasant change to the ranchman's somewhat monotonous diet.

To make any large bag of water fowl, however, it is necessary to take a trip of several days and get over in the farming country, whose western edge lies many miles to the eastward of the broad pastoral belt, whose easternmost border comes within the Dakota Territory. In this farm region there are many hills, lakes and ponds, with reed-grown borders branching out into large slews, and connected by winding, often sluggish streams. A man with a light boat can even by himself make a really very large bag in localities such as these, and his bag will be greatly increased if he is able to take with him a good dog. Out in the West, of course, a sportsman cannot be by any means so particular in reference to the fine points of his animal as is the case in the East; and many a mongrel does duty as a duck retriever which an Eastern sportsman would scorn to look at, and I may mention, by the way, that these ill-looking beasts often do their work uncommonly well. The usual course for a sportsman to follow in such a locality, is to find out where the flight of ducks passes in the evening or morning. A reedy passage-way between two lakes, or the borders of a favorite feeding ground are especially good stations. The gunner has his boat in the lake, and paddles over its broad, shallow surface, or pushes it through the reeds until he finds a spot where there is plenty of cover, and where he will be in the line of the flight. There he remains until the flight begins; once the ducks have begun to come in, if the place is a good one, he may expect almost continuous shooting, as flock follows flock with really remarkable rapidity. A strong close shooting gun is a necessity for one who wishes to make a big bag. Personally, i have never done anything to speak of at duck shooting, my practice with the shotgun having been comparatively limited. Still I know a number of places where even an indifferent shot may get ten or fifteen couple of birds in an afternoon.

  Besides water fowl, the dvotee of the shot gun can also have some sport, in the cattle country, with prairie chickens. The proper name of the prairie chicken found with us is the Sharp-tailed Grouse. It is a somewhat different bird from the Pinnated Grouse or prairie chicken of Illinois and Iowa, being a little smaller, and affording hardly as good eating. The Sharptails are pretty common with us, and, unlike the larger game, seem to be growing more plenty yearly, owing to the fact that the cattle men, with their firearms, and still more with their poison, destroy numbers of the wolves, wild cats, skunks, and other carnivorous animals, who are the chief foes of ground-lying birds. For many years to come, the plains will afford fine sport to those fond of wing-shooting. Average ranchmen, whose favorite weapon is invariably the rifle, are not apt to go out much after prairie chickens. Still, I every now and then take a day after them, both for the sake of the sport, and also for the sake of the addition they make to our bill of fare. Of course, the best way of proceeding is to take a buckboard and a couple of good, far-ranging pointers, but usually we simply go out on horseback, or else take a stroll on foot through ground which we know contains one or more coveys. Last August, we were cutting hay on a great plateau, and noticed that every afternoon numbers of prairie fowl, in small coveys, each one probably consisting of an old hen and hear nearly grown brood of chicks, came up round the edges of the plateau. Toward eventide, accordingly, one afternoon, an hour before sunset, I took the number-ten chokebore and strolled off to the plateau,m which the haymakers had left some days before. Walking around its edge, across the spurs and the heads of the little brush coulies, I came across plenty of grouse. Some were very shy, and would not let me get anywhere near them; others, again, would squat down in the brush or long grass at my approach, and permit themselves to be walked up to, offering easy marks as they flew off, sometimes the whole covery rising together, while on other occasions the birds rose one by one. Although the time was short, i yet had as many plump grouse as I could carry by the time the sun had sunk, and that, too, in spite of making many more misses than should have been the case with such very easy shooting.

In the wild and more barren part of the plains country, we find another kind of grouse, the largest species inabiting America. This is the great Sage Cock, a bird of fine appearance, and one which, contrary to the generally received opinion, afford excellent eating. Its food consists, at different times of the year, of sage leaves or og grasshoppers. Young birds, in August or september, that have been feeding mainly upon grasshoppers, are exceedingly tender and well flavored, quite as good as any other grouse. An old cock or hen that has been feeding exclusively upon sage, of course, would offer very poor eating. In shooting these large and fine birds, it is almost impossible to go on foot or with a dog, owing to the dryness and remoteness of the haunts which they mostly affect and those that I have gotten have almost invariably been procured while riding on horseback through ground containing them, and, when I came across a covey, dismounting to do what execution I could, while my companion held the horses.

Forest and Stream
December 15, 1887

Big Game in Dakota

ELKHORN RANGE, Medora, Dakota, Dec. 1.—Editor Forest and Stream: During the past season my bag has been two mountain sheep, four antelope and eight deer, all shot round the ranch, as I have made no regular hunting trip. One ram had very fine horns.

My old .49-75 being rather the worse for five years hard service, I have taken up the new Winchester model, the .45-90, the so called model of 1886. It has proved most satisfactory; the first weapon for which I have ever been satisfied to exchange the old .45-.75. It has a lower trajectory, a stronger breech action, is absolutely accurate for any range at which game can be killed with the least certainty, and is as handy and capable of standing rough work as the old gun. I use the regular cartridge, 90 grs. of powder and a 300 gr. Solid ball, but I am inclined to think that for shooting bear at close quarters it would be better to take a Keene bullet, half as heavy again. With such a bullet it would be impossible to find a better weapon for dangerous game, and the effectiveness of the Keene principle I have tested with the old .45-.75, having been attracted to it by the mention made of it by General Wingate, in his interesting "Horseback Tour through the Yellowstone."

It is worth while carrying a few such bullets for occasions when hunting dangerous game in thick brush, and the new 1886 model Winchester seems to me the most satisfactory rifle I have ever yet come across for the wilder kinds of hunting in the United States. With the possible exception of the nearly extinct buffalo there is no game for which I would not recommend it, and personally I should use it for buffalo, too.

Bear and cougar seems to be getting more plentiful than ever round the ranch, but without properly trained dogs it is nearly impossible to get them out of the dense thickets and heavy timbered bottoms.

Century Magazine
February, 1888

Ranch Life in the Far West

In the Cattle Country

THE great grazing lands of the West lie in what is known as the arid belt, which stretches from British America on the north to Mexico on the south, through the middle of the United States. It includes New Mexico, part of Arizona, Colorado, Wyoming, Montana, and the western portion of Texas, Kansas, Nebraska, and Dakota. It must not be understood by this that more cattle are to be found here than elsewhere, for the contrary is true, it being a fact often lost sight of that the number of cattle raised on the small, thick-lying farms of the fertile Eastern States is actually many times greater than that of those scattered over the vast, barren ranches of the far West; for stock will always be most plentiful in districts where corn and other winter food can be grown. But in this arid belt, and in this arid belt only,—save in a few similar tracts on the Pacific slope,—stock-raising is almost the sole industry, except in the mountain districts where there is mining. The whole region is one vast stretch of grazing country, with only here and there spots of farm-land, in most places there being nothing more like agriculture than is implied in the cutting of some tons of wild hay or the planting of a garden patch for home use. This is especially true of the northern portion of the region, which comprises the basin of the Upper Missouri, and with which alone I am familiar. Here there are no fences to speak of, and all the land north of the Black Hills and the Big Horn Mountains and between the Rockies and the Dakota wheat-fields might be spoken of as one gigantic, unbroken pasture, where cowboys and branding-irons take the place of fences.

The country throughout this great Upper Missouri basin has a wonderful sameness of character; and the rest of the arid belt, lying to the southward, is closely akin to it in its main features. A traveler seeing it for the first time is especially struck by its look of parched, barren desolation; he can with difficulty believe that it will support cattle at all. It is a region of light rainfall; the grass is short and comparatively scanty; there is no timber except along the beds of the streams, and in many places there are alkali deserts where nothing grows but sage-brush and cactus. Now the land stretches out into level, seemingly endless plains or into rolling prairies; again it is broken by abrupt hills and deep, winding valleys; or else it is crossed by chains of buttes, usually bare, but often clad with a dense growth of dwarfed pines or gnarled, stunted cedars. The muddy rivers run in broad, shallow beds, which after heavy rainfalls are filled to the brim by the swollen torrents, while in droughts the larger streams dwindle into sluggish trickles of clearer water, and the smaller ones dry up entirely, save in occasional deep pools.

All through the region, except on the great Indian reservations, there has been a scanty and sparse settlement, quite peculiar in its character. In the forest the woodchopper comes first; on the fertile prairies the granger is the pioneer; but on the long, stretching uplands of the far West it is the men who guard and follow the horned herds that prepare the way for the settlers who come after. The high plains of the Upper Missouri and its tributary rivers were first opened, and are still held, by the stockmen, and the whole civilization of the region has received the stamp of their marked and individual characteristics. They were from the South, not from the East, although many men from the latter region came out along the great transcontinental railway lines and joined them in their northern migration.

They were not dwellers in towns, and from the nature of their industry lived as far apart from each other as possible. In choosing new ranges, old cow-hands, who are also seasoned plainsmen, are invariably sent ahead, perhaps a year in advance, to spy out the land and pick the best places. One of these may go by himself, or more often, especially if they have to penetrate little known or entirely unknown tracts, two or three will go together, the owner or manager of the herd himself being one of them. Perhaps their herds may already be on the border of the wild and uninhabited country: in that case they may have to take but a few days' journey before finding the stretches of sheltered, long-grass land that they seek. For instance, when I wished to move my own elkhorn steer brand on to a new ranch I had to spend barely a week in traveling north among the Little Missouri Bad Lands before finding what was then untrodden ground far outside the range of any of my neighbors' cattle. But if a large outfit is going to shift its quarters it must go much farther; and both the necessity and the chance for long wanderings were especially great when the final overthrow of the northern Horse Indians opened the whole Upper Missouri basin at one sweep to the stockmen. Then the advance-guards or explorers, each on one horse and leading another with food and bedding, were often absent months at a time, threading their way through the trackless wastes of plain, plateau, and river-bottom. If possible they would choose a country that would be good for winter and summer alike; but often this could not be done, and then they would try to find a well-watered tract on which the cattle could be summered, and from which they could be driven in fall to their sheltered winter range—for the cattle in winter eat snow, and an entirely waterless region, if broken, and with good pasturage, is often the best possible winter ground, as it is sure not to have been eaten off at all during the summer; while in the bottoms the grass is always cropped down soonest. Many outfits regularly shift their herds every spring and fall; but with us in the Bad Lands all we do, when cold weather sets in, is to drive our beasts off the scantily grassed river-bottom back ten miles or more among the broken buttes and plateaus of the uplands to where the brown hay, cured on the stalk, stands thick in the winding coulees.

    These lookouts or forerunners having returned, the herds are set in motion as early in the spring as may be, so as to get on the ground in time to let the travel-worn beasts rest and gain flesh before winter sets in. Each herd is accompanied by a dozen, or a score, or a couple of score, of cowboys, according to its size, and beside it rumble and jolt the heavy four-horse wagons that hold the food and bedding of the men and the few implements they will need at the end of their journey. As long as possible they follow the trails made by the herds that have already traveled in the same direction, and when these end they strike out for themselves. In the Upper Missouri basin, the pioneer herds soon had to scatter out and each find its own way among the great dreary solitudes, creeping carefully along so that the cattle should not be overdriven and should have water at the halting-places. An outfit might thus be months on its lonely journey, slowly making its way over melancholy, pathless plains, or down the valleys of the lonely rivers. It was tedious, harassing work, as the weary cattle had to be driven carefully and quietly during the day and strictly guarded at night, with a perpetual watch kept for Indians or white horse-thieves. Often they would skirt the edges of the streams for days at a time, seeking for a ford or a good swimming crossing, and if the water was up and the quicksand deep the danger to the riders was serious and the risk of loss among the cattle very great.

At last, after days of excitement and danger and after months of weary, monotonous toil, the chosen ground is reached and the final camp pitched. The footsore animals are turned loose to shift for themselves, outlying camps of two or three men each being established to hem them in. Meanwhile the primitive ranch-house, out-buildings, and corrals are built, the unhewn cottonwood logs being chinked with moss and mud, while the roofs are of branches covered with dirt, spades and axes being the only tools needed for the work. Bunks, chairs, and tables are all home-made, and as rough as the houses they are in. The supplies of coarse, rude food are carried perhaps two or three hundred miles from the nearest town, either in the ranch-wagons or else by some regular freighting outfit, the huge canvas-topped prairie schooners of which are each drawn by several yoke of oxen, or perhaps by six or eight mules. To guard against the numerous mishaps of prairie travel, two or three of these prairie schooners usually go together, the brawny teamsters, known either as "bull-whackers" or as "mule-skinners," stalking beside their slow-moving teams.

The small outlying camps are often tents, or mere dug-outs in the ground. But at the main ranch there will be a cluster of log buildings, including a separate cabin for the foreman or ranchman; often another in which to cook and eat; a long house for the men to sleep in; stables, sheds, a blacksmith's shop, etc.,—the whole group forming quite a little settlement, with the corrals, the stacks of natural hay, and the patches of fenced land for gardens or horse pastures. This little settlement may be situated right out in the treeless, nearly level open, but much more often is placed in the partly wooded bottom of a creek or river, sheltered by the usual background of somber brown hills.

When the northern plains began to be settled, such a ranch would at first be absolutely alone in the wilderness, but others of the same sort were sure soon to be established within twenty or thirty miles on one side or the other. The lives of the men in such places were strangely cut off from the outside world, and, indeed, the same is true to a hardly less extent at the present day. Sometimes the wagons are sent for provisions, and the beef-steers are at stated times driven off for shipment. Parties of hunters and trappers call now and then. More rarely small bands of emigrants go by in search of new homes, impelled by the restless, aimless craving for change so deeply grafted in the breast of the American borderer: the white-topped wagons are loaded with domestic goods, with sallow, dispirited-looking women, and with tow-headed children; while the gaunt, moody frontiersmen slouch alongside, rifle on shoulder, lank, homely, uncouth, and yet with a curious suggestion of grim strength under-lying it all. Or cowboys from neighboring ranches will ride over, looking for lost horses, or seeing if their cattle have strayed off the range. But this is all. Civilization seems as remote as if we were living in an age long past. The whole existence is patriarchal in character: it is the life of men who live in the open, who tend their herds on horseback, who go armed and ready to guard their lives by their own prowess, whose wants are very simple, and who call no man master. Ranching is an occupation like those of vigorous, primitive pastoral peoples, having little in common with the humdrum, workaday business world of the nineteenth century; and the free ranchman in his manner of life shows more kinship to an Arab sheik than to a sleek city merchant or tradesman.

By degrees the country becomes what in a stock-raising region passes for well settled. In addition to the great ranches smaller ones are established, with a few hundred, or even a few score, head of cattle apiece; and now and then miserable farmers straggle in to fight a losing and desperate battle with drought, cold, and grasshoppers. The wheels of the heavy wagons, driven always over the same course from one ranch to another, or to the remote frontier towns from which they get their goods, wear ruts in the soil, and roads are soon formed, perhaps originally following the deep trails made by the vanished buffalo. These roads lead down the river-bottoms or along the crests of the divides or else strike out fairly across the prairie, and a man may sometimes journey a hundred miles along one without coming to a house or a camp of any sort. If they lead to a shipping point whence the beeves are sent to market, the cattle, traveling in single file, will have worn many and deep paths on each side of the wheel-marks; and the roads between important places which are regularly used either by the United States Government, by stage-coach lines, or by freight teams become deeply worn landmarks—as, for instance, near us, the Deadwood and the old Fort Keogh trails.

    Cattle-ranching can only be carried on in its present form while the population is scanty; and so in stock-raising regions, pure and simple, there are usually few towns, and these are almost always at the shipping points for cattle. But, on the other hand, wealthy cattlemen, like miners who have done well, always spend their money freely; and accordingly towns like Denver, Cheyenne, and Helena, where these two classes are the most influential in the community, are far pleasanter places of residence than cities of five times their population in the exclusively agricultural States to the eastward.

    A true "cow town" is worth seeing,—such a one as Miles City, for instance, especially at the time of the annual meeting of the great Montana Stock-raisers' Association. Then the whole place is full to over-flowing, the importance of the meeting and the fun of the attendant frolics, especially the horse-races, drawing from the surrounding ranch country many hundreds of men of every degree, from the rich stock-owner worth his millions to the ordinary cowboy who works for forty dollars a month. It would be impossible to imagine a more typically American assemblage, for although there are always a certain number of foreigners, usually English, Irish, or German, yet they have become completely Americanized; and on the whole it would be difficult to gather a finer body of men, in spite of their numerous shortcomings. The ranch-owners differ more from each other than do the cowboys; and the former certainly compare very favorably with similar classes of capitalists in the East. Anything more foolish than the demagogic outcry against "cattle kings" it would be difficult to imagine. Indeed, there are very few businesses so absolutely legitimate as stock-raising and so beneficial to the nation at large; and a successful stock-grower must not only be shrewd, thrifty, patient, and enterprising, but he must also possess qualities of personal bravery, hardihood, and self-reliance to a degree not demanded in the least by any mercantile occupation in a community long settled. Stockmen are in the West the pioneers of civilization, and their daring and adventurousness make the after settlement of the region possible. The whole country owes them a great debt.

The most successful ranchmen are those, usually Southwesterners, who have been bred to the business and have grown up with it; but many Eastern men, including not a few college graduates, have also done excellently by devoting their whole time and energy to their work,—although Easterners who invest their money in cattle without knowing anything of the business, or who trust all to their subordinates, are naturally enough likely to incur heavy losses. Stockmen are learning more and more to act together; and certainly the meetings of their associations are conducted with a dignity and good sense that would do credit to any parliamentary body.

But the cowboys resemble one another much more and outsiders much less than is the case even with their employers, the ranchmen. A town in the cattle country, when for some cause it is thronged with men from the neighborhood, always presents a picturesque sight. On the wooden sidewalks of the broad, dusty streets the men who ply the various industries known only to frontier existence jostle one another as they saunter to and fro or lounge lazily in front of the straggling, cheap-looking board houses. Hunters come in from the plains and the mountains, clad in buckskin shirts and fur caps, greasy and unkempt, but with resolute faces and sullen, watchful eyes, that are ever on the alert. The teamsters, surly and self-contained, wear slouch hats and great cowhide boots; while the stage-drivers, their faces seamed by the hardship and exposure of their long drives with every kind of team, through every kind of country, and in every kind of weather, proud of their really wonderful skill as reinsmen and conscious of their high standing in any frontier community, look down on and sneer at the "skin hunters" and the plodding drivers of the white-topped prairie schooners. Besides these there are trappers, and wolfers, whose business is to poison wolves, with shaggy, knock-kneed ponies to carry their small bales and bundles of furs—beaver, wolf, fox, and occasionally otter; and silent sheep-herders, with cast-down faces, never able to forget the absolute solitude and monotony of their dreary lives, nor to rid their minds of the thought of the woolly idiots they pass all their days in tending. Such are the men who have come to town, either on business or else to frequent the flaunting saloons and gaudy hells of all kinds in search of the coarse, vicious excitement that in the minds of many of them does duty as pleasure—the only form of pleasure they have ever had a chance to know. Indians too, wrapped in blankets, with stolid, emotionless faces, stalk silently round among the whites, or join in the gambling and horse-racing. If the town is on the borders of the mountain country, there will also be sinewy lumbermen, rough-looking miners, and packers, whose business it is to guide the long mule and pony trains that go where wagons can not and whose work in packing needs special and peculiar skill; and mingled with and drawn from all these classes are desperadoes of every grade, from the gambler up through the horse-thief to the murderous professional bully, or, as he is locally called, "bad man"—now, however, a much less conspicuous object than formerly.

But everywhere among these plainsmen and mountain-men, and more important than any, are the cowboys,—the men who follow the calling that has brought such towns into being. Singly, or in twos or threes, they gallop their wiry little horses down the street, their lithe, supple figures erect or swaying slightly as they sit loosely in the saddle; while their stirrups are so long that their knees are hardly bent, the bridles not taut enough to keep the chains from clanking. They are smaller and less muscular than the wielders of ax and pick; but they are as hardy and self-reliant as any men who ever breathed—with bronzed, set faces, and keen eyes that look all the world straight in the face without flinching as they flash out from under the broad-brimmed hats. Peril and hardship, and years of long toil broken by weeks of brutal dissipation, draw haggard lines across their eager faces, but never dim their reckless eyes nor break their bearing of defiant self-confidence. They do not walk well, partly because they so rarely do any work out of the saddle, partly because their chaperajos or leather overalls hamper them when on the ground; but their appearance is striking for all that, and picturesque too, with their jingling spurs, the big revolvers stuck in their belts, and bright silk handkerchiefs knotted loosely round their necks over the open collars of the flannel shirts. When drunk on the villainous whisky of the frontier towns, they cut mad antics, riding their horses into the saloons, firing their pistols right and left, from boisterous light-heartedness rather than from any viciousness, and indulging too often in deadly shooting affrays, brought on either by the accidental contact of the moment or on account of some long-standing grudge, or perhaps because of bad blood between two ranches or localities; but except while on such sprees they are quiet, rather self-contained men, perfectly frank and simple, and on their own ground treat a stranger with the most whole-souled hospitality, doing all in their power for him and scorning to take any reward in return. Although prompt to resent an injury, they are not at all apt to be rude to outsiders, treating them with what can almost be called a grave courtesy. They are much better fellows and pleasanter companions than small farmers or agricultural laborers; nor are the mechanics and workmen of a great city to be mentioned in the same breath.

    The bulk of the cowboys themselves are South-westerners; but there are also many from the Eastern and the Northern States, who, if they begin young, do quite as well as the Southerners. The best hands are fairly bred to the work and follow it from their youth up. Nothing can be more foolish than for an Easterner to think he can become a cowboy in a few months' time. Many a young fellow comes out hot with enthusiasm for life on the plains, only to learn that his clumsiness is greater than he could have believed possible; that the cowboy business is like any other and has to be learned by serving a painful apprenticeship; and that this apprenticeship implies the endurance of rough fare, hard living, dirt, exposure of every kind, no little toil, and month after month of the dullest monotony. For cowboy work there is need of special traits and special training, and young Easterners should be sure of themselves before trying it: the struggle for existence is very keen in the far West, and it is no place for men who lack the ruder, coarser virtues and physical qualities, no matter how intellectual or how refined and delicate their sensibilities. Such are more likely to fail there than in older communities. Probably during the past few years more than half of the young Easterners who have come West with a little money to learn the cattle business have failed signally and lost what they had in the beginning. The West, especially the far West, needs men who have been bred on the farm or in the workshop far more than it does clerks or college graduates.

Some of the cowboys are Mexicans, who generally do the actual work well enough, but are not trustworthy; moreover, they are always regarded with extreme disfavor by the Texans in an outfit, among whom the intolerant caste spirit is very strong. Southern-born whites will never work under them, and look down upon all colored or half-caste races. One spring I had with my wagon a Pueblo Indian, an excellent rider and roper, but a drunken, worthless, lazy devil; and in the summer of 1886 there were with us a Sioux half-breed, a quiet, hard-working, faithful fellow, and a mulatto, who was one of the best cow-hands in the whole round-up.

Cowboys, like most Westerners, occasionally show remarkable versatility in their tastes and pursuits. One whom I know has abandoned his regular occupation for the past nine months, during which time he has been in succession a bartender, a school-teacher, and a probate judge! Another, whom I once employed for a short while, had passed through even more varied experiences, including those of a barber, a sailor, an apothecary, and a buffalo-hunter.

As a rule the cowboys are known to each other only by their first names, with, perhaps, as a prefix, the title of the brand for which they are working. Thus I remember once overhearing a casual remark to the effect that "Bar Y Harry" had married "the Seven Open A girl," the latter being the daughter of a neighboring ranchman. Often they receive nicknames, as, for instance, Dutch Wannigan, Windy Jack, and Kid Williams, all of whom are on the list of my personal acquaintances.

No man traveling through or living in the country need fear molestation from the cowboys unless he himself accompanies them on their drinking-bouts, or in other ways plays the fool, for they are, with us at any rate, very good fellows, and the most determined and effective foes of real law-breakers, such as horse and cattle thieves, murderers, etc. Few of the outrages quoted in Eastern papers as their handiwork are such in reality, the average Easterner apparently considering every individual who wears a broad hat and carries a six-shooter a cowboy. These outrages are, as a rule, the work of the roughs and criminals who always gather on the outskirts of civilization, and who infest every frontier town until the decent citizens become sufficiently numerous and determined to take the law into their own hands and drive them out. The old buffalo-hunters, who formed a distinct class, became powerful forces for evil once they had destroyed the vast herds of mighty beasts the pursuit of which had been their means of livelihood. They were absolutely shiftless and improvident; they had no settled habits; they were inured to peril and hardship, but entirely unaccustomed to steady work; and so they afforded just the materials from which to make the bolder and more desperate kinds of criminals. When the game was gone they hung round the settlements for some little time, and then many of them naturally took to horse-stealing, cattle-killing, and highway robbery, although others, of course, went into honest pursuits. They were men who died off rapidly, however; for it is curious to see how many of these plainsmen, in spite of their iron nerves and thews, have their constitutions completely undermined, as much by the terrible hardships they have endured as by the fits of prolonged and bestial revelry with which they have varied them.

The "bad men," or professional fighters and man-killers, are of a different stamp, quite a number of them being, according to their light, perfectly honest. These are the men who do most of the killing in frontier communities; yet it is a noteworthy fact that the men who are killed generally deserve their fate. These men are, of course, used to brawling, and are not only sure shots, but, what is equally important, able to "draw" their weapons with marvelous quickness. They think nothing whatever of murder, and are the dread and terror of their associates; yet they are very chary of taking the life of a man of good standing, and will often weaken and back down at once if confronted fearlessly. With many of them their courage arises from confidence in their own powers and knowledge of the fear in which they are held; and men of this type often show the white feather when they get in a tight place. Others, however, will face any odds without flinching; and I have known of these men fighting, when mortally wounded, with a cool, ferocious despair that was terrible. As elsewhere, so here, very quiet men are often those who in an emergency show themselves best able to hold their own. These desperadoes always try to "get the drop" on a foe—that is, to take him at a disadvantage before he can use his own weapon. I have known more men killed in this way, when the affair was wholly one-sided, than I have known to be shot in fair fight; and I have known fully as many who were shot by accident. It is wonderful, in the event of a street fight, how few bullets seem to hit the men they are aimed at.

During the last two or three years the stockmen have united to put down all these dangerous characters, often by the most summary exercise of lynch law. Notorious bullies and murderers have been taken out and hung, while the bands of horse and cattle thieves have been regularly hunted down and destroyed in pitched fights by parties of armed cowboys; and as a consequence most of our territory is now perfectly law-abiding. One such fight occurred north of me early last spring. The horse-thieves were overtaken on the banks of the Missouri; two of their number were slain, and the others were driven on the ice, which broke, and two more were drowned. A few months previously another gang, whose headquarters were near the Canadian line, were surprised in their hut; two or three were shot down by the cowboys as they tried to come out, while the rest barricaded themselves in and fought until the great log-hut was set on fire, when they broke forth in a body, and nearly all were killed at once, only one or two making their escape. A little over two years ago one committee of vigilantes in eastern Montana shot or hung nearly sixty—not, however, with the best judgment in all cases.

A stranger in the Northwestern cattle country is especially struck by the resemblance the settlers show in their pursuits and habits to the Southern people. Nebraska and Dakota, east of the Missouri, resemble Minnesota and Iowa and the States farther east, but Montana and the Dakota cow country show more kinship with Texas; for while elsewhere in America settlement has advanced along the parallels of latitude, on the great plains it has followed the meridians of longitude and has gone northerly rather than westerly. The business is carried on as it is in the South. The rough-rider of the plains, the hero of rope and revolver, is first cousin to the backwoodsman of the southern Alleghanies, the man of the ax and the rifle; he is only a unique offshoot of the frontier stock of the South-west. The very term "round-up" is used by the cowboys in the exact sense in which it is employed by the hill people and mountaineers of Kentucky, Tennessee, and North Carolina, with whom also labor is dear and poor land cheap, and whose few cattle are consequently branded and turned loose in the woods exactly as is done with the great herds on the plains.

But the ranching industry itself was copied from the Mexicans, of whose land and herds the South-western frontiersmen of Texas took forcible possession; and the traveler in the North-west will see at a glance that the terms and practices of our business are largely of Spanish origin. The cruel curb-bit and heavy stock-saddle, with its high horn and cantle, prove that we have adopted Spanish-American horse-gear; and the broad hat, huge blunt spurs, and leather chaperajos of the rider, as well as the corral in which the stock are penned, all alike show the same ancestry. Throughout the cattle country east of the Rocky Mountains, from the Rio Grande to the Saskatchewan, the same terms are in use and the same system is followed; but on the Pacific slope, in California, there are certain small differences, even in nomenclature. Thus, we of the great plains all use the double cinch saddle, with one girth behind the horse's fore legs and another farther back, while Californians prefer one with a single cinch, which seems to us much inferior for stock-work. Again, Californians use the Spanish word "lasso," which with us has been entirely dropped, no plainsman with pretensions to the title thinking of any word but "rope," either as noun or verb.

  The rope, whether leather lariat or made of grass, is the one essential feature of every cowboy's equipment. Loosely coiled, it hangs from the horn or is tied to one side of the saddle in front of the thigh, and is used for every conceivable emergency, a twist being taken round the stout saddle-horn the second the noose settles over the neck or around the legs of a chased animal. In helping pull a wagon up a steep pitch, in dragging an animal by the horns out of a bog-hole, in hauling logs for the fire, and in a hundred other ways aside from its legitimate purpose, the rope is of invaluable service, and dexterity with it is prized almost or quite as highly as good horsemanship, and is much rarer. Once a cowboy is a good roper and rider, the only other accomplishment he values is skill with his great army revolver, it being taken for granted that he is already a thorough plainsman and has long mastered the details of cattle-work; for the best roper and rider alive is of little use unless he is hard-working, honest, keenly alive to his employer's interest, and very careful in the management of the cattle.

  All cowboys can handle the rope with more or less ease and precision, but great skill in its use is only attained after long practice, and for its highest development needs that the man should have begun in earliest youth. Mexicans literally practice from infancy; the boy can hardly toddle before he gets a string and begins to render life a burden to the hens, goats, and pigs. A really first-class roper can command his own price, and is usually fit for little but his own special work.

  It is much the same with riding. The cowboy is an excellent rider in his own way, but his way differs from that of a trained school horseman or cross-country fox-hunter as much as it does from the horsemanship of an Arab or of a Sioux Indian, and, as with all these, it has its special merits and special defects—schoolman, fox-hunter, cowboy, Arab, and Indian being all alike admirable riders in their respective styles, and each cherishing the same profound and ignorant contempt for every method but his own. The flash riders, or horse-breakers, always called "bronco busters," can perform really marvelous feats, riding with ease the most vicious and unbroken beasts, that no ordinary cowboy would dare to tackle. Although sitting seemingly so loose in the saddle, such a rider cannot be jarred out of it by the wildest plunges, it being a favorite feat to sit out the antics of a bucking horse with silver half-dollars under each knee or in the stirrups under each foot. But their method of breaking is very rough, consisting only in saddling and bridling a beast by main force and then riding him, also by main force, until he is exhausted, when he is turned over as "broken." Later on the cowboy himself may train his horse to stop or wheel instantly at a touch of the reins or bit, to start at top speed at a signal, and to stand motionless when left. An intelligent pony soon picks up a good deal of knowledge about the cow business on his own account.

    All cattle are branded, usually on the hip, shoulder, and side, or on any one of them, with letters, numbers, or figures, in every combination, the outfit being known by its brand. Near me, for instance, are the Three Sevens, the Thistle, the Bellows, the OX, the VI., the Seventy-six Bar , and the Quarter Circle Diamondoutfits. The dew-lap and the ears may also be cut, notched, or slit. All brands are registered, and are thus protected against imitators, any man tampering with them being punished as severely as possible. Unbranded animals are called mavericks, and when found on the round-up are either branded by the owner of the range on which they are, or else are sold for the benefit of the association. At every shipping point, as well as where the beef cattle are received, there are stock inspectors who jealously examine all the brands on the live animals or on the hides of the slaughtered ones, so as to detect any foul play, which is immediately reported to the association. It becomes second nature with a cowboy to inspect and note the brands of every bunch of animals he comes across.

Perhaps the thing that seems strangest to the traveler who for the first time crosses the bleak plains of this Upper Missouri grazing country is the small number of cattle seen. He can hardly believe he is in the great stock region, where for miles upon miles he will not see a single head, and will then come only upon a straggling herd of a few score. As a matter of fact, where there is no artificial food put up for winter use cattle always need a good deal of ground per head; and this is peculiarly the case with us in the North-west, where much of the ground is bare of vegetation and where what pasture there is is both short and sparse. It is a matter of absolute necessity, where beasts are left to shift for themselves in the open during the bitter winter weather, that they then should have grass that they have not cropped too far down; and to insure this it is necessary with us to allow on the average about twenty-five acres of ground to each animal. This means that a range of country ten miles square will keep between two and three thousand head of stock only, and if more are put on, it is at the risk of seeing a severe winter kill off half or three-quarters of the whole number. So a range may be in reality overstocked when to an Eastern and unpracticed eye it seems hardly to have on it a number worth taking into account.

Overstocking is the great danger threatening the stock-raising industry on the plains. This industry has only risen to be of more than local consequence during the past score of years, as before that time it was confined to Texas and California; but during these two decades of its existence the stockmen in different localities have again and again suffered the most ruinous losses, usually with overstocking as the ultimate cause. In the south the drought, and in the north the deep snows, and everywhere unusually bad winters, do immense damage; still, if the land is fitted for stock at all, they will, averaging one year with another, do very well so long as the feed is not cropped down too close.

But, of course, no amount of feed will make some countries worth anything for cattle that are not housed during the winter; and stockmen in choosing new ranges for their herds pay almost as much attention to the capacity of the land for yielding shelter as they do to the abundant and good quality of the grass. High up among the foot-hills of the mountains cattle will not live through the winter; and an open, rolling prairie land of heavy rainfall, where in consequence the snow lies deep and there is no protection from the furious cold winds, is useless for winter grazing, no matter how thick and high the feed. The three essentials for a range are grass, water, and shelter: the water is only needed in summer and the shelter in winter, while it may be doubted if drought during the hot months has ever killed off more cattle than have died of exposure on shelterless ground to the icy weather, lasting from November to April.

    The finest summer range may be valueless either on account of its lack of shelter or because it is in a region of heavy snowfall—portions of territory lying in the same latitude and not very far apart often differing widely in this respect, or extraordinarily severe weather may cause a heavy death-rate utterly unconnected with overstocking. This was true of the loss that visited the few herds which spent the very hard winter of 1880 on the northern cattle plains. These were the pioneers of their kind, and the grass was all that could be desired; yet the extraordinary severity of the weather proved too much for the cattle. This was especially the case with those herds consisting of "pilgrims," as they are called—that is, of animals driven up on to the range from the south, and therefore in poor condition. One such herd of pilgrims on the Powder River suffered a loss of thirty-six hundred out of a total of four thousand, and the survivors kept alive only by browsing on the tops of cottonwoods felled for them. Even seasoned animals fared very badly. One great herd in the Yellowstone Valley lost about a fourth of its number, the loss falling mainly on the breeding cows, calves, and bulls,— always the chief sufferers, as the steers, and also the dry cows, will get through almost anything. The loss here would have been far heavier than it was had it not been for a curious trait shown by the cattle. They kept in bands of several hundred each, and during the time of the deep snows a band would make a start and travel several miles in a straight line, plowing their way through the drifts and beating out a broad track; then, when stopped by a frozen water-course or chain of buttes, they would turn back and graze over the trail thus made, the only place where they could get at the grass.

A drenching rain, followed by a severe snap of cold, is even more destructive than deep snow, for the saturated coats of the poor beasts are turned into sheets of icy mail, and the grass-blades, frozen at the roots as well as above, change into sheaves of brittle spears as uneatable as so many icicles. Entire herds have perished in consequence of such a storm. Mere cold, however, will kill only very weak animals, which is fortunate for us, as the spirit in the thermometer during winter often sinks to fifty degrees below zero, the cold being literally arctic; yet though the cattle become thin during such a snap of weather, and sometimes have their ears, tails, and even horns frozen off, they nevertheless rarely die from the cold alone. But if there is a blizzard blowing at such a time, the cattle need shelter, and if caught in the open, will travel for scores of miles before the storm, until they reach a break in the ground, or some stretch of dense woodland, which will shield them from the blasts. If cattle traveling in this manner come to some obstacle that they cannot pass, as, for instance, a wire fence or a steep railway embankment, they will not try to make their way back against the storm, but will simply stand with their tails to it until they drop dead in their tracks; and, accordingly, in some parts of the country—but luckily far to the south of us—the railways are fringed with countless skeletons of beasts that have thus perished, while many of the long wire fences make an almost equally bad showing. In some of the very open country of Kansas and Indian Territory, many of the herds during the past two years have suffered a loss of from sixty to eighty per cent., although this was from a variety of causes, including drought as well as severe winter weather. Too much rain is quite as bad as too little, especially if it falls after the 1st of August, for then, though the growth of grass is very rank and luxuriant, it yet has little strength and does not cure well on the stalk; and it is only possible to winter cattle at large at all because of the way in which the grass turns into natural hay by this curing on the stalk.

But scantiness of food, due to overstocking, is the one really great danger to us in the north, who do not have to fear the droughts that occasionally devastate portions of the southern ranges. In a fairly good country, if the feed is plenty, the natural increase of a herd is sure shortly to repair any damage that may be done by an unusually severe winter—unless, indeed, the latter should be one such as occurs but two or three times in a century. When, however, the grass becomes cropped down, then the loss in even an ordinary year is heavy among the weaker animals, and if the winter is at all severe it becomes simply appalling. The snow covers the shorter grass much quicker, and even when there is enough, the cattle, weak and unfit to travel around, have to work hard to get it; their exertions tending to enfeeble them and to render them less able to cope with the exposure and cold. The large patches of brushwood, into which the cattle crowd and which to a small number afford ample shelter and some food, become trodden down and yield neither when the beasts become too plentiful. Again, the grass is, of course, soonest eaten off where there is shelter; and, accordingly, the broken ground to which the animals cling during winter may be grazed bare of vegetation though the open plains, to which only the hardiest will at this season stray, may have plenty; and insufficiency of food, although not such as actually to starve them, weakens them so that they succumb readily to the cold or to one of the numerous accidents to which they are liable—as slipping off an icy butte or getting cast in a frozen washout. The cows in calf are those that suffer most, and so heavy is the loss among these and so light the calf crop that it is yet an open question whether our northern ranges are as a whole fitted for breeding. When the animals get weak they will huddle into some nook or corner and simply stay there till they die. An empty hut, for instance, will often in the spring be found to contain the carcasses of a dozen weak cows or poor steers that have crawled into it for protection from the cold, and once in have never moved out.

     Overstocking may cause little or no harm for two or three years, but sooner or later there comes a winter which means ruin to the ranches that have too many cattle on them; and in our country, which is even now getting crowded, it is merely a question of time as to when a winter will come that will understock the ranges by the summary process of killing off about half of all the cattle throughout the North-west. 1 The herds that have just been put on suffer most in such a case; if they have come on late and are composed of weak animals, very few indeed, perhaps not ten per cent., will survive. The cattle that have been double or single wintered do better; while a range-raised steer is almost as tough as a buffalo.

In our northern country we have "free grass"; that is, the stockmen rarely own more than small portions of the land over which their cattle range, the bulk of it being unsurveyed and still the property of the National Government—for the latter refuses to sell the soil except in small lots, acting on the wise principle of distributing it among as many owners as possible. Here and there some ranchman has acquired title to narrow strips of territory peculiarly valuable as giving water-right; but the amount of land thus occupied is small with us,—although the reverse is the case farther south,—and there is practically no fencing to speak of. As a consequence, the land is one vast pasture, and the man who overstocks his own range damages his neighbors as much as himself. These huge northern pastures are too dry and the soil too poor to be used for agriculture until the rich, wet lands to the east and west are occupied; and at present we have little to fear from grangers. Of course, in the end much of the ground will be taken up for small farms, but the farmers that so far have come in have absolutely failed to make even a living, except now and then by raising a few vegetables for the use of the stockmen; and we are inclined to welcome the incoming of an occasional settler, if he is a decent man, especially as, by the laws of the Territories in which the great grazing plains lie, he is obliged to fence in his own patch of cleared ground, and we do not have to keep our cattle out of it.

At present we are far more afraid of each other. There are always plenty of men who for the sake of the chance of gain they themselves run are willing to jeopardize the interests of their neighbors by putting on more cattle than the land will support—for the loss, of course, falls as heavily on the man who has put on the right number as on him who has put on too many; and it is against these individuals that we have to guard so far as we are able. To protect ourselves completely is impossible, but the very identity of interest that renders all of us liable to suffer for the fault of a few also renders us as a whole able to take some rough measures to guard against the wrong-doing of a portion of our number; for the fact that the cattle wander intermixed over the ranges forces all the ranchmen of a locality to combine if they wish to do their work effectively. Accordingly, the stockmen of a neighborhood, when it holds as many cattle as it safely can, usually unitedly refuse to work with any one who puts in another herd. In the cow country a man is peculiarly dependent upon his neighbors, and a small outfit is wholly unable to work without their assistance when once the cattle have mingled completely with those of other brands. A large outfit is much more master of its destiny, and can do its own work quite by itself; but even such a one can be injured in countless ways if the hostility of the neighboring ranchmen is incurred.

The best days of ranching are over; and though there are many ranchmen who still make money, yet during the past two or three years the majority have certainly lost. This is especially true of the numerous Easterners who went into the business without any experience and trusted themselves entirely to their Western representatives; although, on the other hand, many of those who have made most money at it are Easterners, who, however, have happened to be naturally fitted for the work and who have deliberately settled down to learning the business as they would have learned any other, devoting their whole time and energy to it. Stock-raising, as now carried on, is characteristic of a young and wild land. As the country grows older, it will in some places die out, and in others entirely change its character; the ranches will be broken up, will be gradually modified into stock-farms, or, if on good soil, may even fall under the sway of the husbandman.

In its present form stock-raising on the plains is doomed, and can hardly outlast the century. The great free ranches, with their barbarous, picturesque, and curiously fascinating surroundings, mark a primitive stage of existence as surely as do the great tracts of primeval forests, and like the latter must pass away before the onward march of our people; and we who have felt the charm of the life, and have exulted in its abounding vigor and its bold, restless freedom, will not only regret its passing for our own sakes, but must also feel real sorrow that those who come after us are not to see, as we have seen, what is perhaps the pleasantest, healthiest, and most exciting phase of American existence.

Century Magazine
March, 1888

Ranch Life in the Far West

The Home Ranch

MY home ranch lies on both sides of the Little Missouri, the nearest ranchman above me being about twelve, and the nearest below me about ten miles distant. The general course of the stream here is northerly, but, while flowing through my ranch, it takes a great westerly reach of some three miles, walled in, as always, between chains of steep, high bluffs half a mile or more apart. The stream twists down through the valley in long sweeps, leaving oval wooded bottoms, first on one side and then on the other; and in an open glade among the thick-growing timber stands the long, low house of hewn logs.

Just in front of the ranch veranda is a line of old cottonwoods that shade it during the fierce heats of summer, rendering it always cool and pleasant. But a few feet beyond these trees conies the cut-off bank of the river, through whose broad, sandy bed the shallow stream winds as if lost, except when a freshet fills it from brim to brim with foaming yellow water. The bluffs that wall in the river-valley curve back in semicircles, rising from its alluvial bottom generally as abrupt cliffs, but often as steep, grassy slopes that lead up to great level plateaus; and the line is broken every mile or two by the entrance of a coulee, or dry creek, whose head branches may be twenty miles back. Above us, where the river comes round the bend, the valley is very narrow, and the high buttes bounding it rise, sheer and barren, into scalped hill-peaks and naked knife-blade ridges.

The other buildings stand in the same open glade with the ranch house, the dense growth of cottonwoods and matted, thorny underbrush making a wall all about, through which we have chopped our wagon roads and trodden out our own bridle-paths. The cattle have now trampled down this brush a little, but deer still lie in it, only a couple of hundred yards from the house; and from the door sometimes in the evening one can see them peer out into the open, or make their way down, timidly and cautiously, to drink at the river. The stable, sheds, and other outbuildings, with the hayricks and the pens for such cattle as we bring in during winter, are near the house; the patch of fenced garden land is on the edge of the woods; and near the middle of the glade stands the high, circular horse-corral, with a snubbing-post in the center, and a wing built out from one side of the gate entrance, so that the saddle band can be driven in without trouble. As it is very hard to work cattle where there is much brush, the larger cow-corral is some four miles off on an open bottom.

  A ranchman's life is certainly a very pleasant one, albeit generally varied with plenty of hardship and anxiety. Although occasionally he passes days of severe toil, for example, if he goes on the round-up he works as hard as any of his men, yet he no longer has to undergo the monotonous drudgery attendant upon the tasks of the cowboy or of the apprentice in the business. His fare is simple; but, if he chooses, it is good enough. Many ranches are provided with nothing at all but salt pork, canned goods, and bread; indeed, it is a curious fact that in traveling through this cow country it is often impossible to get any milk or butter; but this is only because the owners or managers are too lazy to take enough trouble to insure their own comfort. We ourselves always keep up two or three cows, choosing such as are naturally tame, and so we invariably have plenty of milk and, when there is time for churning, a good deal of butter. We also keep hens, which, in spite of the damaging inroads of hawks, bob-cats, and foxes, supply us with eggs, and in time of need, when our rifles have failed to keep us in game, with stewed, roast, or fried chicken also. From our garden we get potatoes, and unless drought, frost, or grasshoppers interfere (which they do about every second year), other vegetables as well. For fresh meat we depend chiefly upon our prowess as hunters.

  During much of the time we are away on the different round-ups, that "wheeled house," the great four-horse wagon, being then our home; but when at the ranch our routine of life is always much the same, save during the scattered groups of the saddle band, our six or eight mares, with their colts, keep by themselves, and are rarely bothered by us, as no cowboy ever rides anything but horses, because mares give great trouble where all the animals have to be herded together. Once every two or three days somebody rides round and finds out where each of these smaller bands is, but the man who goes out in the morning merely gathers one bunch. He drives these into the corral, the other men (who have been lolling idly about the house or stable, fixing their saddles or doing any odd job) coming out with their ropes as soon as they hear the patter of the unshod hoofs and the shouts of the cowboy driver. Going into the corral, and standing near the center, each of us picks out some one of his own string from among the animals that are trotting and running in a compact mass round the circle; and after one or more trials, according to his skill, ropes it and leads it out. When all have caught their horses the rest are again turned loose, together with those that have been kept up overnight. Some horses soon get tame and do not need to be roped; my pet cutting pony, little Muley, and good old Manitou, my companion in so many the excessively bitter weather of midwinter, when there is little to do except to hunt, if the days are fine enough. We breakfast early before dawn when the nights have grown long, and rarely later than sunrise, even in midsummer. Perhaps before this meal, certainly the instant it is over, the man whose duty it is rides off to hunt up and drive in the saddle band. Each of us has his own string of horses, eight or ten in number, and the whole band usually split up into two or three companies. In addition to hunting trips, will neither of them stay with the rest of their fellows that are jamming and jostling each other as they rush round in the dust of the corral, but they very sensibly walk up and stand quietly with the men in the middle, by the snubbing-post. Both are great pets, Manitou in particular; the wise old fellow being very fond of bread and sometimes coming up of his own accord to the ranch house and even putting his head into the door to beg for it.

    Once saddled, the men ride off on their different tasks; for almost everything is done in the saddle, except that in winter we cut our firewood and quarry our coal, both on the ranch, and in summer attend to the garden and put up what wild hay we need.

If any horses have strayed, one or two of the men will be sent off to look for them; for hunting lost horses is one of the commonest and most irksome of our duties. Every outfit always has certain of its horses at large; and if they remain out long enough they become as wild and wary as deer and have to be regularly surrounded and run down. On one occasion, when three of mine had been running loose for a couple of months, we had to follow at full speed for at least fifteen miles before exhausting them enough to enable us to get some control over them and head them towards a corral. Twice I have had horses absent nearly a year before they were recovered. One of them, after being on the ranch nine months, went off one night and traveled about two hundred miles in a straight line back to its old haunts, swimming the Yellowstone on the way. Two others were at one time away nearly eighteen months, during which time we saw them twice, and on one occasion a couple of the men fairly ran their horses down in following them. We began to think they were lost for good, as they were all the time going farther down towards the Sioux country, but we finally recovered them.

If the men do not go horse-hunting they may ride off over the range; for there is generally some work to be done among the cattle, such as driving in and branding calves that have been overlooked by the round-up, or getting some animal out of a bog-hole. During the early spring months, before the round-up begins, the chief work is in hauling out mired cows and steers; and if we did not keep a sharp lookout, the losses at this season would be very serious. As long as everything is frozen solid there is, of course, no danger from miring; but when the thaw comes, along towards the beginning of March, a period of new danger to the cattle sets in. When the ice breaks up, the streams are left with an edging of deep bog, while the quicksand is at its worst. As the frost goes out of the soil, the ground round every little alkali-spring changes into a trembling quagmire, and deep holes of slimy, tenacious mud form in the bottom of all the gullies. The cattle, which have had to live on snow for three or four months, are very eager for water, and are weak and in poor condition. They rush heedlessly into any pool and stand there, drinking gallons of the icy water and sinking steadily into the mud. When they try to get out they are already too deep down, and are too weak to make a prolonged struggle. After one or two fits of desperate floundering, they resign themselves to their fate with dumb apathy and are lost, unless some one of us riding about discovers and hauls them out. They may be thus lost in wonderfully small mud-holes; often they will be found dead in a gulch but two or three feet across, or in the quicksand of a creek so narrow that it could almost be jumped. An alkali hole, where the water oozes out through the thick clay, is the worst of all, owing to the ropy tenacity with which the horrible substance sticks and clings to any unfortunate beast that gets into it.

In the spring these mud-holes cause very serious losses among the cattle, and are at all times fruitful sources of danger; indeed, during an ordinary year more cattle die from getting mired than from any other cause. In addition to this they also often prove very annoying to the rider himself, as getting his steed mired or caught in a quicksand is one of the commonest of the accidents that beset a horseman in the far West. This usually happens in fording a river, if the latter is at all high, or else in crossing one of the numerous creeks; although I once saw a horse and rider suddenly engulfed while leisurely walking over what appeared to be dry land. They had come to an alkali mud-hole, an old buffalo wallow, which had filled up and was covered with a sun-baked crust, that let them through as if they had stepped on a trap-door. There being several of us along, we got down our ropes and dragged both unfortunates out in short order. When the river is up it is a very common thing for a horseman to have great difficulty in crossing, for the swift, brown water runs over a bed of deep quicksand that is ever shifting. An inexperienced horse, or a mule--for a mule is useless in mud or quicksand--becomes mad with fright in such a crossing, and, after speedily exhausting its strength in wild struggles, will throw itself on its side and drown unless the rider gets it out. An old horse used to such work will, on the contrary, take matters quietly and often push along through really dangerous quicksand. Old Manitou never loses his head for an instant; but, now resting a few seconds, now feeling his way cautiously forward, and now making two or three desperate plunges, will go on wherever a horse possibly can. It is really dangerous crossing some of the creeks, as the bottom may give way where it seems hardest; and if one is alone he may work hours in vain before getting his horse out, even after taking off both saddle and bridle, the only hope being to head it so that every plunge takes it an inch or two in the right direction.

Nor are mud-holes the only danger the horseman has to fear; for in much of the Bad Lands the buttes are so steep and broken that it needs genuine mountaineering skill to get through them, and no horse but a Western one, bred to the business, could accomplish the feat. In many parts of our country it is impossible for a horseman who does not know the land to cross it, and it is difficult enough even for an experienced hand. For a stretch of nearly ten miles along the Little Missouri above my range, and where it passes through it, there are but three or four places where it is possible for a horseman to get out to the eastern prairie through the exceedingly broken country lying back from the river. In places this very rough ground comes down to the water; elsewhere it lies back near the heads of the creeks. In such very bad ground the whole country seems to be one tangled chaos of canon-like valleys, winding gullies, and washouts, with abrupt, unbroken sides, isolated peaks of sandstone, marl, or "gumbo" clay, which rain turns into slippery glue, and hill chains whose ridges always end in sheer cliffs. After a man has made his way with infinite toil for half a mile, a point will be reached around which it is an absolute impossibility to go, and the adventurer has nothing to do but painfully retrace his steps and try again in a new direction, as likely as not with the same result. In such a place the rider dismounts and leads his horse, the latter climbing with cat-like agility up seemingly inaccessible heights, scrambling across the steep, sloping shoulders of the bluffs, sliding down the faces of the clay cliffs with all four legs rigid, or dropping from ledge to ledge like a goat, and accepting with unruffled composure an occasional roll from top to bottom. But, in spite of the climbing abilities of the ponies, it is difficult, and at times for our steeds, at any rate dangerous work to go through such places, and we only do it when it cannot be avoided. Once I was overtaken by darkness while trying to get through a great tract of very rough land, and, after once or twice nearly breaking my neck, in despair had to give up all attempts to get out, and until daybreak simply staid where I was, in a kind of ledge or pocket on the side of the cliff, luckily sheltered from the wind. It was midsummer and the nights were short, but this particular one seemed quite long enough; and though I was on the move by dawn, it was three hours later before I led the horse, as hungry, numb, and stiff as myself, out on the prairie again.

Occasionally, it is imperatively necessary to cross some of the worst parts of the Bad Lands with a wagon, and such a trip is exhausting and laborious beyond belief. Often the wagon will have to be taken to pieces every few hundred yards in order to get it over a ravine, lower it into a valley, or drag it up a cliff. One outfit, that a year ago tried to take a short cut through some of the Bad Lands of the Powder River, made just four miles in three days, and then had to come back to their starting-point after all. But with only saddle-horses we feel that it must be a very extraordinary country indeed if, in case of necessity, we cannot go through it.

The long forenoon's work, with its attendant mishaps to man and beast, being over, the men who have been out among the horses and cattle come riding in, to be joined by their fellows--if any there be--who have been hunting, or haying, or chopping wood. The midday dinner is variable as to time, for it comes when the men have returned from their work; but, whatever be the hour, it is the most substantial meal of the day, and we feel that we have little fault to find with a table on whose clean cloth are spread platters of smoked elk meat, loaves of good bread, jugs and bowls of milk, saddles of venison or broiled antelope steaks, perhaps roast and fried prairie chickens, with eggs, butter, wild plums, and tea or coffee.

The afternoon's tasks are usually much the same as the morning's, but this time is often spent in doing the odds and ends; as, for instance, it may be devoted to breaking-in a new horse. Large outfits generally hire a bronco-buster to do this; but we ourselves almost always break our own horses, two or three of my men being very good riders, although none of them can claim to be anything out of the common. A first-class flash rider or bronco-buster receives high wages and deserves them, for he follows a most dangerous trade, at which no man can hope to grow old; his work being infinitely harder than that of an Eastern horse-breaker or rough-rider, because he has to do it in such a limited time. A good rider is a good rider all the world over; but an Eastern or English horse-breaker and Western bronco-buster have so little in common with each other as regards style or surroundings, and are so totally out of place in doing each other's work, that it is almost impossible to get either to admit that the other has any merits at all as a horseman, for neither could sit in the saddle of the other or could without great difficulty perform his task. The ordinary Eastern seat, which approaches more or less the seat of a cross-country rider or fox-hunter, is nearly as different from the cowboy's seat as from that of a man who rides bareback. The stirrups on a stock saddle are much farther back than they are on an ordinary English one (a difference far more important than the high horn and cantle of the former, and the man stands nearly erect in them, instead of having his legs bent; and he grips with the thighs and not with the knees, throwing his feet well out. Some of the things he teaches his horse would be wholly useless to an Eastern equestrian: for example, one of the first lessons the newly caught animal has to learn is not to "run on a rope"; and he is taught this by being violently snubbed up, probably turning a somersault, the first two or three times that he feels the noose settle round his neck, and makes a mad rush for liberty. The snubbing-post is the usual adjunct in teaching such a lesson; but a skillful man can do without any help and throw a horse clean over by holding the rope tight against the left haunch, at the same time leaning so far back, with the legs straight in front, that the heels dig deep into the ground when the strain comes, and the horse, running out with the slack of the rope, is brought up standing, or even turned head over heels by the shock. Cowboys are probably the only men in the world who invariably wear gloves, buckskin gauntlets being preferred, as otherwise the ropes would soon take every particle of skin off their hands.

    A bronco-buster has to work by such violent methods in consequence of the short amount of time at his command. Horses are cheap, each outfit has a great many, and the wages for breaking an animal are but five or ten dollars. Three rides, of an hour or two each, on as many consecutive days, are the outside number a bronco-buster deems necessary before turning an animal over as "broken." The average bronco-buster, however, handles horses so very rudely that we prefer, aside from motives of economy, to break our own; and this is always possible, if we take enough time. The best and most quiet horses on the ranch are far from being those broken by the best riders; on the contrary, they are those that have been handled most gently, although firmly, and that have had the greatest number of days devoted to their education.

Some horses, of course, are almost incurably vicious, and must be conquered by main force. One pleasing brute on my ranch will at times rush at a man open-mouthed like a wolf, and this is a regular trick of the range-stallions. In a great many indeed, in most localities there are wild horses to be found, which, although invariably of domestic descent, being either themselves runaways from some ranch or Indian outfit, or else claiming such for their sires and dams, yet are quite as wild as the antelope on whose domain they have intruded. Ranchmen run in these wild horses whenever possible, and they are but little more difficult to break than the so-called "tame" animals. But the wild stallions are, whenever possible, shot; both because of their propensity for driving off the ranch mares, and because their incurable viciousness makes them always unsafe companions for other horses still more than for men. A wild stallion fears no beast except the grizzly, and will not always flinch from an encounter with it; yet it is a curious fact that a jack will almost always kill one in a fair fight. The particulars of a fight of this sort were related to me by a cattle man who was engaged in bringing out blooded stock from the East. Among the animals under his charge were two great stallions, one gray and one black, and a fine jackass, not much over half the size of either of the former. The animals were kept in separate pens, but one day both horses got into the same enclosure, next to the jack-pen, and began to fight as only enraged stallions can, striking like boxers with their fore feet, and biting with their teeth. The gray was getting the best of it; but while clinched with his antagonist in one tussle they rolled against the jack-pen, breaking it in. No sooner was the jack at liberty than, with ears laid back and mouth wide open, he made straight for the two horses, who had for the moment separated. The gray turned to meet him, rearing on his hind legs and striking at him with his fore feet; but the jack slipped in, and in a minute grasped his antagonist by the throat with his wide-open jaws, and then held on like a bull-dog, all four feet planted stiffly in the soil. The stallion made tremendous efforts to shake him off; he would try to whirl round and kick him, but for that the jack was too short; then he would rise up, lifting the jack off the ground, and strike at him with his fore feet; but all that he gained by this was to skin his foe's front legs without making him loose his hold. Twice they fell, and twice the stallion rose, by main strength dragging the jack with him; but all in vain. Meanwhile the black horse attacked both the combatants with perfect impartiality, striking and kicking them with his hoofs, while his teeth, as they slipped off the tough hides, met with a snap like that of a bear-trap. Undoubtedly the jack would have killed at least one of the horses had not the men come up, and with no small difficulty separated the maddened brutes.

If not breaking horses, mending saddles, or doing something else of the sort, the cowboys will often while away their leisure moments by practicing with the rope. A man cannot practice too much with this if he wishes to attain even moderate proficiency; and as a matter of fact he soon gets to wish to practice the whole time. A cowboy is always roping something, and it especially delights him to try his skill at game. A friend of mine, a young ranchman in the Judith basin, about three years ago roped a buffalo, and by the exercise of the greatest skill, both on his own part and on his steed's, actually succeeded, by alternate bullying and coaxing, in getting the huge brute almost into camp. I have occasionally known men on fast horses to rope deer, and even antelope, when circumstances all joined to favor them; and last summer one of the cowboys on a ranch about thirty miles off ran into and roped a wounded elk. A forty-foot lariat is the one commonly used, for the ordinary range at which a man can use it is only about twenty-five feet. Few men can throw forty feet; and to do this, taking into account the coil, needs a sixty-foot rope.

When the day's work is over we take supper, and bedtime comes soon afterward, for the men who live on ranches sleep well and soundly. As a rule, the nights are cool and bracing, even in midsummer; except when we occasionally have a spell of burning weather, with a steady, hot wind that blows in our faces like a furnace blast, sending the thermometer far up above a hundred and making us gasp for breath, even at night, in the dry-baked heat of the air. But it is only rarely that we get a few days of this sort; generally, no matter how unbearable the heat of the day has been, we can at least sleep pleasantly at night.

A ranchman's work is, of course, free from much of the sameness attendant upon that of a mere cowboy. One day he will ride out with his men among the cattle, or after strayed horses; the next he may hunt, so as to keep the ranch in meat; then he can make the tour of his outlying camps; or, again, may join one of the round-ups for a week or two, perhaps keeping with it the entire time it is working. On occasions he will have a good deal of spare time on his hands, which, if he chooses, he can spend in reading or writing. If he cares for books, there will be many a worn volume in the primitive little sitting-room, with its log walls and huge fireplace; but after a hard day's work a man will not read much, but will rock to and fro in the flickering firelight, talking sleepily over his success in the day's chase and the difficulty he has had with the cattle; or else may simply lie stretched at full length on the elk-hides and wolf-skins in front of the hearthstone, listening in drowsy silence to the roar and crackle of the blazing logs and to the moaning of the wind outside.

In the sharp fall weather the riding is delicious all day long; but even in the late spring, and all through the summer, we try, if we can, to do our work before the heat of the day, and if going on a long ride, whether to hunt or for other purposes, leave the ranch house by dawn.

The early rides in the spring mornings have a charm all their own, for they are taken when, for the one and only time during the year, the same brown landscape of these high plains turns to a vivid green, as the new grass sprouts and the trees and bushes thrust forth the young leaves; and at dawn, with the dew glittering everywhere, all things show at their best and freshest.

The flowers are out and a man may gallop for miles at a stretch with his horse's hoofs sinking at every stride into the carpet of prairie roses, whose short stalks lift the beautiful blossoms but a few inches from the ground. Even in the waste places the cactuses are blooming; and one kind in particular, a dwarfish, globular plant, with its mass of splendid crimson flowers, glows against the sides of the gray buttes like a splash of flame.

    The ravines, winding about and splitting into a labyrinth of coulees, with chairs of rounded hills to separate them, have groves of trees in their bottoms, over the sides of the water courses. In these are found the blacktail deer, and his cousin, the whitetail, too, with his flaunting flag but in the springtime, when we are after antelope only, we must go out farther to the flat prairie land on the divide. Here, in places, the level, grassy plains are strewn with mounds and hillocks of red or gray scoria, that stand singly or clustered into little groups, their tops crested, or their sides covered, by queer, detached masses of volcanic rock, wrought into strange shapes by the dead forces whose blind, hidden strength long ago called them into being. The road our wagons take, when the water is too high for us to come down the river bottom, stretches far ahead--two dark, straight, parallel furrows which merge into one in the distance. Quaint little horned frogs crawl sluggishly along in the wheel tracks, and the sickle-billed curlews run over the ground or soar above and around the horsemen, uttering their mournful, never-ceasing clamor. The grass-land stretches out in the sunlight like a sea, every wind bending the blades into a ripple, and flecking the prairie with shifting patches of a different green from that around, exactly as the touch of a light squall or wind-gust will fleck the smooth surface of the ocean. Our Western plains differ widely in detail from those of Asia; yet they always call to mind

       .... The Scythian
       On the wide steppe.

    In the spring mornings the rider on the plains will hear bird songs unknown in the East. The Missouri sky-lark sings while soaring above the great plateaus so high in the air that it is impossible to see the bird; and this habit of singing while soaring it shares with some sparrow-like birds that are often found in company with it. The white-shouldered lark-bunting, in its livery of black, has rich, full notes, and as it sings on the wing it reminds one of the bobolink; and the sweet-voiced lark-finch also utters its song in the air. These birds, and most of the sparrows of the plains, are characteristic of this region.

But many of our birds, especially those found in the wooded river bottoms, answer to those of the East; only almost each one has some marked point of difference from its Eastern representative. The bluebird out West is very much of a blue bird indeed, for it has no "earth tinge" on its breast at all; while the indigo-bird, on the contrary, has gained the ruddy markings that the other has lost. The flicker has the shafts of its wing and tail quills colored orange instead of yellow. The towhee has lost all title to its name, for its only cry is a mew like that of a cat-bird; while, most wonderful of all, the meadow-lark has found a rich, strong voice, and is one of the sweetest and most incessant singers we have.

Throughout June the thickets and groves about the ranch house are loud with bird music from before dawn till long after sunrise. The thrashers have sung all the night through from among the thorn-bushes if there has been a moon, or even if there has been bright starlight; and before the first glimmer of gray the bell-like, silvery songs of the shy woodland thrushes chime in; while meadow-lark, robin, bluebird, and song sparrow, together with many rarer singers, like the grosbeak, join in swelling the chorus. There are some would-be singers whose intention is better than their execution. Blackbirds of several kinds are plenty round the house and stables, walking about with a knowing air, like so many dwarf crows; and now and then a flock of yellow-heads will mix for a few days with their purple or rusty-colored brethren. The males of these yellow-headed grakles are really handsome, their orange and yellow heads contrasting finely with the black of the rest of their plumage; but their voices are discordant to a degree. When a flock has done feeding it will often light in straggling order among the trees in front of the veranda, and then the males will begin to sing, or rather to utter the most extraordinary collection of broken sounds creakings, gurglings, hisses, twitters, and every now and then a liquid note or two. It is like an accentuated representation of the noise made by a flock of common blackbirds. At nightfall the poor-wills begin to utter their boding call from the wooded ravines back in the hills; not "whip-poorwill," as in the East, but with two syllables only. They often come round the ranch house. Late one evening I had been sitting motionless on the veranda, looking out across the water and watching the green and brown of the hilltops change to purple and umber and then fade off into shadowy gray as the somber darkness deepened. Suddenly a poorwill lit on the floor beside me and stayed some little time; now and then uttering its mournful cries, then ceasing for a few moments as it flitted round after insects, and again returning to the same place to begin anew. The little owls, too, call to each other with tremulous, quavering voices throughout the livelong night, as they sit in the creaking trees that overhang the roof. Now and then we hear the wilder voices of the wilderness, from animals that in the hours of darkness do not fear the neighborhood of man; the coyotes wail like dismal ventriloquists, or the silence may be broken by the strident challenge of a lynx, or by the snorting and stamping of a deer that has come to the edge of the open.

    In the hot noontide hours of midsummer the broad ranch veranda, always in the shade, is almost the only spot where a man can be comfortable; but here he can sit for hours at a time, leaning back in his rocking-chair as he reads or smokes, or with half-closed, dreamy eyes gazes across the shallow, nearly dry riverbed to the wooded bottoms opposite, and to the plateaus lying back of them. Against the sheer white faces of the cliffs that come down without a break, the dark green treetops stand out in bold relief. In the hot, lifeless air all objects that are not near by seem to sway and waver. There are few sounds to break the stillness. From the upper branches of the cottonwood trees overhead, whose shimmering, tremulous leaves are hardly ever quiet, but if the wind stirs at all, rustle and quaver and sigh all day long, comes every now and then the soft, melancholy cooing of the mourning dove, whose voice always seems far away and expresses more than any other sound in nature the sadness of gentle, hopeless, never-ending grief. The other birds are still; and very few animals move about. Now and then the black shadow of a wheeling vulture falls on the sun-scorched ground. The cattle, that have strung down in long files from the hills, lie quietly on the sand-bars, except that some of the bulls keep traveling up and down, bellowing and routing or giving vent to long, surly grumblings as they paw the sand and toss it up with their horns. At times the horses, too, will come down to drink, and to splash and roll in the water.

The prairie-dogs alone are not daunted by the heat, but sit at the mouths of their burrows with their usual pert curiosity. They are bothersome little fellows, and most prolific, increasing in spite of the perpetual war made on them by every carnivorous bird and beast. One of their worst foes is the black-footed ferret, a handsome, rather rare animal, somewhat like a mink, with a yellow-brown body and dark feet and mask. It is a most blood-thirsty little brute, feeding on all small animals and ground birds. It will readily master a jack-rabbit, will kill very young fawns if it finds them in the mother's absence, and work extraordinary havoc in a dog town, as it can follow the wretched little beasts down into the burrows. In one instance, I knew of a black-footed ferret making a succession of inroads on a ranchman's poultry, killing and carrying off most of them before it was trapped. Coyotes, foxes, swifts, badgers, and skunks also like to lurk about the dog towns. Of the skunks, by the way, we had last year altogether too much; there was a perfect plague of them all along the river, and they took to trying to get into the huts, with the stupid pertinacity of the species. At every ranch house dozens were killed, we ourselves bagging thirty-three, all slain near the house, and one, to our unspeakable sorrow, in it.

In making a journey over ground we know, during the hot weather we often prefer to ride by moonlight. The moon shines very brightly through the dry, clear night air, turning the gray buttes into glimmering silver; and the horses travel far more readily and easily than under the glaring noonday sun. The road between my upper and lower ranch houses is about forty miles long, sometimes following the river-bed, and then again branching off inland, crossing the great plateaus and winding through the ravines of the broken country. It is a five-hours' fair ride; and so, in a hot spell, we like to take it during the cool of the night, starting at sunset. After nightfall the face of the country seems to alter marvelously, and the cool moonlight only intensifies the change. The river gleams like running quicksilver, and the moonbeams play over the grassy stretches of the plateaus and glance off the wind-rippled blades as they would from water. The Bad Lands seem to be stranger and wilder than ever, the silvery rays turning the country into a kind of grim fairy-land. The grotesque, fantastic outlines of the higher cliffs stand out with startling clearness, while the lower buttes have become formless, misshapen masses, and the deep gorges are in black shadow; in the darkness there will be no sound but the rhythmic echo of the hoof-beats of the horses, and the steady, metallic clank of the steel bridle-chains.

But the fall is the time for riding; for in the keen, frosty air neither man nor beast will tire, though out from the dawn until the shadows have again waxed long and the daylight has begun to wane, warning all to push straight for home without drawing rein. Then deer saddles and elk haunches hang from the trees near the house; and one can have good sport right on the sand of the river-bed, for we always keep shot-gun or rifle at hand, to be ready for any prairie chickens, or for such of the passing water-fowl as light in the river near us. Occasionally we take a shot at a flock of waders, among which the pretty avocets are the most striking in looks and manners. Prairie fowl are quite plenty all round us, and occasionally small flocks come fairly down into the yard, or perch among the trees near by. At evening they fly down to the river to drink, and as they sit on the sand-bars offer fine marks for the rifles. So do the geese and ducks when they occasionally light on the same places or paddle leisurely down stream in the middle of the river; but to make much of a bag of these we have to use the heavy No. 10, choke-bore shot-gun, while the little i6-bore fowling-piece is much the handiest for prairie fowl. A good many different kinds of water-fowl pass, ranging in size from a teal duck to a Canada goose, and all of them at times help to eke out our bill of fare. Last fall a white-fronted goose lit on the river in front of the ranch house, and three of us, armed with miscellaneous weapons, went out after him; we disabled him, and then after much bad shooting, and more violent running through thick sand and thick underbrush, finally overtook and most foully butchered him. The snow geese and common wild geese are what we usually kill, however.

Sometimes strings of sandhill cranes fly along the river, their guttural clangor being heard very far off. They usually light on a plateau, where sometimes they form rings and go through a series of queer antics, dancing and posturing to each other. They are exceedingly wide-awake birds, and more shy and wary than antelope, so that they are rarely shot; yet once I succeeded in stalking up to a group in the early morning, and firing into them rather at random, my bullet killed a full-grown female. Its breast, when roasted, proved to be very good eating.

Sometimes we vary our diet with fish--wall-eyed pike, ugly, slimy catfish, and other uncouth finny things, looking very fit denizens of the mud-choked water; but they are good eating withal, in spite of their uncanny appearance. We usually catch them with set lines, left out overnight in the deeper pools.

The cattle are fattest and in best condition during the fall, and it is then that the bulk of the beef steers are gathered and shipped--four-year-olds as a rule, though some threes and some fives go along with them. Cattle are a nuisance while hunting on foot, as they either take fright and run off when they see the hunter, scaring all game within sight, or else, what is worse, follow him, blustering and bullying and pretending that they are on the point of charging, but rarely actually doing so. Still, they are occasionally really dangerous, and it is never entirely safe for a man to be on foot when there is a chance of meeting the droves of long-horned steers. But they will always bluster rather than fight, whether with men or beasts, or with one another. The bulls and some of the steers are forever traveling and challenging each other, never ceasing their hoarse rumbling and moaning and their long-drawn, savage bellowing, tearing up the banks with their horns and sending little spurts of dust above their shoulders with their fore hoofs; yet they do not seem especially fond of real fighting, although, of course, they do occasionally have most desperate and obstinate set-tos with one another. A large bear will make short work of a bull: a few months ago one of the former killed a very big bull near a ranch house a score of miles or so distant, and during one night tore up and devoured a large part of his victim. The ranchman poisoned the carcass and killed the bear.

In the winter there is much less work than at any other season, but what there is involves great hardship and exposure. Many of the men are discharged after the summer is over, and during much of the cold weather there is little to do except hunt now and then, and in very bitter days lounge about the house. But some of the men are out in the line camps, and the ranchman has occasionally to make the round of these; and besides that, one or more of the cowboys who are at home ought to be out every day when the cattle have become weak, so as to pick up and drive in any beast that will otherwise evidently fail to get through the season a cow that has had an unusually early calf being particularly apt to need attention. The horses shift for themselves and need no help. Often, in winter, the Indians cut down the cottonwood trees and feed the tops to their ponies; but this is not done to keep them from starving, but only to keep them from wandering off in search of grass. Besides, the ponies are very fond of the bark of the young cottonwood shoots, and it is healthy for them.

The men in the line camps lead a hard life, for they have to be out in every kind of weather, and should be especially active and watchful during the storms. The camps are established along some line which it is proposed to make the boundary of the cattle's drift in a given direction. For example, we care very little whether our cattle wander to the Yellowstone; but we strongly object to their drifting east and south-east towards the granger country and the Sioux reservation, especially as when they drift that way they come out on flat, bare plains where there is danger of perishing. Accordingly, the cowmen along the Little Missouri have united in establishing a row of camps to the east of the river, along the line where the broken ground meets the prairie. The camps are usually for two men each, and some fifteen or twenty miles apart; then, in the morning, its two men start out in opposite ways, each riding till he meets his neighbor of the next camp nearest on that side, when he returns. The camp itself is sometimes merely a tent pitched in a sheltered coulee, but ought to be either made of logs or else a dug-out in the ground. A small corral and horse-shed is nearby with enough hay for the ponies, of which each rider has two or three. In riding over the beat each man drives any cattle that have come near it back into the Bad Lands, and if he sees by the hoof-marks that a few have strayed out over the line very recently, he will follow and fetch them home. They must be shoved well back into the Bad Lands before a great storm strikes them; for if they once begin to drift in masses before an icy gale it is impossible for a small number of men to hold them, and the only thing is to let them go, and then to organize an expedition to follow them as soon as possible. Line riding is very cold work, and dangerous too, when the men have to be out in a blinding snowstorm, or in a savage blizzard that takes the spirit in the thermometer far down below zero. In the worst storms it is impossible for any man to be out.

    But other kinds of work besides line riding necessitate exposure to bitter weather. Once, while spending a few days over on Beaver Creek hunting up a lost horse, I happened to meet a cowboy who was out on the same errand, and made friends with him. We started home together across the open prairies, but were caught in a very heavy snow-storm almost immediately after leaving the ranch where we had spent the night. We were soon completely turned round, the great soft flakes--for, luckily, it was not cold--almost blinding us, and we had to travel entirely by compass. After feeling our way along for eight or nine hours, we finally got down into the broken country near Sentinel Butte and came across an empty hut, a welcome sight to men as cold, hungry, and tired as we were. In this hut we passed the night very comfortably, picketing our horses in a sheltered nook near by, with plenty of hay from an old stack. To while away the long evening, I read Hamlet aloud, from a little pocket Shakespere. The cowboy, a Texan--one of the best riders I have seen, and also a very intelligent as well as a thoroughly good fellow in every way--was greatly interested in it and commented most shrewdly on the parts he liked, especially Polonius's advice to Laertes, which he translated into more homely language with great relish, and ended with the just criticism that "old Shakespere saveyed human natur' some"--savey being a verb presumably adapted into the limited plains' vocabulary from the French.

    Even for those who do not have to look up stray horses, and who are not forced to ride the line day in and day out, there is apt to be some hardship and danger in being abroad during the bitter weather; yet a ride in midwinter is certainly fascinating. The great white country wrapped in the powdery snowdrift seems like another land; and the familiar landmarks are so changed that a man must be careful lest he lose his way, for the discomfort of a night in the open during such weather is very great indeed. When the sun is out the glare from the endless white stretches dazzles the eyes; and if the gray snow-clouds hang low and only let a pale, wan light struggle through, the lonely wastes become fairly appalling in their desolation. For hour after hour a man may go on and see ho sign of life except, perhaps, a big white owl sweeping noiselessly by, so that in the dark it looks like a snow-wreath; the cold gradually chilling the rider to the bones, as he draws his fur cap tight over his ears and muffles his face in the huge collar of his wolf-skin coat, and making the shaggy little steed drop head and tail as it picks its way over the frozen soil. There are few moments more pleasant than the home-coming, when, in the gathering darkness, after crossing the last chain of ice-covered buttes, or after coming round the last turn in the wind-swept valley, we see, through the leafless trees, or across the frozen river, the red gleam of the firelight as it shines through the ranch windows and flickers over the trunks of the cottonwoods outside, warming a man's blood by the mere hint of the warmth awaiting him within.

Century Magazine
April, 1888

Ranch Life in the Far West

The Round-Up

DURING the winter-time there is ordinarily but little work done among the cattle. There is some line riding, and a continual lookout is kept for the very weak animals; but most of the stock are left to shift for themselves, undisturbed. Almost every stock-grower's association forbids branding any calves before the spring round-up. If great bands of cattle wander off the range, parties may be fitted out to go after them and bring them back; but this is only done when absolutely necessary, as when the drift of the cattle has been towards an Indian reservation or a settled granger country, for the weather is very severe, and the horses are so poor that their food must be carried along. The bulk of the work is done during the summer, including the late spring and early fall, and consists mainly in a succession of round-ups, beginning, with us, in May and ending towards the last of October. But a good deal may be done by riding over one's range. Frequently, too, herding will be practiced on a large scale.

More important than herding is "trail" work; cattle, while driven from one range to another, or to a shipping point for beef, being said to be "on the trail." For years, the oversupply from the vast breeding ranches to the south, especially in Texas, has been driven northward in large herds, either to the shipping towns along the great railroads, or else to the fattening ranges of the Northwest; it having been found, so far, that while the calf crop is larger in the South, beeves become much heavier in the North. Such cattle, for the most part, went along tolerably well-marked routes or trails, which became for the time being of great importance, flourishing and extremely lawless towns growing up along them; but with the growth of the railroad system, and above all with the filling-up of the northern ranges, these trails have steadily become of less and less consequence, though many herds still travel them on their way to the already crowded ranges of western Dakota and Montana, or to the Canadian regions beyond. The trail work is something by itself. The herds may be on the trail several months, averaging fifteen miles or less a day. The cowboys accompanying each have to undergo much hard toil, of a peculiarly same and wearisome kind, on account of the extreme slowness with which everything must be done, as trail cattle should never be hurried. The foreman of a trail outfit must be not only a veteran cowhand, but also a miracle of patience and resolution.

    Round-up work is far less irksome, there being an immense amount of dash and excitement connected with it; and when once the cattle are on the range, the important work is done during the round-up. On cow ranches, or wherever there is breeding stock, the spring round-up is the great event of the season, as it is then that the bulk of the calves are branded. It usually lasts six weeks, or thereabouts; but its end by no means implies rest for the stockman. On the contrary, as soon as it is over, wagons are sent to work out-of-the-way parts of the country that have been passed over, but where cattle are supposed to have drifted; and by the time these have come back the first beef round-up has begun, and thereafter beeves are steadily gathered and shipped, at least from among the larger herds, until cold weather sets in; and in the fall there is another round-up, to brand the late calves and see that the stock is got back on the range. As all of these round-ups are of one character, a description of the most important, taking place in the spring, will be enough.

    In April we begin to get up the horses. Throughout the winter very few have been kept for use, as they are then poor and weak, and must be given grain and hay if they are to be worked. The men in the line camps need two or three apiece, and each man at the home ranch has a couple more; but the rest are left out to shift for themselves, which the tough, hardy little fellows are well able to do. Ponies can pick up a living where cattle die; though the scanty feed, which they may have to uncover by pawing off the snow, and the bitter weather often make them look very gaunt by spring-time. But the first warm rains bring up the green grass, and then all the live-stock gain flesh with wonderful rapidity. When the spring round-up begins the horses should be as fat and sleek as possible. After running all winter free, even the most sober pony is apt to betray an inclination to buck; and, if possible, we like to ride every animal once or twice before we begin to do real work with him. Animals that have escaped for any length of time are almost as bad to handle as if they had never been broken. One of the two horses mentioned in a preceding article as having been gone eighteen months has, since his return, been suggestively dubbed "Dynamite Jimmy," on account of the incessant and eruptive energy with which he bucks. Many of our horses, by the way, are thus named from some feat or peculiarity. Wire Fence, when being broken, ran into one of the abominations after which he is now called; Hackamore once got away and remained out for three weeks with a hackamore, or breaking halter, on him; Macaulay contracted the habit of regularly getting rid of the huge Scotchman to whom he was entrusted; Bulberry Johnny spent the hour or two after he was first mounted in a large patch of thorny bulberry bushes, his distracted rider unable to get him to do anything but move round sidewise in a circle; Fall Back would never get to the front; Water Skip always jumps mud-puddles; and there are a dozen others with names as purely descriptive.

The stock-growers of Montana, of the western part of Dakota, and even of portions of extreme northern Wyoming--that is, of all the grazing lands lying in the basin of the Upper Missouri--have united, and formed themselves into the great Montana Stock-growers' Association. Among the countless benefits they have derived from this course, not the least has been the way in which the various round-ups work in with and supplement one another. At the spring meeting of the association, the entire territory mentioned above, including perhaps a hundred thousand square miles, is mapped out into round-up districts, which generally are changed but slightly from year to year, and the times and places for the round-ups to begin refixed so that those of adjacent districts may be run with a view to the best interests of all. Thus the stockmen along the Yellowstone have one round-up; we along the Little Missouri have another; and the country lying between, through which the Big Beaver flows, is almost equally important to both. Accordingly, one spring, the Little Missouri round-up, beginning May 25 and working down-stream, was timed so as to reach the mouth of the Big Beaver about June 1, the Yellowstone round-up beginning at that date and place. Both then worked up the Beaver together to its head, when the Yellowstone men turned to the west and we bent back to our own river; thus the bulk of the strayed cattle of each were brought back to their respective ranges. Our own round-up district covers the Big and Little Beaver creeks, which rise near each other, but empty into the Little Missouri nearly a hundred and fifty miles apart, and so much of the latter river as lies between their mouths.

The captain or foreman of the round-up, upon whom very much of its efficiency and success depends, is chosen beforehand. He is, of course, an expert cowman, thoroughly acquainted with the country; and he must also be able to command and to keep control of the wild rough-riders he has under him--a feat needing both tact and firmness.

At the appointed day all meet at the place from which the round-up is to start. Each ranch, of course, has most work to be done in its own round-up district, but it is also necessary to have representatives in all those surrounding it. A large outfit may employ a dozen cowboys, or over, in the home district, and yet have nearly as many more representing its interest in the various ones adjoining. Smaller outfits generally club together to run a wagon and send outside representatives, or else go along with their stronger neighbors, they paying part of the expenses. A large outfit, with a herd of twenty thousand cattle or more, can, if necessary, run a round-up entirely by itself, and is able to act independently of outside help; it is therefore at a great advantage compared with those that can take no step effectively without their neighbors' consent and assistance.

If the starting-point is some distance off, it may be necessary to leave home three or four days in advance. Before this we have got everything in readiness; have overhauled the wagons, shod any horse whose fore feet are tender--as a rule, all our ponies go barefooted--and left things in order at the ranch.

Our outfit may be taken as a sample of everyone else's. We have a stout four-horse wagon to carry the bedding and the food; in its rear a messchest is rigged to hold the knives, forks, cans, etc. All our four team-horses are strong, willing animals, though of no great size, being originally just "broncos," or unbroken native horses, like the others. The teamster is also cook: a man who is a really first-rate hand at both driving and cooking--and our present teamster is both--can always command his price. Besides our own men, some cowboys from neighboring ranches and two or three representatives from other round-up districts are always along, and we generally have at least a dozen "riders," as they are termed--that is, cowboys, or "cowpunchers," who do the actual cattle-work--with the wagon. Each of these has a string of eight or ten ponies; and to take charge of the saddle-band, thus consisting of a hundred odd head, there are two herders, always known as "horse-wranglers" one for the day and one for the night. Occasionally there will be two wagons, one to carry the bedding and one the food, known, respectively, as the bed and the mess wagon; but this is not usual.

While traveling to the meeting-point the pace is always slow, as it is an object to bring the horses on the ground as fresh as possible. Accordingly, we keep at a walk almost all day, and the riders, having nothing else to do, assist the wranglers in driving the saddle-band, three or four going in front, and others on the side, so that the horses shall keep on a walk. There is always some trouble with the animals at the starting out, as they are very fresh and are restive under the saddle. The herd is likely to stampede, and any beast that is frisky or vicious is sure to show its worst side. To do really effective cow-work a pony should be well broken; but many even of the old ones have vicious traits, and almost every man will have in his string one or two young horses, or broncos, hardly broken at all. In consequence, very many of my horses have to this day traits not calculated to set a timid or a clumsy rider at his ease. One or two run away and cannot be held by even the strongest bit; others can hardly be bridled or saddled until they have been thrown; two or three have a tendency to fall over backward; and half of them buck more or less, some so hard that only an expert can sit them.

In riding these wild, vicious horses, and in careering over such very bad ground, especially at night, accidents are always occurring. A man who is merely an ordinary rider is certain to have a pretty hard time. On my first round-up I had a string of nine horses, four of them broncos, only broken to the extent of having each been saddled once or twice. One of them it was an impossibility to bridle or to saddle single-handed; it was very difficult to get on or off him, and he was exceedingly nervous if a man moved his hands or feet; but he had no bad tricks. The second soon became perfectly quiet. The third turned out to be one of the worst buckers on the ranch; once, when he bucked me off, I managed to fall on a stone and broke a rib. The fourth had a still worse habit, for he would balk and then throw himself over backward; once, when I was not quick enough, he caught me and broke something in the point of my shoulder, so that it was some weeks before I could raise the arm freely. My hurts were far from serious, and did not interfere with my riding and working as usual through the round-up; but I was heartily glad when it ended, and ever since have religiously done my best to get none but gentle horses in my own string. However, every one gets falls from or with his horse now and then in the cow country; and even my men, good riders though they are, are sometimes injured. One of them once broke his ankle; another a rib; another was on one occasion stunned, remaining unconscious for some hours; and yet another had certain of his horses buck under him so hard and long as finally to hurt his lungs and make him cough blood. Fatal accidents occur annually in almost every district, especially if there is much work to be done among stampeded cattle at night; but on my own ranch none of my men have ever been seriously hurt, though on one occasion a cowboy from another ranch, who was with my wagon, was killed, his horse falling and pitching him heavily on his head.

For bedding, each man has two or three pairs of blankets, and a tarpaulin or small wagon-sheet. Usually, two or three sleep together. Even in June the nights are generally cool and pleasant, and it is chilly in the early mornings; although this is not always so, and when the weather stays hot and mosquitoes are plenty, the hours of darkness, even in midsummer, seem painfully long.

In the Bad Lands proper we are not often bothered very seriously by these winged pests; but in the low bottoms of the Big Missouri, and beside many of the reedy ponds and great sloughs out on the prairie, they are a perfect scourge. During the very hot nights, when they are especially active, the bed-clothes make a man feel absolutely smothered, and yet his only chance for sleep is to wrap himself tightly up, head and all; and even then some of the pests will usually force their way in. At sunset I have seen the mosquitoes rise up from the land like a dense cloud, to make the hot, stifling night one long torture; the horses would neither lie down nor graze, traveling restlessly to and fro till daybreak, their bodies streaked and bloody, and the insects settling on them so as to make them all one color, a uniform gray; while the men, after a few hours' tossing about in the vain attempt to sleep, rose, built a little fire of damp sage brush, and thus endured the misery as best they could until it was light enough to work.

But if the weather is fine, a man will never sleep better nor more pleasantly than in the open air after a hard day's work on the roundup; nor will an ordinary shower or gust of wind disturb him in the least, for he simply draws the tarpaulin over his head and goes on sleeping. But now and then we have a windstorm that might better be called a whirlwind and has to be met very differently; and two or three days or nights of rain insure the wetting of the blankets, and therefore shivering discomfort on the part of the would-be sleeper. For two or three hours all goes well; and it is rather soothing to listen to the steady patter of the great raindrops on the canvas. But then it will be found that a corner has been left open through which the water can get in, or else the tarpaulin will begin to leak somewhere; or perhaps the water wilt have collected in a hollow underneath and have begun to soak through. Soon a little stream trickles in, and every effort to remedy matters merely results in a change for the worse. To move out of the way insures getting wet in a fresh spot; and the best course is to lie still and accept the evils that have come with what fortitude one can. Even thus, the first night a man can sleep pretty well; but if the rain continues, the second night, when the blankets are already damp, and when the water comes through more easily, is apt to be most unpleasant.

Of course, a man can take little spare clothing on a round-up; at the very outside two or three clean handkerchiefs, a pair of socks, a change of underclothes, and the most primitive kind of washing apparatus, all wrapped up in a stout jacket which is to be worn when night-herding. The inevitable "slicker," or oilskin coat, which gives complete protection from the wet, is always carried behind the saddle.

At the meeting-place there is usually a delay of a day or two to let every one come in; and the plain on which the encampment is made becomes a scene of great bustle and turmoil. The heavy four-horse wagons jolt in from different quarters, the horse wranglers rushing madly to and fro in the endeavor to keep the different saddle-bands from mingling, while the "riders," or cowboys, with each wagon jog along in a body. The representatives from outside districts ride in singly or by twos and threes, every man driving before him his own horses, one of them loaded with his bedding. Each wagon wheels out of the way into some camping-place not too near the others, the bedding is tossed out on the ground, and then every one is left to do what he wishes, while the different wagon bosses, or foremen, seek out the captain of the round-up to learn what his plans are.

There is a good deal of rough but effective discipline and method in the way in which a round-up is carried on. The captain of the whole has as lieutenants the various wagon foremen, and in making demands for men to do some special service he will usually merely designate some foreman to take charge of the work and let him parcel it out among his men to suit himself. The captain of the round-up or the foreman of a wagon may himself be a ranchman; if such is not the case, and the ranchman nevertheless comes along, he works and fares precisely as do the other cowboys.

While the head men are gathered in a little knot, planning out the work, the others are dispersed over the plain in every direction, racing, breaking rough horses, or simply larking with one another. If a man has an especially bad horse, he usually takes such an opportunity, when he has plenty of time, to ride him; and while saddling he is surrounded by a crowd of most unsympathetic associates who greet with uproarious mirth any misadventure. A man on a bucking horse is always considered fair game, every squeal and jump of the bronco being nailed with cheers of delighted irony for the rider and shouts to "stay with him." The antics of a vicious bronco show infinite variety of detail, but are ah l modeled on one general plan. When the rope settles round his neck the fight begins, and it is only after much plunging and snorting that a twist is taken over his nose, or else a hackamore--a species of severe halter, usually made of plaited hair slipped on his head. While being bridled he strikes viciously with his fore feet, and perhaps has to be blindfolded or thrown down; and to get the saddle on him is quite as difficult. When saddled, he may get rid of his exuberant spirits by bucking under the saddle, or may reserve all his energies for the rider. In the last case, the man, keeping tight hold with his left hand of the cheek-strap, so as to prevent the horse from getting his head down until he is fairly seated, swings himself quickly into the saddle. Up rises the bronco's back into an arch; his head, the ears laid straight back, goes down between his fore feet, and, squealing savagely, he makes a succession of rapid, stiff-legged, jarring bounds. Sometimes he is a "plunging" bucker, who runs forward all the time while bucking; or he may buck steadily in one place, or "sunfish"--that is, bring first one shoulder down almost to the ground and then the other--or else he may change ends while in the air. A first-class rider will sit throughout it all without moving from the saddle, quirting his horse all the time, though his hat may be jarred off his head and his revolver out of its sheath. After a few jumps, however, the average man grasps hold of the horn of the saddle--the delighted onlookers meanwhile earnestly advising him not to "go to leather"--and is contented to get through the affair in any shape provided he can escape without being thrown off. An accident is of necessity borne with a broad grin, as any attempt to resent the raillery of the bystanders--which is perfectly good-humored--would be apt to result disastrously. Cowboys are certainly extremely good riders. As a class they have no superiors. Of course, they would at first be at a disadvantage in steeple-chasing or fox-hunting, but their average of horsemanship is without doubt higher than that of the men who take part in these latter amusements. A cowboy would learn to ride across country in a quarter of the time it would take a cross-country rider to learn to handle a vicious bronco or to do good cow-work round and in a herd.

On such a day, when there is no regular work, there will often also be horse-races, as each outfit is pretty sure to have some running pony which it believes can outpace any other. These contests are always short-distance dashes, for but a few hundred yards. Horse-racing is a mania with most plainsmen, white or red. A man with a good racing pony will travel all about with it, often winning large sums, visiting alike cow ranches, frontier towns, and Indian encampments. Sometimes the race is "pony against pony," the victor taking both steeds. In racing the men ride bareback, as there are hardly any light saddles in the cow country. There will be intense excitement and very heavy betting over a race between two well-known horses, together with a good chance of blood being shed in the attendant quarrels. Indians and whites often race against each other as well as among themselves. I have seen several such contests, and in every case but one the white man happened to win. A race is usually run between two thick rows of spectators, on foot and on horseback, and as the racers pass, these rows close in behind them, every man yelling and shouting with all the strength of his lungs, and all waving their hats and cloaks to encourage the contestants, or firing off their revolvers and saddle guns. The little horses are fairly maddened, as is natural enough, and run as if they were crazy; were the distances longer, some would be sure to drop in their tracks.

Besides the horse-races, which are, of course, the main attraction, the men at a round-up will often get up wrestling matches or footraces. In fact, everyone feels that he is off for a holiday; for after the monotony of a long winter, the cowboys look forward eagerly to the round-up, where the work is hard, it is true, but exciting and varied, and treated a good deal as a frolic. There is no eight-hour law in cowboy land; during round-up time we often count ourselves lucky if we get off with much less than sixteen hours; but the work is done in the saddle, and the men are spurred on all the time by the desire to outdo one another in feats of daring and skillful horsemanship. There is very little quarreling or fighting; and though the fun often takes the form of rather rough horse-play, yet the practice of carrying dangerous weapons makes cowboys show far more rough courtesy to each other and far less rudeness to strangers than is the case among, for instance, Eastern miners, or even lumbermen. When a quarrel may very probably result fatally, a man thinks twice before going into it; warlike people or classes always treat one another with a certain amount of consideration and politeness. The moral tone of a cow-camp, indeed, is rather high than otherwise. Meanness, cowardice, and dishonesty are not tolerated. There is a high regard for truthfulness and keeping one's word, intense contempt for any kind of hypocrisy, and a hearty dislike for a man who shirks his work. Many of the men gamble and drink, but many do neither; and the conversation is not worse than in most bodies composed wholly of male human beings. A cowboy will not submit tamely to an insult, and is very ready to avenge his own wrongs; nor has he an overwrought fear of shedding blood. He possesses, in fact, few of the emasculated, milk-and-water moralities admired by the pseudo-philanthropists; but he does possess, to a very high degree, the stern, manly qualities that are so valuable to a nation.

    The method of work is simple. The mess-wagons and loose horses, after breaking camp in the morning, move on in a straight line for some few miles, going into camp again before midday; and the day herd, consisting of all the cattle that have been found far off their range, and which are to be brought back there, and of any others that it is necessary to gather, follows on afterwards. Meanwhile the cowboys scatter out and drive in all the cattle from the country round about, going perhaps ten or fifteen miles back from the line of march, and meeting at the place where camp has already been pitched. The wagons always keep some little distance from one another, and the saddle-bands do the same, so that the horses may not get mixed. It is rather picturesque to see the four-horse teams filing down at a trot through a pass among the buttes--the saddle-bands being driven along at a smart pace to one side or behind, the teamsters cracking their whips, and the horse-wranglers calling and shouting as they ride rapidly from side to side behind the horses, urging on the stragglers by dexterous touches with the knotted ends of their long lariats that are left trailing from the saddle. The country driven over is very rough, and it is often necessary to double up teams and put on eight horses to each wagon in going up an unusually steep pitch, or hauling through a deep mud-hole, or over a river crossing where there is quicksand.

The speed and thoroughness with which a country can be worked depends, of course, very largely upon the number of riders. Ours is probably about an average round-up as regards size. The last spring I was out, there were half a dozen wagons along; the saddle-bands numbered about a hundred each; and the morning we started, sixty men in the saddle splashed across the shallow ford of the river that divided the plain where we had camped from the valley of the long winding creek up which we were first to work.

In the morning, the cook is preparing breakfast long before the first glimmer of dawn. As soon as it is ready, probably about 3 o'clock, he utters a long-drawn shout, and all the sleepers feel it is time to be up on the instant, for they know there can be no such thing as delay on the round-up, under penalty of being set afoot. Accordingly, they bundle out, rubbing their eyes and yawning, draw on their boots and trousers--if they have taken the latter off--roll up and cord their bedding, and usually without any attempt at washing crowd over to the little smoldering fire, which is placed in a hole dug in the ground, so that there may be no risk of its spreading. The men are rarely very hungry at breakfast, and it is a meal that has to be eaten in shortest order, so it is perhaps the least important. Each man, as he comes up, grasps a tin cup and plate from the mess-box, pours out his tea or coffee, with sugar, but of course no milk, helps himself to one or two of the biscuits that have been baked in a Dutch oven, and perhaps also to a slice of the fat pork swimming in the grease of the frying-pan, ladles himself out some beans, if there are any, and squats down on the ground to eat his breakfast. The meal is not an elaborate one; nevertheless a man will have to hurry if he wishes to eat it before hearing the foreman sing out, "Come, boys, catch your horses"; when he must drop everything and run out to the wagon with his lariat. The night wrangler is now bring-

The Round-Up / 89

ing in the saddle-band, which he has been up all night guarding. A rope corral is rigged up by stretching a rope from each wheel of one side of the wagon, making a V-shaped space, into which the saddle-horses are driven. Certain men stand around to keep them inside, while the others catch the horses; many outfits have one man to do all the roping. As soon as each has caught his horse--usually a strong, tough animal, the small, quick ponies being reserved for the work round the herd in the afternoon--the band, now in charge of the day wrangler, is turned loose, and every one saddles up as fast as possible. It still lacks some time of being sunrise, and the air has in it the peculiar chill of the early morning. When all are saddled, many of the horses bucking and dancing about, the riders from the different wagons all assemble at the one where the captain is sitting, already mounted. He waits a very short time--for laggards receive but scant mercy--before announcing the proposed camping-place and parceling out the work among those present. If, as is usually the case, the line of march is along a river or creek, he appoints some man to take a dozen others and drive down (or up) it ahead of the day herd, so that the latter will not have to travel through other cattle; the day herd itself being driven and guarded by a dozen men detached for that purpose. The rest of the riders are divided into two bands, placed under men who know the country, and start out, one on each side, to bring in every head for fifteen miles back. The captain then himself rides down to the new camping-place, so as to be there as soon as any cattle are brought in.

Meanwhile the two bands, a score of riders in each, separate and make their way in opposite directions. The leader of each tries to get such a "scatter" on his men that they will cover completely all the land gone over. This morning work is called circle riding, and is peculiarly hard in the Badlands on account of the remarkably broken, rugged nature of the country. The men come in on lines that tend to a common center--as if the sticks of a fan were curved. As the band goes out, the leader from time to time detaches one or two men to ride down through certain sections of the country, making the shorter, or what are called inside, circles, while he keeps on; and finally, retaining as companions the two or three whose horses are toughest, makes the longest or outside circle himself, going clear back to the divide, or whatever the point may be that marks the limit of the round-up work, and then turning and working straight to the meeting-place. Each man, of course, brings in every head of cattle he can see.

    These long, swift rides in the glorious spring mornings are not soon to be forgotten. The sweet, fresh air, with a touch of sharpness thus early in the day, and the rapid motion of the fiery little horse combine to make a man's blood thrill and leap with sheer buoyant light-heartedness and eager, exultant pleasure in the boldness and freedom of the life he is leading. As we climb the steep sides of the first range of buttes, wisps of wavering mist still cling in the hollows of the valley; when we come out on the top of the first great plateau, the sun flames up over its edge, and in the level, red beams the galloping horsemen throw long fantastic shadows. Black care rarely sits behind a rider whose pace is fast enough; at any rate, not when he first feels the horse move under him.

    Sometimes we trot or pace, and again we lope or gallop; the few who are to take the outside circle must needs ride both hard and fast. Although only grass-fed, the horses are tough and wiry; and, moreover, are each used but once in four days, or thereabouts, so they stand the work well. The course out lies across great grassy plateaus, along knife-like ridge crests, among winding valleys and ravines, and over acres of barren, sun-scorched buttes, that look grimly grotesque and forbidding, while in the Badlands the riders unhesitatingly go down and over places where it seems impossible that a horse should even stand . The line of horsemen will quarter down the side of a butte, where every pony has to drop from ledge to ledge like a goat, and will go over the shoulder of a soapstone cliff, when wet and slippery, with a series of plunges and scrambles which if unsuccessful would land horses and riders in the bottom of the canyon-like washout below. In descending a clay butte after a rain, the pony will put all four feet together and slide down to the bottom almost or quite on his haunches. In very wet weather the Badlands are absolutely impassable; but if the ground is not slippery, it is a remarkable place that can shake the matter-of-course confidence felt by the rider in the capacity of his steed to go anywhere.

When the men on the outside circle have reached the bound set them--whether it is a low divide, a group of jagged hills, the edge of the rolling, limitless prairie, or the long, waste reaches of alkali and sage brush--they turn their horses' heads and begin to work down the branches of the creeks, one or two riding down the bottom, while the others keep off to the right and the left, a little ahead and fairly high up on the side hills, so as to command as much of a view as possible. On the level or rolling prairies the cattle can be seen a long way off, and it is an easy matter to gather and to drive them; but in the Badlands every little pocket, basin, and coulee has to be searched, every gorge or ravine entered, and the dense patches of brushwood and spindling, wind-beaten trees closely examined. All the cattle are carried on ahead down the creek; and it is curious to watch the different behavior of the different breeds. A cowboy riding off to one side of the creek, and seeing a number of long-horned Texans grazing in the branches of a set of coulees, has merely to ride across the upper ends of these, uttering the drawn-out "ei-koh-h-h," so familiar to the cattle-men, and the long-horns will stop grazing, stare fixedly at him, and then, wheeling, strike off down the coulees at a trot, tails in air, to be carried along by the center riders when they reach the main creek into which the coulees lead. Our own range cattle are not so wild, but nevertheless are easy to drive; while Eastern-raised beasts have little fear of a horseman, and merely stare stupidly at him until he rides directly towards them. Every little bunch of stock is thus collected, and all are driven along together. At the place where some large fork joins the main creek another band may be met, driven by some of the men who have left earlier in the day to take one of the shorter circles; and thus, before coming down to the bottom where the wagons are camped and where the actual "round-up" itself is to take place, this one herd may include a couple of thousand head; or, on the other hand, the longest ride may not result in the finding of a dozen animals. As soon as the riders are in, they disperse to their respective wagons to get dinner and change horses, leaving the cattle to be held by one or two of their number. If only a small number of cattle have been gathered, they will all be run into one herd; if there are many of them, however, the different herds will be held separate.

A plain where a round-up is taking place offers a picturesque sight. I well remember one such. It was on a level bottom in the bend of the river, which here made an almost semicircular sweep. The bottom was in shape a long oval, hemmed in by an unbroken line of steep bluffs so that it looked like an amphitheater. Across the faces of the dazzling white cliffs there were sharp bands of black and red, drawn by the coal seams and the layers of burned clay; the leaves of the trees and the grass had the vivid green of spring-time. The wagons were camped among the cottonwood trees fringing the river, a thin column of smoke rising up from beside each. The horses were grazing round the outskirts, those of each wagon by themselves and kept from going too near the others by their watchful guard. In the great circular corral, towards one end, the men were already branding calves, while the whole middle of the bottom was covered with lowing herds of cattle and shouting, galloping cowboys. Apparently there was nothing but dust, noise, and confusion; but in reality the work was proceeding all the while with the utmost rapidity and certainty.

As soon as, or even before, the last circle riders have come in and have snatched a few hasty mouthfuls to serve as their midday meal, we begin to work the herd--or herds, if the one herd would be of too unwieldy size. The animals are held in a compact bunch, most of the riders forming a ring outside, while a couple from each ranch successively look the herds through and cut out those marked with their own brand. It is difficult, in such a mass of moving beasts--for they do not stay still, but keep weaving in and out among each other--to find all of one's own animals: a man must have natural gifts, as well as great experience, before he becomes a good brand reader and is able to really "clean up a herd"--that is, be sure he has left nothing of his own in it.

To do good work in cutting out from a herd, not only should the rider be a good horseman, but he should also have a skillful, thoroughly trained horse. A good cutting pony is not common, and is generally too valuable to be used anywhere but in the herd. Such a one enters thoroughly into the spirit of the thing, and finds out immediately the animal his master is after;

he will then follow it closely of his own accord through every wheel and double, at top speed. When looking through the herd, it is necessary to move slowly; and when any animal is found it is taken to the outskirts at a walk, so as not to alarm the others. Once at the outside, however, the cowboy has to ride like lightning; for as soon as the beast he is after finds itself separated from its companions it endeavors to break back among them, and a young, range-raised steer or heifer runs like a deer. In cutting out a cow and a calf two men have to work together. As the animals of a brand are cut out they are received and held apart by some rider detailed for the purpose, who is said to be "holding the cut."

All this time the men holding the herd have their hands full, for some animal is continually trying to break out, when the nearest man flies at it at once and after a smart chase brings it back to its fellows. As soon as all the cows, calves, and whatever else is being gathered have been cut out, the rest are driven clear off the ground and turned loose, being headed in the direction contrary to that in which we travel the following day. Then the riders surround the next herd, the men holding cuts move them up near it, and the work is begun anew.

If it is necessary to throw an animal, either to examine a brand or for any other reason, half a dozen men will have their ropes down at once; and then it is spur and quirt in the rivalry to see which can outdo the other until the beast is roped and thrown. A first-class hand will, unaided, rope, throw, and tie down a cow or steer in wonderfully short time; one of the favorite tests of competitive skill among the cowboys is the speed with which this feat can be accomplished. Usually, however, one man ropes the animal by the head and another at the same time gets the loop of his lariat over one or both its hind legs, when it is twisted over and stretched out in a second. In following an animal on horseback the man keeps steadily swinging the rope round his head, by a dexterous motion of the wrist only, until he gets a chance to throw it; when on foot, especially if catching horses in a corral, the loop is allowed to drag loosely on the ground. A good roper will hurl out the coil with marvelous accuracy and force; it fairly whistles through the air, and settles round the object with almost infallible certainty. Mexicans make the best ropers; but some Texans are very little behind them. A good horse takes as much interest in the work as does his rider, and the instant the noose settles over the victim wheels and braces himself to meet the shock, standing with his legs firmly planted, the steer or cow being thrown with a jerk. An unskillful rider and an untrained horse will often themselves be thrown when the strain comes.

Sometimes an animal--usually a cow or steer, but, strangely enough, very rarely a bull--will get fighting mad, and turn on the men. If on the drive, such a beast usually is simply dropped out; but if they have time, nothing delights the cowboys more than an encounter of this sort, and the charging brute is roped and tied down in short order. Often such a one will make a very vicious fight, and is most dangerous. Once a fighting cow kept several of us busy for nearly an hour; she gored two ponies, one of them, which was, luckily, hurt but slightly, being my own pet cutting horse. If a steer is hauled out of a mud-hole, its first act is usually to charge the rescuer.

As soon as all the brands of cattle are worked, and the animals that are to be driven along have been put in the day herd, attention is turned to the cows and calves, which are already gathered in different bands, consisting each of all the cows of a certain brand and all the calves that are following them. If there is a corral, each band is in turn driven into it; if there is none, a ring of riders does duty in its place. A fire is built, the irons heated, and a dozen men dismount to, as it is called, "wrestle" the calves. The best two ropers go in on their horses to catch the latter; one man keeps tally, a couple put on the brands, and the others seize, throw, and hold the little unfortunates. A first-class roper invariably catches the calf by both hind feet, and then, having taken a twist with his lariat round the horn of the saddle, drags the bawling little creature, extended at full length, up to the fire, where it is held before it can make a struggle. A less skillful roper catches round the neck, and then, if the calf is a large one, the man who seizes it has his hands full, as the bleating, bucking animal develops astonishing strength, cuts the wildest capers, and resists frantically and with all its power. If there are seventy or eighty calves in a corral, the scene is one of the greatest confusion. The ropers, spurring and checking the fierce little horses, drag the calves up so quickly that a dozen men can hardly hold them; the men with the irons, blackened with soot, run to and fro; the calf-wrestlers, grimy with blood, dust, and sweat, work like beavers; while with the voice of a stentor the tally-man shouts out the number and sex of each calf. The dust rises in clouds, and the shouts, cheers, curses, and laughter of the men unite with the lowing of the cows and the frantic bleating of the roped calves to make a perfect babel. Now and then an old cow turns vicious and puts every one out of the corral. Or a maverick bull--that is, an unbranded bull--a yearling or a two-years-old, is caught, thrown, and branded; when he is let up, there is sure to be a fine scatter. Down goes his head, and he bolts at the nearest man, who makes out of the way at top speed, amidst roars of laughter from all of his companions; while the men holding down calves swear savagely as they dodge charging mavericks, trampling horses, and taut lariats with frantic, plunging little beasts at the farther ends.

Every morning certain riders are detached to drive and to guard the day herd, which is most monotonous work, the men being on from 4 in the morning till 8 in the evening, the only rest coming at dinner-time, when they change horses. When the herd has reached the camping-ground there is nothing to do but to loll listlessly over the saddle-bow in the blazing sun, watching the cattle feed and sleep, and seeing that they do not spread out too much. Plodding slowly along on the trail through the columns of dust stirred up by the hoofs is not much better. Cattle travel best and fastest strung out in long lines; the swiftest taking the lead in single file, while the weak and the lazy, the young calves and the poor cows, crowd together in the rear. Two men travel along with the leaders, one on each side, to point them in the right direction; one or two others keep by the flanks, and the rest are in the rear to act as "drag-drivers" and hurry up the phalanx of reluctant weaklings. If the foremost of the string travels too fast, one rider will go along on the trail a few rods ahead, and thus keep them back so that those in the rear will not be left behind.

Generally all this is very tame and irksome; but by fits and starts there will be little flurries of excitement. Two or three of the circle riders may unexpectedly come over a butte near by with a bunch of cattle, which at once start for the day herd, and then there will be a few minutes' furious riding hither and thither to keep them out. Or the cattle may begin to run, and then get "milling"--that is, all crowd together into a mass like a ball, wherein they move round and round, trying to keep their heads towards the center, and refusing to leave it. The only way to start them is to force one's horse in among them and cut out some of their number, which then begin to travel off by themselves, when the others will probably follow. But in spite of occasional incidents of this kind, day-herding has a dreary sameness about it that makes the men dislike and seek to avoid it.

    From 8 in the evening till 4 in the morning the day herd becomes a night herd. Each wagon in succession undertakes to guard it for a night, dividing the time into watches of two hours apiece, a couple of riders taking each watch. This is generally chilly and tedious; but at times it is accompanied by intense excitement and danger, when the cattle become stampeded, whether by storm or otherwise. The first and the last watches are those chosen by preference; the others are disagreeable, the men having to turn out cold and sleepy, in the pitchy darkness, the two hours of chilly wakefulness completely breaking the night's rest. The first guards have to bed the cattle down, though the day-herders often do this themselves it simply consists in hemming them into as small a space as possible, and then riding round them until they lie down and fall asleep. Often, especially at first, this takes some time--the beasts will keep rising and lying down again. When at last most become quiet, some perverse brute of a steer will deliberately hook them all up; they keep moving in and out among one another, and long strings of animals suddenly start out from the herd at a stretching walk, and are turned back by the nearest cowboy only to break forth at a new spot. When finally they have lain down and are chewing their cud or slumbering, the two night guards begin riding round them in opposite ways, often, on very dark nights, calling or singing to them, as the sound of the human voice on such occasions seems to have a tendency to quiet them. In inky black weather, especially when rainy, it is both difficult and unpleasant work; the main trust must be placed in the horse, which, if old at the business, will of its own accord keep pacing steadily round the herd, and head off any animals that, unseen by the rider's eyes in the darkness, are trying to break out. Usually the watch passes off without incident, but on rare occasions the cattle become restless and prone to stampede. Anything may then start them--the plunge of a horse, the sudden approach of a coyote, or the arrival of some outside steers or cows that have smelt them and come up. Every animal in the herd will be on its feet in an instant, as if by an electric shock, and off with a rush, horns and tail up. Then, no matter how rough the ground nor how pitchy black the night, the cowboys must ride for all there is in them and spare neither their own nor their horses' necks. Perhaps their charges break away and are lost altogether; perhaps, by desperate galloping, they may head them off, get them running in a circle, and finally stop them. Once stopped, they may break again, and possibly divide up, one cowboy, perhaps, following each band. I have known six such stops and renewed stampedes to take place in one night, the cowboy staying with his ever-diminishing herd of steers until daybreak, when he managed to get them under control again, and, by careful humoring of his jaded, staggering horse, finally brought those that were left back to the camp several miles distant. The riding in these night stampedes is wild and dangerous to a degree, especially if the man gets caught in the rush of the beasts. It also frequently necessitates an immense amount of work in collecting the scattered animals. On one such occasion a small party of us were thirty-six hours in the saddle, dismounting only to change horses or to eat. We were almost worn out at the end of the time; but it must be kept in mind that for a long spell of such work a stock-saddle is far less tiring than the ordinary Eastern or English one, and in every way superior to it.

  By very hard riding, such a stampede may sometimes be prevented. Once we were bringing a thousand head of young cattle down to my lower ranch, and as the river was high were obliged to take the inland trail. The third night we were forced to make a dry camp, the cattle having had no water since the morning. Nevertheless, we got them bedded down without difficulty, and one of the cowboys and myself stood first guard. But very soon after nightfall, when the darkness had become complete, the thirsty brutes of one accord got on their feet and tried to break out. The only salvation was to keep them close together, as, if they once got scattered, we knew they could never be gathered; so I kept on one side, and the cowboy on the other, and never in my life did I ride so hard. In the darkness I could but dimly see the shadowy outlines of the herd, as with whip and spurs I ran the pony along its edge, turning back the beasts at one point barely in time to wheel and keep them in at another. The ground was cut up by numerous little gullies, and each of us got several falls, horses and riders turning complete somersaults. We were dripping with sweat, and our ponies quivering and trembling like quaking aspens, when, after more than an hour of the most violent exertion, we finally got the herd quieted again.

On another occasion while with the roundup we were spared an excessively unpleasant night only because there happened to be two or three great corrals not more than a mile or so away. All day long it had been raining heavily, and we were well drenched; but towards evening it lulled a little, and the day herd, a very large one, of some two thousand head, was gathered on an open bottom. We had turned the horses loose, and in our oilskin slickers cowered, soaked and comfortless, under the lee of the wagon, to take a meal of damp bread and lukewarm tea, the sizzling embers of the fire having about given up the ghost after a fruitless struggle with the steady downpour. Suddenly the wind began to come in quick, sharp gusts, and soon a regular blizzard was blowing, driving the rain in stinging level sheets before it. Just as we were preparing to turn into bed, with the certainty of a night of more or less chilly misery ahead of us, one of my men, an iron-faced personage, whom no one would ever have dreamed had a weakness for poetry, looked towards the plain where the cattle were, and remarked, "I guess there's 'racing and chasing on Cannobie Lea' now, sure." Following his gaze, I saw that the cattle had begun to drift before the storm, the night guards being evidently unable to cope with them, while at the other wagons riders were saddling in hot haste and spurring off to their help through the blinding rain. Some of us at once ran out to our own saddleband. All of the ponies were standing huddled together, with their heads down and their tails to the wind. They were wild and restive enough usually; but the storm had cowed them, and we were able to catch them without either rope or halter. We made quick work of saddling; and the second each man was ready, away he loped through the dusk, splashing and slipping in the pools of water that studded the muddy plain. Most of the riders were already out when we arrived. The cattle were gathered in a compact, wedge-shaped, or rather fan-shaped mass, with their tails to the wind--that is, towards the thin end of the wedge or fan. In front of this fan-shaped mass of frightened, maddened beasts was a long line of cowboys, each muffled in his slicker and with his broad hat pulled down over his eyes, to shield him from the pelting rain. When the cattle were quiet for a moment every horseman at once turned round with his back to the wind, and the whole line stood as motionless as so many sentries. Then, if the cattle began to spread out and overlap at the ends, or made a rush and broke through at one part of the lines, there would be a change into wild activity. The men, shouting and swaying in their saddles, darted to and fro with reckless speed, utterly heedless of danger now racing to the threatened point, now checking and wheeling their horses so sharply as to bring them square on their haunches, or even throw them flat down, while the hoofs plowed long furrows in the slippery soil, until, after some minutes of this mad galloping hither and thither, the herd, having drifted a hundred yards or so, would be once more brought up standing. We always had to let them drift a little to prevent their spreading out too much. The din of the thunder was terrific, peal following peal until they mingled in one continuous, rumbling roar; and at every thunder-clap louder than its fellows the cattle would try to break away. Darkness had set in, but each flash of lightning showed us a dense array of tossing horns and staring eyes. It grew always harder to hold in the herd; but the drift took us along to the corrals already spoken of, whose entrances were luckily to windward. As soon as we reached the first we cut off part of the herd, and turned it within; and after again doing this with the second, we were able to put all the remaining animals into the third. The instant the cattle were housed five-sixths of the horsemen started back at full speed for the wagons;

the rest of us barely waited to put up the bars and make the corrals secure before galloping after them. We had to ride right in the teeth of the driving storm; and once at the wagons we made small delay in crawling in under our blankets, damp though the latter were, for we were ourselves far too wet, stiff, and cold not to hail with grateful welcome any kind of shelter from the wind and the rain.

All animals were benumbed by the violence of this gale of cold rain; a prairie-chicken rose from under my horse's feet so heavily that, thoughtlessly striking at it, I cut it down with my whip; while when a jack rabbit got up ahead of us, it was barely able to limp clumsily out of our way.

But though there is much work and hardship, rough fare, monotony, and exposure connected with the round-up, yet there are few men who do not look forward to it and back to it with pleasure. The only fault to be found is that the hours of work are so long that one does not usually have enough time to sleep. The food, if rough, is good. The men are good-humored, bold, and thoroughly interested in their business, continually vying with one another in the effort to see which can do the work best. It is superbly health-giving, and is full of excitement and adventure, calling for the exhibition of pluck, self-reliance, hardihood, and dashing horsemanship; and of all forms of physical labor the easiest and pleasantest is to sit in the saddle.

The scenery is often exceedingly striking in character, especially in the Badlands, with their queer fantastic formations. Among the most interesting features are the burning mines. These are formed by the coal seams that get on fire. They vary greatly in size. Some send up smoke-columns that are visible miles away, while others are not noticeable a few rods off. The old ones gradually burn away, while new ones unexpectedly break out. Thus, last fall, one suddenly appeared but half a mile from the ranch house. We never knew it was there until one cold moonlight night, when we were riding home, we rounded the corner of a ravine and saw in our path a tall white column of smoke rising from a rift in the snowy crags ahead of us. As the trail was over perfectly familiar ground, we were for a moment almost as startled as if we had seen a ghost.

The burning mines are uncanny places, anyhow. A strong smell of sulphur hangs round them, the heated earth crumbles and cracks, and through the long clefts that form in it we can see the lurid glow of the subterranean fires, with here and there tongues of blue or cherry colored flame dancing up to the surface.

The winters vary greatly in severity with us. During some seasons men can go lightly clad even in January and February, and the cattle hardly suffer at all; during others there will be spells of bitter weather, accompanied by furious blizzards, which render it impossible for days and weeks at a time for men to stir out-of-doors at all, save at the risk of their lives. Then line rider, ranchman, hunter, and teamster alike all have to keep within doors. I have known of several cases of men freezing to death when caught in shelterless places by such a blizzard, a strange fact being that in about half of them the doomed man had evidently gone mad before dying, and had stripped himself of most of his clothes, the body when found being nearly naked. On our ranch we have never had any bad accidents, although every winter some of us get more or less frost-bitten. My last experience in this line was while returning by moonlight from a successful hunt after mountain sheep. The thermometer was 26 below zero, and we had had no food for twelve hours. I got numbed, and before I was aware of it had frozen my face, one foot, both knees, and one hand. Luckily, I reached the ranch before serious damage was done. About once every six or seven years we have a season when these storms follow one another almost without interval throughout the winter months, and then the loss among the stock is frightful. One such winter occurred in 1880-81. This was when there were very few ranchmen in the country. The next severe winter was that of 1886-87, when the rush of incoming herds had overstocked the ranges, and the loss was in consequence fairly appalling.

The snow-fall was unprecedented, both for its depth and for the way it lasted; and it was this, and not the cold, that caused the loss. About the middle of November the storms began. Day after day the snow came down, thawing and then freezing and piling itself higher and higher. By January the drifts had filled the ravines and coulees almost level. The snow lay in great masses on the plateaus and river bottoms; and this lasted until the end of February. The preceding summer we had been visited by a prolonged drought, so that the short, scanty grass was already well cropped down; the snow covered what pasturage there was to the depth of several feet, and the cattle could not get at it at all, and could hardly move round. It was all but impossible to travel on horseback, except on a few well-beaten trails. It was dangerous to attempt to penetrate the Bad Lands, whose shape had been completely altered by the great white mounds and drifts. The starving cattle died by scores of thousands before their helpless owners' eyes. The bulls, the cows who were suckling calves, or who were heavy with calf, the weak cattle that had just been driven up on the trail, and the late calves suffered most; the old range animals did better, and the steers best of all; but the best was bad enough. Even many of the horses died. An outfit near me lost half its saddle-band, the animals having been worked so hard that they were very thin when fall came.

In the thick brush the stock got some shelter and sustenance. They gnawed every twig and bough they could get at. They browsed the bitter sage brush down to where the branches were the thickness of a man's finger. When near a ranch they crowded into the out-houses and sheds to die, and fences had to be built around the windows to keep the wild-eyed, desperate beasts from thrusting their heads through the glass panes. In most cases it was impossible either to drive them to the haystacks or to haul the hay out to them. The deer even were so weak as to be easily run down; and on one or two of the plateaus where there were bands of antelope, these wary creatures grew so numbed and feeble that they could have been slaughtered like rabbits. But the hunters could hardly get out, and could bring home neither hide nor meat, so the game went unharmed. The way in which the cattle got through the winter depended largely on the different localities in which the bands were caught when the first heavy snows came. A group of animals in a bare valley, without underbrush and with steepish sides, would all die, weak and strong alike; they could get no food and no shelter, and so there would not be a hoof left. On the other hand, hundreds wintered on the great thickly wooded bottoms near my ranch house with little more than ordinary loss, though a skinny sorry-looking crew by the time the snow melted. In intermediate places the strong survived and the weak perished.

It would be impossible to imagine any sight more dreary and melancholy than that offered by the ranges when the snow went off in March. The land was a mere barren waste; not a green thing to be seen; the dead grass eaten off till the country looked as if it had been shaved with a razor. Occasionally among the desolate hills a rider would come across a band of gaunt, hollow-flanked cattle feebly cropping the sparse, dry pasturage, too listless to move out of the way; and the blackened carcasses lay in the sheltered spots, some stretched out, others in as natural a position as if the animals had merely lain down to rest. It was small wonder that cheerful stockmen were rare objects that spring. Our only comfort was that we did not, as usual, suffer a heavy loss from weak cattle getting mired down in the springs and mud-holes when the ice broke up--for all the weak animals were dead already. The truth is, ours is a primitive industry, and we suffer the reverses as well as enjoy the successes only known to primitive peoples. A hard winter is to us in the north what a dry summer is to Texas or Australia what seasons of famine once were to all peoples. We still live in an iron age that the old civilized world has long passed by. The men of the border reckon upon stern and unending struggles with their iron-bound surroundings; against the grim harshness of their existence they set the strength and the abounding vitality that come with it. They run risks to life and limb that are unknown to the dwellers in cities; and what the men freely brave, the beasts that they own must also sometimes suffer.

Century Magazine
May, 1888

Sheriff's Work on a Ranch

UP to 1880 the country through which the Little Missouri flows remained as wild and almost as unknown as it was when the old explorers and fur traders crossed it in the early part of the century. It was the last great Indian hunting ground across which Grosventres and Mandans, Sioux and Cheyennes, and even Crows and Rees wandered in chase of game, and where they fought one another and plundered the small parties of white trappers and hunters that occasionally ventured into it. Once or twice generals like Sully and Custer had penetrated it in the course of the long, tedious, and bloody campaigns that finally broke the strength of the northern Horse Indians; indeed, the trail made by Custer's baggage train is to this day one of the well-known landmarks, for the deep ruts worn by the wheels of the heavy wagons are in many places still as distinctly to be seen as ever. In 1883 a regular long-range skirmish took place just south of us between some Cheyennes and some cowboys, with bloodshed on both sides, while about the same time a band of Sioux plundered a party of buffalo hunters of everything they owned, and some Crows who attempted the same feat with another party were driven off with the loss of two of their number. Since then there have been in our neighborhood no stand-up fights or regular raids; but the Indians have at different times proved more or less troublesome, burning the grass, and occasionally killing stock or carrying off horses that have wandered some distance away. They have also themselves suffered somewhat at the hands of white horse-thieves. Bands of them, accompanied by their squaws and children, often come into the ranch country, either to trade or to hunt, and are then, of course, perfectly meek and peaceable. If they stay any time they build themselves quite comfortable tepees (wigwams, as they would be styled in the East), and an Indian camp is a rather interesting, though very dirty, place to visit. On our ranch we get along particularly well with them, as it is a rule that they shall be treated as fairly as if they were whites: we neither wrong them ourselves nor allow others to wrong them. We have always, for example, been as keen in putting down horse-stealing from Indians as from whites--which indicates rather an advanced stage of frontier morality, as theft from the "redskins" or the "Government" is usually held to be a very trivial matter compared with the heinous crime of theft from "citizens."

There is always danger in meeting a band of young bucks in lonely, uninhabited country--those that have barely reached manhood being the most truculent, insolent, and reckless. A man meeting such a party runs great risk of losing his horse, his rifle, and all else he has. This has happened quite frequently during the past few years to hunters or cowboys who have wandered into the debatable territory where our country borders on the Indian lands; and in at least one such instance, that took place two years ago, the unfortunate individual lost his life as well as his belongings. But a frontiersman of any experience can generally "stand off" a small number of such assailants, unless he loses his nerve or is taken by surprise.

My only adventure with Indians was of a very mild kind. It was in the course of a solitary trip to the north and east of our range, to what was then practically unknown country, although now containing many herds of cattle. One morning I had been traveling along the edge of the prairie, and about noon I rode Manitou up a slight rise and came out on a plateau that was perhaps half a mile broad. When near the middle, four or five Indians suddenly came up over the edge, directly in front of me. The second they saw me they whipped their guns out of their slings, started their horses into a run, and came on at full tilt, whooping and brandishing their weapons. I instantly reined up and dismounted. The level plain where we were was of all places the one on which such an onslaught could best be met. In any broken country, or where there is much cover, a white man is at a great disadvantage if pitted against such adepts in the art of hiding as

Indians; while, on the other hand, the latter will rarely rush in on a foe who, even if overpowered in the end, will probably inflict severe loss on his assailants. The fury of an Indian charge, and the whoops by which it is accompanied, often scare horses so as to stampede them; but in Manitou I had perfect trust, and the old fellow stood as steady as a rock, merely cocking his ears and looking round at the noise. I waited until the Indians were a hundred yards off, and then threw up my rifle and drew a bead on the foremost. The effect was like magic. The whole party scattered out as wild pigeons or teal ducks sometimes do when shot at, and doubled back on their tracks, the men bending over alongside their horses. When some distance off they halted and gathered together to consult, and after a minute one came forward alone, ostentatiously dropping his rifle and waving a blanket over his head. When he came to within fifty yards I stopped him, and he pulled out a piece of paper--all Indians, when absent from their reservations, are supposed to carry passes--and called out, "How! Me good Indian!" I answered "How," and assured him most sincerely I was very glad he was a good Indian, but I would not let him come closer; and when his companions began to draw near, I covered him with the rifle and made him move off, which he did with a sudden lapse into the most canonical Anglo-Saxon profanity. I then started to lead my horse out to the prairie; and after hovering round a short time they rode off, while I followed suit, but in the opposite direction. It had all passed too quickly for me to have time to get frightened; but during the rest of my ride I was exceedingly uneasy, and pushed tough, speedy old Manitou along at a rapid rate, keeping well out on the level. However, I never saw the Indians again. They may not have intended any mischief beyond giving me a fright; but I did not dare to let them come to close quarters, for they would have probably taken my horse and rifle, and not impossibly my scalp as well. Towards nightfall I fell in with two old trappers who lived near Killdeer Mountains, and they informed me that my assailants were some young Sioux bucks, at whose hands they themselves had just suffered the loss of a couple of horses.

However, in our own immediate locality, we have had more difficulty with white desperadoes than with the redskins.

At times there has been a good deal of cattle-killing and horse-stealing, and occasionally a murder or two. But as regards the last, a man has very little more to fear in the West than in the East, in spite of all the lawless acts one reads about. Undoubtedly a long-standing quarrel sometimes ends in a shooting-match; and of course savage affrays occasionally take place in the barrooms; in which, be it remarked, that, inasmuch as the men are generally drunk, and, furthermore, as the revolver is at best a rather inaccurate weapon, outsiders are nearly as apt to get hurt as are the participants. But if a man minds his own business and does not go into barrooms, gambling saloons, and the like, he need have no fear of being molested; while a revolver is a mere foolish encumbrance for any but a trained expert, and need never be carried.

Against horse-thieves, cattle-thieves, claim-jumpers, and the like, however, every ranchman has to be on his guard; and armed collisions with these gentry are sometimes inevitable.

The fact of such scoundrels being able to ply their trade with impunity for any length of time can only be understood if the absolute wildness of our land is taken into account.

The country is yet unsurveyed and unmapped; the course of the river itself, as put down on the various Government and railroad maps, is very much a mere piece of guesswork, its bed being in many parts--as by my ranch--ten or fifteen miles, or more, away from where these maps make it.

White hunters came into the land by 1880; but the actual settlement only began in 1882, when the first cattlemen drove in their herds, all of Northern stock, the Texans not passing north of the country around the headwaters of the river until the following year, while until 1885 the territory through which it ran for the final hundred and fifty miles before entering the Big Missouri remained as little known as ever.

Some of us had always been anxious to run down the river in a boat during the time of the spring floods, as we thought we might get good duck and goose shooting, and also kill some beaver, while the trip would, in addition, have all the charm of an exploring expedition. Twice, so far as we knew, the feat had been performed, both times by hunters, and in one instance with very good luck in shooting and trapping. A third attempt, by a couple of men on a raft, made the spring preceding that on which we made ours, had been less successful; for when a score or so of miles below our ranch, a bear killed one of the two adventurers, and the survivor returned.

We could only go down during a freshet; for the Little Missouri, like most plains rivers, is usually either a dwindling streamlet, a mere slender thread of sluggish water, or else a boiling, muddy torrent, running over a bed of shifting quicksand, that neither man nor beast can cross. It rises and falls with extraordinary suddenness and intensity; an instance of which has just occurred as this very page is being written. Last evening, when the moon rose, from the ranch veranda we could see the river-bed almost dry, the stream having shrunk under the drought till it was little but a string of shallow pools, with between them a trickle of water that was not ankle deep, and hardly wet the fetlocks of the saddle-band when driven across it; yet at daybreak this morning, without any rain having fallen near us, but doubtless in consequence of some heavy cloudburst near its head, the swift, swollen current was foaming brim high between the banks, and even the fords were swimming deep for the horses.

Accordingly we had planned to run down the river sometime towards the end of April, taking advantage of a rise; but an accident made us start three or four weeks sooner than we had intended.

In 1886 the ice went out of the upper river very early, during the first part of February; but it at times almost froze over again, the bottom ice did not break up, and a huge gorge, scores of miles in length, formed in and above the bend known as the Ox-bow, a long distance upstream from my ranch. About the middle of March this great October jam came down past us. It moved slowly, its front forming a high, crumbling wall, and creaming over like an immense breaker on the seashore; we could hear the dull roaring and crunching as it plowed down the riverbed long before it came in sight round the bend above us. The ice kept piling and tossing up in the middle, and not only heaped itself above the level of the banks, but also in many places spread out on each side beyond them, grinding against the cotton wood trees in front of the ranch veranda, and at one moment bidding fair to overwhelm the house itself. It did not, however, but moved slowly down past us with that look of vast, resistless, relentless force that any great body of moving ice, as a glacier, or an iceberg, always conveys to the beholder. The heaviest pressure from the water that was backed up behind being, of course, always in the middle, this part kept breaking away, and finally was pushed on clear through, leaving the river so changed that it could hardly be known. On each bank, and for a couple of hundred feet out from it into the stream, was a solid mass of ice, edging the river along most of its length, at least as far as its course lay through lands that we knew; and in the narrow channel between the sheer ice-walls the water ran like a mill-race.

At night the snowy, glittering masses, tossed and heaped up into fantastic forms, shone like crystal in the moonlight; but they soon lost their beauty, becoming fouled and blackened, and at the same time melted and settled down until it was possible to clamber out across the slippery hummocks.

We had brought out a clinker-built boat especially to ferry ourselves over the river when it was high, and were keeping our ponies on the opposite side, where there was a good range shut in by some very broken country that we knew they would not be apt to cross. This boat had already proved very useful and now came in handier than ever, as without it we could take no care of our horses. We kept it on the bank tied to a tree, and every day would carry it or slide it across the hither ice bank, usually with not a little tumbling and scrambling on our part, lower it gently into the swift current, pole it across to the ice on the farther bank, and then drag it over that, repeating the operation when we came back. One day we crossed and walked off about ten miles to a tract of wild and rugged country, cleft in every direction by ravines and cedar canyons, in the deepest of which we had left four deer hanging a fortnight before, as game thus hung up in cold weather keeps indefinitely. The walking was very bad, especially over the clay buttes; for the sun at midday had enough strength to thaw out the soil to the depth of a few inches only, and accordingly the steep hillsides were covered by a crust of slippery mud, with the frozen ground underneath.

It was hard to keep one's footing, and to avoid falling while balancing along the knife-like ridge crests, or while clinging to the stunted sage brush as we went down into the valleys. The deer had been hung in a thicket of dwarfed cedars; but when we reached the place we found nothing save scattered pieces of their carcasses, and the soft mud was tramped all over with round, deeply marked footprints, some of them but a few hours old, showing that the plunderers of our cache were a pair of cougars--"mountain lions," as they are called by the Westerners. They had evidently been at work for some time, and had eaten almost every scrap of flesh; one of the deer had been carried for some distance to the other side of a deep, narrow, chasm-like gully across which the cougar must have leaped with the carcass in its mouth. We followed the fresh trail of the cougars for some time, as it was well marked, especially in the snow still remaining in the bottoms of the deeper ravines; finally it led into a tangle of rocky hills riven by dark cedar-clad gorges, in which we lost it, and we retraced our steps, intending to return on the morrow with a good track hound.

  But we never carried out our intentions, for next morning one of my men who was out before breakfast came back to the house with the startling news that our boat was gone--stolen, for he brought with him the end of the rope with which it had been tied, evidently cut off with a sharp knife; and also a red woolen mitten with a leather palm, which he had picked up on the ice. We had no doubt as to who had stolen it; for whoever had done so had certainly gone down the river in it, and the only other thing in the shape of a boat on the Little Missouri was a small flat-bottomed scow in the possession of three hard characters who lived in a shack or hut some twenty miles above us, and whom we had shrewdly suspected for some time of wishing to get out of the country, as certain of the cattlemen had begun openly to threaten to lynch them. They belonged to a class that always holds sway during the raw youth of a frontier community, and the putting down of which is the first step towards decent government. Dakota, west of the Missouri, has been settled very recently, and every town within it has seen strange antics performed during the past five or six years. Medora, in particular, has had more than its full share of shooting and stabbing affrays, horse-stealing and cattle-killing. But the time for such things was passing away; and during the preceding fall the vigilantes--locally known as "stranglers," in happy allusion to their summary method of doing justice--had made a clean sweep of the cattle country along the Yellowstone and that part of the Big Missouri around and below its mouth. Be it remarked, in passing, that while the outcome of their efforts had been in the main wholesome, yet, as is always the case in an extended raid of vigilantes, several of the sixty-odd victims had been perfectly innocent men who had been hung or shot in company with the real scoundrels, either through carelessness and misapprehension or on account of some personal spite.

The three men we suspected had long been accused justly or unjustly of being implicated both in cattle-killing and in that worst of frontier crimes, horse-stealing: it was only by an accident that they had escaped the clutches of the vigilantes the preceding fall. Their leader was a well-built fellow named Finnigan, who had long red hair reaching to his shoulders, and always wore a broad hat and a fringed buckskin shirt. He was rather a hard case, and had been chief actor in a number of shooting scrapes. The other two were a half-breed, a stout, muscular man, and an old German, whose viciousness was of the weak and shiftless type.

We knew that these three men were becoming uneasy and were anxious to leave the locality; and we also knew that traveling on horseback, in the direction in which they would wish to go, was almost impossible, as the swollen, ice-fringed rivers could not be crossed at all, and the stretches of broken ground would form nearly as impassable barriers. So we had little doubt that it was they who had taken our boat; and as they knew there was then no boat left on the river, and as the country along its banks was entirely impracticable for horses, we felt sure they would be confident that there could be no pursuit.

Accordingly we at once set to work in our turn to build a flat-bottomed scow, wherein to follow them. Our loss was very annoying, and might prove a serious one if we were long prevented from crossing over to look after the saddle-band; but the determining motive in our minds was neither chagrin nor anxiety to recover our property. In any wild country where the power of the law is little felt or heeded, and where everyone has to rely upon himself for protection, men soon get to feel that it is in the highest degree unwise to submit to any wrong without making an immediate and resolute effort to avenge it upon the wrong-doers, at no matter what cost of risk or trouble. To submit tamely and meekly to theft, or to any other injury, is to invite almost certain repetition of the offense, in a place where self-reliant hardihood and the ability to hold one's own under all circumstances rank as the first of virtues.

Two of my cowboys, Seawall and Dow, were originally from Maine, and were mighty men of their hands, skilled in woodcraft and the use of the ax, paddle, and rifle. They set to work with a will, and, as by good luck there were plenty of boards, in two or three days they had turned out a first-class flat-bottom, which was roomy, drew very little water, and was dry as a bone; and though, of course, not a handy craft, was easily enough managed in going downstream. Into this we packed flour, coffee, and bacon enough to last us a fortnight or so, plenty of warm bedding, and the mess kit; and early one cold March morning slid it into the icy current, took our seats, and shoved off down the river.

There could have been no better men for a trip of this kind than my two companions, Seawall and Dow. They were tough, hardy, resolute fellows, quick as cats, strong as bears, and able to travel like bull moose. We felt very little uneasiness as to the result of a fight with the men we were after, provided we had anything like a fair show; moreover, we intended, if possible, to get them at such a disadvantage that there would not be any fight at all. The only risk of any consequence that we ran was that of being ambushed; for the extraordinary formation of the Bad Lands, with the ground cut up into gullies, serried walls, and battlemented hilltops, makes it the country of all others for hiding-places and ambuscades.

For several days before we started the weather had been bitterly cold, as a furious blizzard was blowing; but on the day we left there was a lull, and we hoped a thaw had set in. We all were most warmly and thickly dressed, with woolen socks and underclothes, heavy jackets and trousers, and great fur coats, so that we felt we could bid defiance to the weather. Each carried his rifle, and we had in addition a double-barreled duck gun, for waterfowl and beaver. To manage the boat, we had paddles, heavy oars, and long iron-shod poles, Seawall steering while Dow sat in the bow. Altogether we felt as if we were off on a holiday trip, and set to work to have as good a time as possible.

The river twisted in every direction, winding to and fro across the alluvial valley bottom, only to be brought up by the rows of great barren buttes that bounded it on each edge. It had worn away the sides of these till they towered up as cliffs of clay, marl, or sandstone. Across their white faces the seams of coal drew sharp black bands, and they were elsewhere blotched and varied with brown, yellow, purple, and red. This fantastic coloring, together with the jagged irregularity of their crests, channeled by the weather into spires, buttresses, and battlements, as well as their barrenness and the distinctness with which they loomed up through the high, dry air, gave them a look that was a singular mixture of the terrible and the grotesque. The bottoms were covered thickly with leafless cottonwood trees, or else with withered brown grass and stunted, sprawling sage bushes. At times the cliffs rose close to us on either hand, and again the valley would widen into a sinuous oval a mile or two long, bounded on every side, as far as our eyes could see, by a bluff line without a break, until, as we floated down close to its other end, there would suddenly appear in one corner a cleft through which the stream rushed out. As it grew dusk the shadowy outlines of the buttes lost nothing of their weirdness; the twilight only made their uncouth shapelessness more grim and forbidding. They looked like the crouching figures of great goblin beasts.

> Those two hills on the right
> Crouched like two bulls locked horn in horn in fight—
> While to the left a tall scalped mountain. . . .
> The dying sunset kindled through a cleft;
> The hills, like giants at a hunting, lay
> Chin upon hand, to see the game at bay—

might well have been written after seeing the strange, desolate lands lying in western Dakota.

All through the early part of the day we drifted swiftly down between the heaped-up piles of ice, the cakes and slabs now dirty and unattractive looking. Towards evening, however, there came long reaches where the banks on either side were bare, though even here there would every now and then be necks where the jam had been crowded into too narrow a spot and had risen over the side as it had done upstream, grinding the bark from the big cottonwoods and snapping the smaller ones short off. In such places the ice-walls were sometimes eight or ten feet high, continually undermined by the restless current; and every, now and then overhanging pieces would break off and slide into the stream with a loud sullen splash, like the plunge of some great water beast. Nor did we dare to go in too close to the high cliffs, as boulders and earth masses, freed by the thaw from the grip of the frost, kept rolling and leaping down their faces and forced us to keep a sharp lookout lest our boat should be swamped.

At nightfall we landed, and made our camp on a point of wood-covered land jutting out into the stream. We had seen very little trace of life until late in the day, for the ducks had not yet arrived; but in the afternoon a sharp-tailed prairie fowl flew across stream ahead of the boat, lighting on a low branch by the water's edge. Shooting him, we landed and picked off two others that were perched high up in leafless cottonwoods, plucking the buds. These three birds served us as supper; and shortly afterward, as the cold grew more and more biting, we rolled in under our furs and blankets and were soon asleep.

In the morning it was evident that instead of thawing it had grown decidedly colder. The anchor ice was running thick in the river, and we spent the first hour or two after sunrise in hunting over the frozen swamp bottom for white-tail deer, of which there were many tracks; but we saw nothing. Then we broke camp--a simple operation, as we had no tent, and all we had to do was to cord up our bedding and gather the mess kit and again started downstream. It was colder than before, and for some time we went along in chilly silence, nor was it until midday that the sun warmed our blood in the least. The crooked bed of the current twisted hither and thither, but whichever way it went the icy north wind, blowing stronger all the time, drew steadily up it. One of us remarking that we bade fair to have it in our faces all day, the steersman announced that we couldn't, unless it was the crookedest wind in Dakota; and half an hour afterward we overheard him muttering to himself that it was the crookedest wind in Dakota. We passed a group of tepees on one bottom, marking the deserted winter camp of some Grosventre Indians, which some of my men had visited a few months previously on a trading expedition. It was almost the last point on the river with which we were acquainted. At midday we landed on a sand-bar for lunch; a simple enough meal, the tea being boiled over a fire of driftwood, that also fried the bacon, while the bread only needed to be baked every other day. Then we again shoved off. As the afternoon waned the cold grew still more bitter, and the wind increased, blowing in fitful gusts against us, until it chilled us to the marrow when we sat still. But we rarely did sit still; for even the rapid current was unable to urge the light-draught scow down in the teeth of the strong blasts, and we only got her along by dint of hard work with pole and paddle. Long before the sun went down the ice had begun to freeze on the handles of the poles, and we were not sorry to haul on shore for the night. For supper we again had prairie fowl, having shot four from a great patch of bulberry bushes late in the afternoon. A man doing hard open-air work in cold weather is always hungry for meat.

    During the night the thermometer went down to zero, and in the morning the anchor ice was running so thickly that we did not care to start at once, for it is most difficult to handle a boat in the deep frozen slush. Accordingly we took a couple of hours for a deer hunt, as there were evidently many whitetail on the bottom. We selected one long, isolated patch of tangled trees and brushwood, two of us beating through it while the other watched one end; but almost before we had begun four deer broke out at one side, loped easily off, evidently not much scared, and took refuge in a deep glen or gorge, densely wooded with cedars, that made a blind pocket in the steep side of one of the great plateaus bounding the bottom. After a short consultation, one of our number crept round to the head of the gorge, making a wide detour, and the other two advanced up it on each side, thus completely surrounding the doomed deer. They attempted to break out past the man at the head of the glen, who shot down a couple, a buck and a yearling doe. The other two made their escape by running off over ground so rough that it looked fitter to be crossed by their upland-loving cousins, the black-tail.

This success gladdened our souls, insuring us plenty of fresh meat. We carried pretty much all of both deer back to camp, and, after a hearty breakfast, loaded our scow and started merrily off once more. The cold still continued intense, and as the day wore away we became numbed by it, until at last an incident occurred that set our blood running freely again.

We were, of course, always on the alert, keeping a sharp lookout ahead and around us, and making as little noise as possible. Finally our watchfulness was rewarded, for in the middle of the afternoon of this, the third day we had been gone, as we came round a bend, we saw in front of us the lost boat, together with a scow, moored against the bank, while from among the bushes some little way back the smoke of a camp-fire curled up through the frosty air. We had come on the camp of the thieves. As I glanced at the faces of my two followers I was struck by the grim, eager look in their eyes. Our overcoats were off in a second, and after exchanging a few muttered words, the boat was hastily and silently shoved towards the bank. As soon as it touched the shore ice I leaped out and ran up behind a clump of bushes, so as to cover the landing of the others, who had to make the boat fast. For a moment we felt a thrill of keen excitement, and our veins tingled as we crept cautiously towards the fire, for it seemed likely there would be a brush; but, as it turned out, this was almost the only moment of much interest, for the capture itself was as tame as possible. The men we were after knew they had taken with them the only craft there was on the river, and so felt perfectly secure; accordingly, we took them absolutely by surprise. The only one in camp was the German, whose weapons were on the ground, and who, of course, gave up at once, his two companions being off hunting. We made him safe, delegating one of our number to look after him particularly and see that he made no noise, and then sat down and waited for the others. The camp was under the lee of a cut bank, behind which we crouched, and, after waiting an hour or over, the men we were after came in. We heard them a long way off and made ready, watching them for some minutes as they walked towards us, their rifles on their shoulders and the sunlight glinting on the steel barrels. When they were within twenty yards or so we straightened up from behind the bank, covering them with our cocked rifles, while I shouted to them to hold up their hands--an order that in such a case, in the West, a man is not apt to disregard if he thinks the giver is in earnest. The half-breed obeyed at once, his knees trembling as if they had been made of whalebone. Finnigan hesitated for a second, his eyes fairly wolfish; then, as I walked up within a few paces, covering the center of his chest so as to avoid overshooting, and repeating the command, he saw he had no show, and, with an oath, let his rifle drop and held his hands up beside his head.

It was nearly dusk, so we camped where we were. The first thing to be done was to collect enough wood to enable us to keep a blazing fire all night long. While Seawall and Dow, thoroughly at home in the use of the ax, chopped down dead cottonwood trees and dragged the logs up into a huge pile, I kept guard over the three prisoners, who were huddled into a sullen group some twenty yards off, just the right distance for the buckshot in the double-barrel. Having captured our men, we were in a quandary how to keep them. The cold was so intense that to tie them tightly hand and foot meant, in all likelihood, freezing both hands and feet off during the night; and it was no use tying them at all unless we tied them tightly enough to stop in part the circulation. So nothing was left for us to do but to keep perpetual guard over them. Of course we had carefully searched them, and taken away not only their firearms and knives, but everything else that could possibly be used as a weapon. By this time they were pretty well cowed, as they found out very quickly that they would be well treated so long as they remained quiet, but would receive some rough handling if they attempted any disturbance.

Our next step was to cord their weapons up in some bedding, which we sat on while we took supper. Immediately afterward we made the men take off their boots--an additional safeguard, as it was a cactus country, in which a man could travel barefoot only at the risk of almost certainly laming himself for life--and go to bed, all three lying on one buffalo robe and being covered by another, in the full light of the blazing fire. We determined to watch in succession a half-night apiece, thus each getting a full rest every third night. I took first watch, my two companions, revolver under head, rolling up in their blankets on the side of the fire opposite that on which the three captives lay; while I, in fur cap, gantlets, and overcoat, took my station a little way back in the circle of firelight, in a position in which I could watch my men with the absolute certainty of being able to stop any movement, no matter how sudden. For this night-watching we always used the double-barrel with buckshot, as a rifle is uncertain in the dark; while with a shot-gun at such a distance, and with men lying down, a person who is watchful may be sure that they cannot get up, no matter how quick they are, without being riddled. The only danger lies in the extreme monotony of sitting still in the dark guarding men who make no motion, and the consequent tendency to go to sleep, especially when one has had a hard day's work and is feeling really tired. But neither on the first night nor on any subsequent one did we ever abate a jot of our watchfulness.

Next morning we started down-stream, having a well-laden flotilla, for the men we had caught had a good deal of plunder in their boats, including some saddles, as they evidently intended to get horses as soon as they reached a part of the country where there were any, and where it was possible to travel. Finnigan, who was the ringleader, and the man I was especially after, I kept by my side in our boat, the other two being put in their own scow, heavily laden and rather leaky, and with only one paddle. We kept them just in front of us, a few yards distant, the river being so broad that we knew, and they knew also, any attempt at escape to be perfectly hopeless.

For some miles we went swiftly downstream, the cold being bitter and the slushy anchor ice choking the space between the boats; then the current grew sluggish, eddies forming along the sides. We paddled on until, coming into a long reach where the water was almost backed up, we saw there was a stoppage at the other end. Working up to this, it proved to be a small ice jam, through which we broke our way only to find ourselves, after a few hundred yards, stopped by another. We had hoped that the first was merely a jam of anchor ice, caused by the cold of the last few days; but the jam we had now come to was black and solid, and, running the boats ashore, one of us went off down the bank to find out what the matter was. On climbing a hill that commanded a view of the valley for several miles, the explanation became only too evident--as far as we could see, the river was choked with black ice. The great Ox-bow jam had stopped and we had come down to its tail.

We had nothing to do but to pitch camp, after which we held a consultation. The Little Missouri has much too swift a current--when it has any current at all--with too bad a bottom, for it to be possible to take a boat up-stream; and to walk, of course, meant abandoning almost all we had. Moreover we knew that a thaw would very soon start the jam, and so made up our minds that we had best simply stay where we were, and work downstream as fast as we could, trusting that the spell of bitter weather would pass before our food gave out.

The next eight days were as irksome and monotonous as any I ever spent; there is very little amusement in combining the functions of a sheriff with those of an arctic explorer. The weather kept as cold as ever. During the night the water in the pail would freeze solid. Ice formed all over the river, thickly along the banks; and the clear, frosty sun gave us so little warmth that the melting hardly began before noon. Each day the great jam would settle down-stream a few miles, only to wedge again, leaving behind it several smaller jams, through which we would work our way until we were as close to the tail of the large one as we dared to go.

We had to be additionally cautious on account of being in the Indian country, having worked down past Killdeer Mountains, where some of my cowboys had run across a band of Sioux--said to be Tetons--the year before. Very probably the Indians would not have harmed us anyhow, but as we were hampered by the prisoners, we preferred not meeting them; nor did we, though we saw plenty of fresh signs, and found, to our sorrow, that they had just made a grand hunt all down the river, and had killed or driven off almost every head of game in the country through which we were passing. As our stock of provisions grew scantier and scantier, we tried in vain to eke it out by the chase; for we saw no game. Two of us would go out hunting at a time, while the third kept guard over the prisoners. The latter would be made to sit down together on a blanket at one side of the fire, while the guard for the time being stood or sat some fifteen or twenty yards off. The prisoners being unarmed, and kept close together, there was no possibility of their escaping, and the guard kept at such a distance that they could not overpower him by springing on him, he having a Winchester or the double-barreled shotgun always in his hands cocked and at the ready. So long as we kept wide-awake and watchful, there was not the least danger, as our three men knew us, and understood perfectly that the slightest attempt at a break would result in their being shot down; but, although there was thus no risk, it was harassing, tedious work, and the strain, day in and day out, without any rest or let up, became very tiresome.

   The days were monotonous to a degree. The endless rows of hills bounding the valley, barren and naked, stretched along without a break. When we rounded a bend, it was only to see on each hand the same lines of broken buttes dwindling off into the distance ahead of us as they had dwindled off into the distance behind. If, in hunting, we climbed to their tops, as far as our eyes could scan there was nothing but the great rolling prairie, bleak and lifeless, reaching off to the horizon. We broke camp in the morning, on a point of land covered with brown, leafless, frozen cottonwoods; and in the afternoon we pitched camp on another point in the midst of a grove of the same stiff, dreary trees. The discolored river, whose eddies boiled into yellow foam, flowed always between the same banks of frozen mud or of muddy ice. And what was, from a practical standpoint, even worse, our diet began to be as same as the scenery. Being able to kill nothing, we exhausted all our stock of provisions and got reduced to flour, without yeast or baking-powder; and unleavened bread, made with exceedingly muddy water, is not, as a steady thing, attractive.

Finding that they were well treated and were also watched with the closest vigilance, our prisoners behaved themselves excellently and gave no trouble, though afterward, when out of our hands and shut up in jail, the half-breed got into a stabbing affray. They conversed freely with my two men on a number of indifferent subjects, and after the first evening no allusion was made to the theft, or anything connected with it; so that an outsider overhearing the conversation would never have guessed what our relations to each other really were. Once, and once only, did Finnigan broach the subject. Somebody had been speaking of a man whom we all knew, known as "Calamity," who had been recently taken by the sheriff on a charge of horse stealing. Calamity had escaped once, but was caught at a disadvantage the next time; nevertheless, when summoned to hold his hands up, he refused, and attempted to draw his own revolver, with the result of having two bullets put through him. Finnigan commented on Calamity as a fool for "not knowing when a man had the drop on him"; and then, suddenly turning to me, said, his weather-beaten face flashing darkly: "If I'd had any show at all, you'd have sure had to fight, Mr. Roosevelt; but there wasn't any use making a break when I'd only have got shot myself, with no chance of harming any one else." I laughed and nodded, and the subject was dropped.

Indeed, if the time was tedious to us, it must have seemed never-ending to our prisoners, who had nothing to do but to lie still and read, or chew the bitter cud of their reflections, always conscious that some pair of eyes was watching them every moment, and that at least one loaded rifle was ever ready to be used against them. They had quite a stock of books, some of a rather unexpected kind. Dime novels and the inevitable "History of the James Brothers"--a book that, together with the "Police Gazette," is to be found in the hands of every professed or putative ruffian in the West--seemed perfectly in place; but it was somewhat surprising to find that a large number of more or less drearily silly "society" novels, ranging from Ouida's to those of The Duchess and Augusta J. Evans, were most greedily devoured.

Our commons grew shorter and shorter; and finally even the flour was nearly gone, and we were again forced to think seriously of abandoning the boats. The Indians had driven all the deer out of the country; occasionally we shot prairie fowl, but they were not plentiful. A flock of geese passed us one morning, and afterward an old gander settled down on the river near our camp; but he was over two hundred yards off, and a rifle-shot missed him.

But when the day was darkest the dawn appeared. At last, having worked down some thirty miles at the tail of the ice jam, we struck an outlying cow-camp of the C Diamond (CO) ranch, and knew that our troubles were almost over. There was but one cowboy in it, but we were certain of his cordial help, for in a stock country all make common cause against either horse-thieves or cattle-thieves. He had no wagon, but told us we could get one up at a ranch near Killdeer Mountains, some fifteen miles off, and lent me a pony to go up there and see about it--which I accordingly did, after a sharp preliminary tussle when I came to mount the wiry bronco. When I reached the solitary ranch spoken of, I was able to hire a large prairie schooner and two tough little bronco mares, driven by the settler himself, a rugged old plainsman, who evidently could hardly understand why I took so much bother with the thieves instead of hanging them off-hand. Returning to the river the next day, we walked our men up to the Killdeer Mountains. Seawall and Dow left me the following morning, went back to the boats, and had no further difficulty, for the weather set in very warm, the ice went through with a rush, and they reached Mandan in about ten days, killing four beaver and five geese on the way, but lacking time to stop and do any regular hunting.

Meanwhile I took the three thieves into Dickinson, the nearest town. The going was bad, and the little mares could only drag the wagon at a walk, so, though we drove during the daylight, it took us two days and a night to make the journey. It was a most desolate drive. The prairie had been burned the fall before, and was a mere bleak waste of blackened earth, and a cold, rainy mist lasted throughout the two days. The only variety was where the road crossed the shallow headwaters of Knife and Green rivers. Here the ice was high along the banks, and the wagon had to be taken to pieces to get it over. My three captives were unarmed, but as I was alone with them, except for the driver, of whom I knew nothing, I had to be doubly on my guard, and never let them come close to me. The little mares went so slowly, and the heavy road rendered any hope of escape by flogging up the horses so entirely out of the question, that I soon found the safest plan was to put the prisoners in the wagon and myself walk behind with the inevitable Winchester. Accordingly I trudged steadily the whole time behind the wagon through the ankle-deep mud. It was a gloomy walk. Hour after hour went by always the same, while I plodded along through the dreary landscape--hunger, cold, and fatigue struggling with a sense of dogged, weary resolution. At night, when we put up at the squalid hut of a frontier granger, the only habitation on our road, it was even worse. I did not dare to go to sleep, but making my three men get into the upper bunk, from which they could get out only with difficulty, I sat up with my back against the cabin door and kept watch over them all night long. So, after thirty-six hours' sleeplessness, I was most heartily glad when we at last jolted into the long, straggling main street of Dickinson, and I was able to give my unwilling companions into the hands of the sheriff.

Forest and Stream
April 11, 1889

Editor, Forest and Stream:

    I trust that through your paper some effective protest will be made against allowing Indians from the reservations to use the Yellowstone National Park for a hunting ground. At present bands of roaming savages bid fair to destroy not only all the game, but also all the forests. Every Indian hunting party habitually starts forest fires, which destroy vast quantities of woodland. The forest fires started by these roving bands have caused such devastation as to become a serious menace to all the settled districts. The water supply is a matter of vital consequence to the settlers on the plains near the Rockies, and nothing interferes with it so seriously as the destruction of the woods. It is urgently necessary that these bands be restrained; they should never be allowed off the reservation unless a responsible white man is with them. Capt. Harris has done all he could for the Park. I hope the Indian Department will back him up more efficiently than it has done for the past four years. The Agent of the Bannocks, Shoshones and Crows must be made to understand that these Indians can no longer be allowed to waste and destroy round the Park at their pleasure.

        THEODORE ROOSEVELT
        New York, April 6

St. Nicholas
December, 1889

Buffalo Hunting

WHEN Independence was declared, in 1776, and the United States of America appeared among the powers of the earth, the continent beyond the Alleghanies was one unbroken -wildemess; and the buffaloes, the first animals to vanish when the wilderness is settled, roved up to the crests of the mountains which mark the western boundaries of Pennsylvania, Virginia, and the Carolinas. They were plentiful in what are now the states of Ohio, Kentucky, and Tennessee. But by the beginning of the present century they had been driven beyond the Mississippi; and for the next eighty years they formed one of the most distinctive and characteristic features of existence on the Great Plains. Their numbers were countless — incredible. In vast herds of hundreds of thousands of individuals, they roamed from the Saskatchewan to the Rio Grande and westward to the Rocky Mountains. They furnished all the means of livelihood to the tribes of Horse Indians, and to the curious population of French Metis, or half-breeds, on the Red River, as well as those dauntless and archtypical wanderers, the white hunters and trappers. Their numbers slowly diminished; but the decrease was very gradual until after the Civil War. They were not destroyed by the settlers, but by the railways and by the skin hunters.

After the ending of the Civil War, the work of constructing transcontinental railway lines was pushed forward with the utmost vigor. These supplied cheap and indispensable, but hitherto wholly lacking, means of transportation to the hunters; and at the same time the demand for buffalo robes and hides became very great, while the enormous numbers of the beasts, and the comparative ease with which they were slaughtered, attracted throngs of adventurers. The result was such a slaughter of big game as the world had never before seen; never before were so many large animals of one species destroyed in so short a time.

Several million buffaloes were slain. In fifteen years from the time the destruction fairly began, the great herds were exterminated. In all probability there are not now, all told, a thousand head of wild buffaloes on the American continent; and no herd of a hundred individuals has been in existence since 1884.

The first great break followed the building of the Union Pacific Railway. All the buffaloes of the middle region were then destroyed, and the others were then split into two vast sets of herds, the northern and the southern. The latter were destroyed first, about 1878; the former not until 1883. My own experience with buffaloes was obtained in the latter year, among small bands and scattered individuals, near my ranch on the Little Missouri; I have related it elsewhere. But two of my relatives were more fortunate, and took part in the chase of these lordly beasts when the herds still darkened the prairie as far as the eye could see.

During the first two months of 1877, my brother Elliott, then a lad not seventeen years old, made a buffalo-hunt toward the edge of the Staked Plains in northern Texas. He was thus in at the death of the southern herds, for all, save a few scattering bands, were destroyed within two years of this time.

My brother was with my cousin, John Roosevelt, and they went out on the range with six other adventurers—a German-American, a Scotchman who had been in the Confederate cavalry and afterward in Maximilian's Mexican bodyguard, and four Irishmen. It was a party of just such young men as frequently drift to the frontier. All were short of cash, and all were hardy, vigorous fellows eager for excitement and adventure. My brother was much the youngest of the party, and the least experienced; but he was well-grown, strong and healthy, and very fond of boxing, wrestling, running, riding, and shooting; moreover, he had served an apprenticeship in hunting deer and turkeys. Their mess-kit, ammunition, bedding, and provisions were carried in two prairie wagons, each drawn by four horses. In addition to the teams they had six saddle-animals—all of them shaggy, unkempt mustangs. Three or four dogs, setters and half-bred greyhounds, trotted along behind the wagons. Each man took his turn for two days as teamster and cook; and there were always two with the wagons, or camp, as the case might be, while the other six were off hunting, usually in couples. The expedition was undertaken partly for sport and partly with the hope of profit; for, after purchasing the horses and wagons, none of the party had any money left, and they were forced to rely upon selling skins and hides and, when near the forts, meat.

They started on January 2d, and shaped their course for the headwaters of the Salt Fork of the Brazos, the center of abundance for the great buffalo herds. During the first few days they were in the outskirts of the settled country, and shot only small game—quail and prairie fowl; then they began to kill turkey, deer, and antelope. These they "swapped" for flour and feed at the ranches or squalid, straggling frontier towns. On several occasions the hunters were lost, spending the night out in the open, or sleeping at a ranch if one was found. Both towns and ranches were filled with rough customers; all of my brother's companions were muscular, hot-headed fellows; and as a consequence they were involved in several savage "free fights," in which, fortunately, nobody was seriously hurt. My brother kept a very brief diary, the entries being fairly startling from their conciseness. A number of times, the mention of their arrival, either at a halting-place, a little village, or a rival buffalo-camp is followed by the laconic remark, "big fight," or "big row"; but once they evidently concluded discretion to be the better part of valor, the entry for January 20th being, "On the road—passed through Belknap—too lively, so kept on to the Brazos—very late." The buffalo-camps in particular were very jealous of one another, each party regarding itself as having exclusive right to the range it was the first to find; and on several occasions this feeling came near involving my brother and his companions in serious trouble.

While slowly driving the heavy wagons to the hunting-grounds they suffered the usual hardships of plains travel. The weather, as in most Texas winters, alternated between the extremes of heat and cold. There had been little rain; in consequence water was scarce. Twice they were forced to cross wild, barren wastes, where the pools had dried up, and they suffered terribly from thirst. On the first occasion the horses were in good condition, and they traveled steadily, with only occasional short halts, for over thirty-six hours, by which time they were across the waterless country. The journal reads: "January 29th—Big hunt — no water and we left Quinn's blockhouse this morning 3 a. m. — on the go all night — hot. January 28th. — No water — hot — at seven we struck water and by eight Stinking Creek — grand 'hurrah.'" On the second occasion, the horses were weak and traveled slowly, so the party went forty-eight hours without drinking. "February 19th. — Pulled on twenty-one miles — trail bad — freezing night, no water, and wolves after our fresh meat. 20th. — Made nineteen miles over prairie; again only mud, no water, freezing hard — frightful thirst. 21st. — Thirty miles to Clear Fork, fresh water." These entries were hurriedly jotted down at the time, by a boy who deemed it unmanly to make any especial note of hardship or suffering; but every plainsman will understand the real agony implied in working hard for two nights, one day, and portions of two others, without water, even in cool weather. During the last few miles the staggering horses were only just able to drag the lightly loaded wagon, — for they had but one with them at the time, — while the men plodded along in sullen silence, their mouths so parched that they could hardly utter a word. My own hunting and ranching were done in the north where there is more water; so I have never had a similar experience. Once I took a team in thirty-six hours across a country where there was no water; but by good luck it rained heavily in the night, so that the horses had plenty of wet grass, and I caught the rain in my slicker, and so had enough water for myself. Personally, I have but once been as long as twenty-six hours without water.

The party pitched their permanent camp in a canon of the Brazos known as Canon Blanco. The last few days of their journey they traveled beside the river through a veritable hunter's paradise. The drought had forced all the animals to come to the larger watercourses, and the country was literally swarming with game. Every day, and all day long, the wagons traveled through the herds of antelopes that grazed on every side, while, whenever they approached the canyon brink, bands of deer started from the timber that fringed the river's course; often, even the deer wandered out on the prairie with the antelopes. Nor was the game shy; for the hunters, both red and white, followed only the buffaloes until the huge, shaggy herds were destroyed, and the smaller beasts were in consequence but little molested.

Once my brother shot five antelopes from a single stand, when the party were short of fresh venison; he was out of sight and to leeward, and the antelopes seemed confused rather than alarmed at the rifle-reports and the fall of their companions. As was to be expected where game was so plenty, wolves and coyotes also abounded. At night they surrounded the camp, wailing and howling in a kind of shrieking chorus throughout the hours of darkness; one night they came up so close that the frightened horses had to be hobbled and guarded. On another occasion a large wolf actually crept into camp, where he was seized by the dogs, and the yelling, writhing knot of combatants rolled over one of the sleepers; finally, the long-toothed prowler managed to shake himself loose, and vanished in the gloom. One evening they were almost as much startled by a visit of a different kind. They were just finishing supper when an Indian stalked suddenly and silently out of the surrounding darkness, squatted down in the circle of firelight, remarked gravely, "Me Tonk," and began helping himself from the stew. He belonged to the friendly tribe of Tonkaways, so his hosts speedily recovered their equanimity; as for him, he had never lost his, and he sat eating by the fire until there was literally nothing left to eat. The panic caused by his appearance was natural; for at that time the Comanches were a scourge to the buffalo-hunters, ambushing them and raiding their camps; and several bloody fights had taken place.

Their camp had been pitched near a deep pool or waterhole. On both sides the bluffs rose like walls, and where they had crumbled and lost their sheerness, the vast buffalo herds, passing and repassing for countless generations, had worn furrowed trails so deep that the backs of the beasts were but little above the surrounding soil. In the bottom, and in places along the crests of the cliffs that hemmed in the canyon-like valley, there were groves of tangled trees, tenanted by great flocks of wild turkeys. Once my brother made two really remarkable shots at a pair of these great birds. It was at dusk, and they were flying directly overhead from one cliff to the other. He had in his hand a thirty-eight-caliber Ballard rifle, and, as the gobblers winged their way heavily by, he brought them both down with two successive bullets. This was of course mainly a piece of mere luck; but it meant good shooting, too. The Ballard was a very accurate, handy little weapon; it belonged to me, and was the first rifle I ever owned or used. With it I had once killed a deer, the only specimen of large game I had then shot; and I presented the rifle to my brother when he went to Texas. In our happy ignorance we deemed it quite good enough for buffalo or anything else; but out on the plains my brother soon found himself forced to procure a heavier and more deadly weapon.

When camp was pitched the horses were turned loose to graze and refresh themselves after their trying journey, during which they had lost flesh woefully. They were watched and tended by the two men who were always left in camp, and, save on rare occasions, were only used to haul in the buffalo-hides. The camp-guards for the time being acted as cooks; and, though coffee and flour both ran short and finally gave out, fresh meat of every kind was abundant. The camp was never without buffalo-beef, deer and antelope venison, wild turkeys, prairie-chickens, quails, ducks, and rabbits. The birds were simply "potted," as occasion required; when the quarry was deer or antelope, the hunters took the dogs with them to run down the wounded animals. But almost the entire attention of the hunters was given to the buffalo. After an evening spent in lounging round the camp-fire, and a sound night's sleep, wrapped in robes and blankets, they would get up before daybreak, snatch a hurried breakfast, and start off in couples through the chilly dawn. The great beasts were very plentiful; in the first day's hunt, twenty were slain; but the herds were restless and ever on the move. Sometimes they would be seen right by the camp, and again it would need an all-day's tramp to find them. There was no difficulty in spying them — the chief trouble with forest game; for on the prairie a buffalo makes no effort to hide, and its black, shaggy bulk looms up as far as the eye can see. Sometimes they were found in small parties of three or four individuals, sometimes in bands of about two hundred, and again in great herds of many thousand; and solitary old bulls, expelled from the herds, were common. If on broken land, among hills and ravines, there was not much dif-

Buffalo Hunting / 131

ficulty in approaching from the leeward; for, though the sense of smell in the buffalo is very acute, they do not see well at a distance through their overhanging frontlets of coarse and matted hair. If, as was generally the case, they were out on the open, rolling prairie, the stalking was far more difficult. Every hollow, every earth hummock and sagebush had to be used as cover. The hunter wriggled through the grass flat on his face, pushing himself along for perhaps a quarter of a mile by his toes and fingers, heedless of the spiny cactus. When near enough to the huge, unconscious quarry the hunter began firing, still keeping himself carefully concealed. If the smoke was blown away by the wind, and if the buffaloes caught no glimpse of the assailant, they would often stand motionless and stupid until many of their number had been slain; the hunter being careful not to fire too high, aiming just behind the shoulder, about a third of the way up the body, that his bullet might go through the lungs. Sometimes, even after they saw the man, they would act as if confused and panic-struck, huddling up together and staring at the smoke puffs — but generally they were off at a lumbering gallop as soon as they had an idea of the point of danger. When once started, they ran for many miles before halting, and their pursuit on foot was extremely laborious.

    One morning my cousin and brother had been left in camp as guards. They were sitting, idly warming themselves in the first sunbeams, when their attention was sharply drawn to four buffaloes who were coming to the pool to drink. The beasts came down a game trail, a deep rut in the bluff, fronting where they were sitting, and they did not dare stir for fear of being discovered. The buffaloes walked into the pool, and, after drinking their fill, stood for some time with the water running out of their mouths, idly lashing their sides with their short tails, enjoying the bright warmth of the early sunshine; then, with much splashing and the gurgling of soft mud, they left the pool and clambered up the bluff with unwieldy agility. As soon as they turned, my brother and cousin ran for their rifles; but before they got back the buffaloes had crossed the bluff crest. Climbing after them, the two hunters found, when they reached the summit, that their game, instead of halting, had struck straight off across the prairie at a slow lope, doubtless intending to rejoin the herd they had left. After a moment's consultation, the men went in pursuit, excitement overcoming their knowledge that they ought not, by rights, to leave the camp. They struck a steady trot, following the animals by sight until they passed over a knoll, and then trailing them. Where the grass was long, as it was for the first four or five miles, this was a work of no difficulty, and they did not break their gait, only glancing now and then at the trail. As the sun rose and the day became warm, their breathing grew quicker; and the sweat rolled off their faces as they ran across the rough prairie sward, up and down the long inclines, now and then shifting their heavy rifles from one shoulder to the other. But they were in good training, and they did not have to halt. At last they reached stretches of bare ground, sun-baked and grassless, where the trail grew dim; and here they had to go very slowly, carefully examining the faint dents and marks made in the soil by the heavy hoofs, and unraveling the trail from the mass of old foot-marks. It was tedious work, but it enabled them to completely recover their breath by the time that they again struck the grass land; and but a few hundred yards from its edge, in a slight hollow, they saw the four buffaloes just entering a herd of fifty or sixty that were scattered out grazing. The herd paid no attention to the newcomers, and these immediately began to feed greedily. After a whispered consultation, the two hunters crept back, and made a long circle that brought them well to leeward of the herd, in line with a slight rise in the ground. They then crawled up to this rise and, peering through the tufts of tall, rank grass, saw the unconscious beasts a hundred and twenty-five or fifty yards away. They fired together, each mortally wounding his animal, and then, rushing in as the herd halted in confusion, and following them as they ran, impeded by numbers, hurry, and panic, they eventually got three more.

  On another occasion, the same two hunters nearly met with a frightful death, being overtaken by a vast herd of stampeded buffaloes. All animals that go in herds are subject to these instantaneous attacks of uncontrollable terror, under the influence of which they become perfectly mad, and rush headlong in dense masses on any form of death. Horses, and more especially cattle, often suffer from stampedes; it is a danger against which the cowboys are compelled to be perpetually on guard. A band of stampeded horses, sweeping in mad terror up a valley, will dash against a rock or tree with such violence as to leave several dead animals at its base, while the survivors race on without halting; they will overturn and destroy tents and wagons, and a man on foot caught in the rush has but a small chance for his life. A buffalo stampede is much worse — or rather was much worse, in the old days — because of the great weight and immense numbers of the beasts, who, in a fury of heedless terror, plunged over cliffs and into rivers, and bore down whatever was in their path. On the occasion in question, my brother and cousin were on their way homeward. They were just mounting one of the long, low swells into which the prairie was broken when they heard a low, muttering, rumbling noise, like far-off thunder. It grew steadily louder, and, not knowing what it meant, they hurried forward to the top of the rise. As they reached it, they stopped short in terror and amazement, for before them the whole prairie was black with madly rushing buffaloes.

Afterward they learned that another couple of hunters, four or five miles off, had fired into and stampeded a large herd. This herd, in its rush, gathered others, all thundering along together in uncontrollable and increasing panic.

The surprised hunters were far away from any broken ground or other place of refuge; while the vast herd of huge, plunging, maddened beasts was charging straight down on them not a quarter of a mile distant. Down they came ! — thousands upon thousands, their front extending a mile in breadth, while the earth shook beneath their thunderous gallop, and as they came closer, their shaggy frontlets loomed dimly through the columns of dust thrown up from the dry soil. The two hunters knew that their only hope for life was to split the herd, which, though it had so broad a front, was not very deep. If they failed they would inevitably be trampled to death.

Waiting until the beasts were in close range, they opened a rapid fire from their heavy breech-loading rifles, yelling at the top of their voices. For a moment the result seemed doubtful. The line thundered steadily down on them; from their foes in front, strove desperately to edge away from the dangerous neighborhood; the shouts and shots were redoubled; the hunters were almost choked by the cloud of dust through which they could see the stream of dark huge bodies passing within rifle-length on either side; and in a moment the peril was over, and the two men were left alone on the plain, unharmed, though with their nerves terribly shaken. The herd careered on toward the horizon, save five individuals who had been killed or disabled by the shots.

On another occasion, when my brother was out with one of his Irish friends, they fired at a small herd containing an old bull; the bull charged the smoke, and the whole herd followed him. Probably they were simply stampeded, and had no hostile intention; at any rate, after the death of their leader, they rushed by without doing any damage.

But buffaloes sometimes charged with the utmost determination, and were then dangerous antagonists. My cousin, a very hardy and resolute hunter, had a narrow escape from a wounded cow which he followed up a steep bluff or sand cliff. Just as he reached the summit, he was charged, and was only saved by the sudden appearance of his dog, which distracted the cow's attention. He thus escaped with only a tumble and a few bruises.

My brother also came in for a charge, while killing the biggest bull that was slain by any of the party. He was out alone, and saw a small herd of cows and calves at some distance, with a huge bull among them, towering above them like a giant. There was no break in the ground nor any tree or bush near them, but by making a half-circle, my brother managed to creep up against the wind behind a slight roll in the prairie surface, until he was within seventy-five yards of the grazing and unconscious beasts. There were some cows and calves between him and the bull, and he had to wait some moments before they shifted positions as the herd grazed onward and gave him a fair shot; in the interval they had moved so far forward that he was in plain view. His first bullet struck just behind the shoulder; the herd started and looked around but the bull merely lifted his head and took a step forward, his tail curled up over his back. The next bullet likewise struck fair, nearly in the same place; telling with a loud "pack!"

against the thick hide, and making the dust fly up from the matted hair. Instantly the great bull wheeled and charged in headlong anger, while the herd fled in the opposite direction. On the bare prairie, with no spot of refuge, it was useless to try and escape, and the hunter, with reloaded rifle, waited until the bull was not far off, then drew up his weapon and fired. Either he was nervous or the bull at the moment bounded over some obstacle, for the ball went a little wild; nevertheless, by good luck, it broke a fore leg, and the great beast came crashing to the earth, and was slain before it could struggle to its feet.

Two days after this event, a war party of Comanches swept down along the river. They "jumped" a neighboring camp, killing one man and wounding two more, and at the same time ran off all but three of the horses belonging to our eight adventurers. With the remaining three horses and one wagon they set out homeward. The march was hard and tedious; they lost their way and were in jeopardy from quicksands and cloudbursts; they suffered from thirst and cold, their shoes gave out and their feet were lamed by cactus spines. At last they reached Fort Sniffin in safety, and great was their ravenous rejoicing when they procured some bread — for during the final fortnight of the hunt they had been without flour or vegetables of any kind, or even coffee, and had subsisted on fresh meat "straight." Nevertheless, it was a very healthy, as well as a very pleasant and exciting experience; and I doubt if any of those who took part in it will ever forget their great buffalo-hunt on the Brazos.

Century Magazine
September, 1892

An Elk-Hunt at Two-Ocean Pass

ONE fall with my ranch-partner, Ferguson, I made an elk-hunt in northwestern Wyoming among the Shoshone Mountains, where they join the Hoodoo and Absoraka ranges. There is no more beautiful game-country in the United States. It is a park-land, where glades, meadows, and high mountain pastures break the evergreen forest: a forest which is open compared to the tangled density of the woodland farther north. It is a high, cold region of many lakes and clear, rushing streams. The steep mountains are generally of the rounded form so often seen in the ranges of the cordilleras of the United States; but the Koodoos, or Goblins, are carved in fantastic and extraordinary shapes; while the Tetons, a group of isolated rock peaks, show a striking boldness in their lofty outlines.

This was one of the pleasantest hunts I ever made. As always in the mountains, save where the country is so rough and so densely wooded that one must go afoot, we had a pack-train; and we took a more complete outfit than we had ever before taken on such a hunt, and so traveled in much comfort. Usually, when in the mountains, I have merely had one companion, or at most two, and two or three pack-ponies; each of us doing his share of the packing, cooking, fetching water, and pitching the small square of canvas which served as tent. In itself packing is both an art and a mystery, and a skilful professional packer, versed in the intricacies of the diamond packs with a speed which no non-professional can hope to rival, and fixes the side packs and top packs with such scientific nicety, and adjusts the doubles and turns of the lash-rope so accurately, that everything stays in place under any but the most adverse conditions. Of course, like most hunters, I myself can in case of need throw the diamond hitch, after a fashion, and pack on either the off or near side. Indeed, unless a man can pack, it is not possible to make a really hard hunt in the mountains, if alone, or with only a single companion. The mere fair-weather hunter, who trusts entirely to the exertions of others, and does nothing more than ride or walk about under favorable circumstances, and shoot at what somebody else shows him, is a hunter in name only. Whoever would really deserve the title must be able at a pinch to shift for himself, to grapple with the difficulties and hardships of wilderness life unaided, and not only to hunt, but at times to travel for days, whether on foot or on horseback, alone. However, after one has passed one's novitiate, it is pleasant to be comfortable when the comfort does not interfere with the sport; and although a man sometimes likes to hunt alone, yet often it is well to be with some old mountain hunter, a master of woodcraft, who is a first-rate hand at finding game, creeping upon it, and tracking it when wounded. With such a companion one gets much more game, and learns many things by observation instead of by painful experience.

On this trip we had with us two hunters, Tazewell Woody and Elwood Hofer, a packer who acted as cook, and a boy to herd the horses. Of the latter there were twenty; six saddle-animals and fourteen for the packs, two or three being spare horses, to be used later in carrying the elk-antlers, sheephorns, and other trophies. Like most hunters' pack-animals, they were either half broken, or else broken down; tough, unkempt, jaded-looking beasts of every color -- sorrel, buckskin, pinto, white, bay, roan. After the day's work was over, they were turned loose to shift for themselves; and about once a week they strayed, and all hands had to spend the better part of the day hunting for them. The worst ones for straying, curiously enough, were three broken-down old "bearbaits," which went by themselves, as is generally the case with the cast-off horses of a herd. There were two sleeping-tents, another for the provisions, in which we ate during bad weather, and a canvas tepee, which was put up with lodge-poles, Indian fashion, like a wigwam. A tepee is more difficult to put up than an ordinary tent; but it is very convenient when there is rain or snow. A small fire kindled in the middle keeps it warm, the smoke escaping through the open top; that is, when it escapes at all. Strings are passed from one pole to another, on which to hang wet clothes and shoes, and the beds are made round the edges. As an offset to the warmth and shelter, the smoke often renders it impossible even to sit upright. We had a very good camp-kit, including plenty of cooking and eating utensils; and among our provisions were some canned goods and sweetmeats, to give a relish to our meals of meat and bread. We had fur coats and warm clothes, which are chiefly needed at night, and plenty of bedding, including water-proof canvas sheeting and two caribou-hide sleeping-bags, procured from the survivors of a party of arctic explorers. Except on rainy days I used my buckskin hunting-shirt or tunic; in dry weather I deem it, because of its color, texture, and durability, the best possible garb for the still-hunter, especially in the woods.

    Starting a day's journey south of Heart Lake, we traveled and hunted on the eastern edge of the great basin, wooded and mountainous, wherein rise the headwaters of the mighty Snake River. There was not so much as a spotted line, that series of blazes made with the ax, man's first highway through the hoary forest, but this we did not mind, as for most of the distance we followed well-worn elk-trails. The train traveled in Indian file. At the head, to pick the path, rode tall, silent old Woody, a true type of the fast-vanishing race of game-hunters and Indian-fighters, a man who had been one of the California forty-niners, and who ever since had lived the restless, reckless life of the wilderness. Then came Ferguson and I; then the pack-animals, strung out in line; while from the rear rose the varied oaths of our three companions, whose miserable duty it was to urge forward the beasts of burden.

    It is heart-breaking work to drive a pack-train through thick timber and over mountains, where there is either a dim trail or none. The animals have a perverse faculty for choosing the wrong turn at critical moments, and they are continually scraping under branches and squeezing between tree-trunks, to the jeopardy or destruction of their burdens. After having been laboriously driven up a very steep incline, at the cost of severe exertion both to them and to the men, the foolish creatures turn and run down to the bottom, so that all the work has to be done over again. Some travel too slow, others travel too fast; yet one cannot but admire the toughness of the animals, and the sure-footedness with which they pick their way along the sheer mountainsides, or among boulders and over fallen logs.

As our way was so rough, we found that we had to halt at least once every hour to fix the packs. Moreover, we at the head of the column were continually being appealed to for help by the unfortunates in the rear. First it would be "that white-eyed cayuse; one side of its pack's down!" then we would be notified that the saddle-blanket of the "lop-eared Indian buckskin" had slipped back; then a shout "Look out for the pinto!" would be followed by that pleasing beast's appearance, bucking and squealing, smashing dead timber, and scattering its load to the four winds. It was no easy task to get the horses across some of the boggy places without miring, or to force them through the denser portions of the forest, where there was much down timber. Riding with a pack-train, day in and day out, becomes both monotonous and irritating, unless one is upheld by the hope of a game-country ahead, or by the delight of exploration of the unknown. Yet when buoyed by such a hope, there is pleasure in taking a train across so beautiful and wild a country as that which lay on the threshold of our hunting-grounds in the Shoshones. We went over mountain passes, with ranges of scalped peaks on each hand; we skirted the edges of lovely lakes, and of streams with boulder-strewn beds; we plunged into depths of somber woodland, broken by wet prairies. It was a picturesque sight to see the loaded pack-train stringing across one of these high mountain meadows, the motley-colored line of ponies winding round the marshy spots through the bright green grass, while beyond rose the dark line of frowning forest, with lofty peaks towering in the background. Some of the meadows were beautiful with many flowers -- goldenrod, purple aster, bluebells, white immortelles, and here and there masses of blood-red Indian pinks. In the park-country, on the edges of the evergreen forest, were groves of delicate quaking-aspen, the trees often growing to a considerable height; their tremulous leaves were already changing to bright green and yellow, occasionally with a reddish blush. In the Rocky Mountains the aspens are almost the only deciduous trees, their foliage offering a pleasant relief to the eye after the monotony of the unending pine and spruce woods, which afford so striking a contrast to the hard-wood forest east of the Mississippi.

For two days our journey was uneventful, save that we came on the camp of a squaw-man, one Beaver Dick, an old mountain hunter, living in a skin tepee, where dwelt his comely Indian wife and half-breed children. He had quite a herd of horses, many of them mares and colts; they had evidently been well treated, and came up to us fearlessly.

The morning of the third day of our journey was gray and lowering. Gusts of rain blew in my face as I rode at the head of the train. It still lacked an hour of noon, as we were plodding up a valley, beside a rapid brook running through narrow willow-flats, with the dark forest crowding down on each hand from the low foot-hills of the mountains. Suddenly the call of a bull elk came echoing down through the wet woodland on our right, beyond the brook, seemingly less than half a mile off, and was answered by a faint, far-off call from a rival on the mountain beyond. Instantly halting the train, Woody and I slipped off our horses, crossed the brook, and started to still-hunt the first bull.

In this place the forest was composed of the western tamarack; the large, tall trees stood well apart, and there was much down timber, but the ground was covered with deep, wet moss, over which we trod silently. The elk was traveling up-wind, but slowly, stopping continually to paw the ground and to thrash the bushes with his antlers. He was very noisy, challenging every minute or two, being doubtless much excited by the neighborhood of his rival on the mountain. We followed, Woody leading, guided by the incessant calling.

It was very exciting as we crept toward the great bull, and the challenge sounded nearer and nearer. While we were still at some distance the pealing notes were like those of a bugle, delivered in two bars, first rising, then abruptly falling; as we drew nearer they took on a harsh, squealing sound. Each call made our veins thrill; it sounded like the cry of some huge beast of prey. At last we heard the roar of the challenge not eighty yards off. Stealing forward three or four rods, I saw the tips of the horns through a mass of dead timber and young growth, and slipped to one side to get a clean shot. Seeing us, but not making out what we were, and full of fierce and insolent excitement, the wapiti bull stepped boldly toward us with a stately, swinging gait. Then he stood motionless, facing us, barely fifty yards away, his handsome twelve-tined antlers tossed aloft, as he held his head with the lordly grace of his kind. I fired into his chest, and as he turned I raced forward and shot him in the flank; but the second bullet was not needed, for the first wound was mortal, and he fell before going fifty yards.

The dead elk lay among the young evergreens. The huge, shapely body was set on legs that were as strong as steel rods, and yet slender, clean, and smooth; they were in color a beautiful dark brown, contrasting well with the yellowish of the body. The neck and throat were garnished with a mane of long hair; the symmetry of the great horns set off the fine, delicate lines of the noble head. He had been wallowing, as elk are fond of doing, and the dried mud clung in patches to his flank; a stab in the haunch showed that he had been overcome in battle by some master bull, who had turned him out of the herd.

We cut off the head, and bore it down to the train. The horses crowded together, snorting, with their ears pricked forward, as they smelled the blood. We also took the loins with us, as we were out of meat, though bull elk in the rutting season is not very good. The rain had changed to a steady downpour when we again got under way. Two or three miles further we pitched camp in a clump of pines on a hillock in the bottom of the valley, starting hot fires of pitchy stumps before the tents, to dry our wet things.

Next day opened with fog and cold rain. The drenched pack-animals, when driven into camp, stood mopingly, with drooping heads and arched backs; they groaned and grunted as the loads were placed on their backs and the cinches tightened, the packers bracing one foot against the pack to get a purchase as they hauled in on the lash-rope. A stormy morning is a trial to temper: the packs are wet and heavy, and the cold makes the work even more than usually hard on the hands. By ten we broke camp. It needs between two and three hours to break camp and to get such a train properly packed; once started, our day's journey was from six to eight hours long, making no halt. We started up a steep, pine-clad mountain- side, broken by cliffs. My hunting-shoes, though comfortable, were old and thin, and let the water through like a sieve. On the top of the first plateau, where black-spruce groves were strewn across the grassy surface, we saw a band of elk, cows and calves, trotting off through the rain. Then we plunged down into a deep valley, and, crossing it, a hard climb took us to the top of a great bare table-land, bleak and wind-swept. We passed little alpine lakes, fringed with scattering dwarf evergreens. Snow lay in drifts on the north sides of the gullies; a cutting wind blew the icy rain in our faces. For two or three hours we traveled toward the farther edge of the table-land. In one place a spike-bull elk stood half a mile off in the open ; he traveled to and fro, watching us.

  As we neared the edge the storm lulled, and pale, watery sunshine gleamed through the rifts in the low-scudding clouds. At last our horses stood on the brink of a bold cliff. Deep down beneath our feet lay the wild and lonely valley of Two-Ocean Pass, walled in on each hand by rugged mountain-chains, their flanks scarred and gashed by precipice and chasm. Beyond, in a wilderness of jagged and barren peaks, stretched the Shoshones. At the middle point of the pass two streams welled down from each side. At first each flowed in but one bed, but soon divided into two; each of the twin branches then joined the like branch of the brook opposite, and swept one to the east and one to the west, on their long journey to the two great oceans. They ran as rapid brooks, through wet meadows and willow-flats, the eastern to the Yellowstone, the western to the Snake. The dark pine forests swept down from the flanks and lower ridges of the mountains to the edges of the marshy valley. Above them jutted gray rock peaks, snow-drifts lying in the rents that seamed their northern faces. Far below us, from a great basin at the foot of the cliff, filled with the pine forest, rose the musical challenge of a bull elk; and we saw a band of cows and calves looking like mice as they ran among the trees.

  It was getting late, and after some search we failed to find any trail leading down; so at last we plunged over the brink at a venture. It was very rough scrambling, dropping from bench to bench, and in places it was not only difficult but dangerous for the loaded pack-animals. Here and there we were helped by well-beaten elk-trails, which we could follow for several hundred yards at a time. On one narrow pine-clad ledge we met a spike-bull face to face, and in scrambling down a very steep, bare, rock-strewn shoulder the loose stones started by the horses' hoofs, bounding in great leaps to the forest below, dislodged two cows.

    As evening fell, we reached the bottom, and pitched camp in a beautiful point of open pine forest thrust out into the meadow. There we found good shelter and plenty of wood, water, and grass; we built a huge fire and put up our tents, scattering them in likely places among the pines, which grew far apart and without undergrowth. We dried our steaming clothes, and ate a hearty supper of elk-meat; then we turned into our beds, warm and dry, and slept soundly under the canvas, while all night long the storm roared without. Next morning it still stormed fitfully; the high peaks and ridges round about were all capped with snow. Woody and I started on foot for an all-day tramp; the amount of game seen the day before showed that we were in a good elk-country, where the elk had been so little disturbed that they were traveling, feeding, and whistling in daylight. For three hours we walked across the forest-clad spurs of the foot-hills. We roused a small band of elk in thick timber; but they rushed off before we saw them, with much smashing of dead branches. Then we climbed to the summit of the range. The wind was light and baffling; it blew from all points, veering every few minutes. There were occasional rain-squalls; our feet and legs were well soaked; and we became chilled through whenever we sat down to listen. We caught a glimpse of a big bull feeding up-hill, and followed him; it needed smart running to overtake him, for an elk, even while feeding, has a ground-covering gait. Finally we got within a hundred and twenty-five yards, but in very thick timber, and all I could see plainly was the hip and the after part of the flank. I waited for a chance at the shoulder, but the bull got my wind and was off before I could pull trigger. It was just one of those occasions when there are two courses to pursue, neither very good, and when one is apt to regret whichever decision is made.

At noon we came to the edge of a deep and wide gorge, and sat down shivering to await what might turn up, our fingers numb, and our wet feet icy. Suddenly the love-challenge of an elk came pealing across the gorge, through the fine, cold rain, from the heart of the forest opposite. An hour's stiff climb, down and up, brought us nearly to him; but the wind forced us to advance from below through a series of open glades. He was lying on a point of the cliff-shoulder, surrounded by his cows: and he saw us, and made off. An hour afterward, as we were trudging up a steep hillside dotted with groves of fir and spruce, a young bull of ten points, roused from his day-bed by our approach, galloped across us some sixty yards off. We were in need of better venison than can be furnished by an old rutting bull, so I instantly took a shot at the fat and tender young ten- pointer. I aimed well ahead, and pulled trigger just as he came to a small gully, and he fell into it in a heap with a resounding crash. On the way back that afternoon I shot off the heads of two blue grouse, as they perched in the pines.

That evening the storm broke, and the weather became clear and very cold, so that the snow made the frosty mountains gleam like silver. The moon was full, and in the flood of light the wild scenery round our camp was very beautiful. As always where we camped for several days, we had fixed long tables and settles, and were most comfortable; and when we came in at nightfall, or sometimes long afterward, cold, tired, and hungry, it was sheer physical delight to get warm before the roaring fire of pitchy stumps, and then to feast ravenously on bread and beans, on stewed or roasted elk venison, on grouse, and sometimes trout, and flapjacks with maple syrup.

Next morning dawned clear and cold, the sky a glorious blue. Woody and I started to hunt over the great table-land, and led our stout horses up the mountain-side by elk-trails so bad that they had to climb like goats. All these elk-trails have one striking peculiarity: they lead through thick timber, but every now and then send off short, well-worn branches to some cliff-edge or jutting crag, commanding a view far and wide over the country beneath. Elk love to stand on these lookout points, and scan the valleys and mountains round about.

Blue grouse rose from beside our path; Clarke's crows flew past us, with a hollow, flapping sound, or lighted in the pine-tops, calling and flirting their tails; the gray-clad whisky-jacks, with multitudinous cries, hopped and fluttered near us. Snow-shoe rabbits scuttled away, the great furry feet which give them their name already turning white. At last we came out on the great plateau, seamed with deep, narrow ravines. Reaches of pasture alternated with groves and open forests of varying size. Almost immediately we heard the bugle of a bull elk, and saw a big band of cows and calves on the other side of a valley. There were three bulls with them, one very large, and we tried to creep up on them: but the wind was baffling and spoiled our stalk. So we returned to our horses, mounted them, and rode a mile further, toward a large open wood on a hillside. When within a hundred yards we heard directly ahead the bugle of a bull, and pulled up short. In a moment I saw him walking through an open glade; he had not seen us. The slight breeze brought us his scent. Elk have a strong characteristic smell; it is usually sweet, like that of a herd of Alderney cows, but in old bulls, while rutting, it is rank, pungent, and lasting. We stood motionless till the bull was out of sight, then stole to the wood, tied our horses, and trotted after him. He was traveling fast, occasionally calling, whereupon others in the neighborhood would answer. Evidently he had been driven out of some herd by the master bull.

He went faster than we did, and while we were vainly trying to overtake him we heard other very loud and sonorous challenge to our left. It came from a ridge-crest at the edge of the woods, among some scattered clumps of the northern nut-pine, or piñon, a queer conifer, growing very high on the mountains, its multiforked trunk and wide-spreading branches giving it the rounded top and, at a distance, the general look of an oak rather than a pine. We at once walked toward the ridge, up-wind. In a minute or two, to our chagrin, we stumbled on an outlying spike-bull, evidently kept on the outskirts of the herd by the master bull. I thought it would alarm all the rest; but, as we stood motionless, it could not see clearly what we were. It stood, ran, stood again, gazed at us, and trotted slowly off. We hurried forward as fast as we dared, and with too little care, for we suddenly came in view of two cows. As they raised their heads to look, Woody squatted down where he was, to keep their attention fixed, while I cautiously tried to slip off to one side unobserved. Favored by the neutral tint of my buckskin hunting-shirt, with which my shoes, leggings, and soft hat matched, I succeeded. As soon as I was out of sight, I ran hard and came up to a hillock crested with piñons, behind which I judged I should find the herd. As I approached the crest, their strong, sweet smell smote my nostrils. In another moment I saw the tips of a pair of mighty antlers, and I peered over the crest with my rifle at the ready. Thirty yards off, behind a clump of piñons, stood a huge bull, his head thrown back as he rubbed his shoulders with his horns. There were several cows around him, and one saw me immediately, and took alarm. I fired into the bull's shoulder, inflicting a mortal wound; but he went off, and I raced after him at top speed, firing twice into his flank; then he stopped, very sick, and I broke his neck with a fourth bullet. An elk often hesitates in the first moments of surprise and fright, and does not get really under way for two or three hundred yards; but when once fairly started, he may go several miles, even though mortally wounded; therefore, the hunter, after his first shot, should run forward as fast as he can, and shoot again and again until the quarry drops. In this way many animals that would otherwise be lost are obtained, especially by the man who has a repeating-rifle. Nevertheless the hunter should beware of being led astray by the ease with which he can fire half a dozen shots from his repeater; and he should aim as carefully with each shot as if it were his last. No possible rapidity of fire can atone for habitual carelessness of aim with the first shot.

The elk I slew was a giant. His body was the size of a steer's, and his antlers, though not unusually long, were very massive and heavy. He lay in a glad, on the edge of a great cliff. Standing on its brink, we overlooked a most beautiful country, the home of all homes for the elk, a wilderness of mountains, the immense evergreen forest broken by park and glade, by meadow and pasture, by bare hillside and barren table-land. Some five miles off lay the sheet of water known to the old hunters as Spotted Lake; two or three shallow, sedgy pplaces, and spots of geyser formation made pale green blotches on its wind-rippled surface. Far to the southwest, in daring beauty and majesty, the grand domes and lofty spires of the Tetons shot into the blue sky. Too sheer for the snow to rest on their sides, it yet filled the rents in their rough flanks, and lay deep between the towering pinnacles of dark rock.

That night, as on more than one night afterward, a bull elk came down whistling to within two or three hundred yards of the tents, and tried to join the horse herd. The moon had set, so I could not go after it. Elk are very restless and active throughout the night in the rutting season; but where undisturbed they feed freely in the daytime, resting for two or three hours about noon.

Next day, which was rainy, we spent in getting in the antlers and meat of the two dead elk, and I shot off the heads of two or three blue grouse on the way home. The following day I killed another bull elk, following him by the strong, not unpleasing, smell, and hitting him twice as he ran, at about eighty yards. So far I had had good luck, killing everything I had shot at; but now the luck changed, through no fault of mine, as far as I could see, and Ferguson had his innings. The day after I killed this bull he shot two fine mountain rams, and during the remainder of our hunt he killed five elk--one cow, for meat, and four good bulls. The two rams were with three others, all old and with fine horns; Ferguson peeped over a lofty precipice and saw them coming up it only fifty yards below him. His two first and finest bulls were obtained by hard running and good shooting; the herds were on the move at the time, and only his speed of foot and soundness of wind enabled him to get near enough for a shot. One herd started before he got close, and he killed the master bull by a shot right through the heart, as it trotted past, a hundred and fifty yards distant.

As for me, during the next ten days I killed nothing save one cow for meat, and this though I hunted hard every day from morning till night, no matter what the weather. It was stormy, with hail and snow almost every day; and after working hard from dawn until nightfall, laboriously climbing the slippery mountain-sides, walking through the wet woods, and struggling across the bare plateaus and cliff-shoulders, while the violent blasts of wind drove the frozen rain in our faces, we would come in after dusk wet through and chilled to the marrow. Even when it rained in the valleys it snowed on the mountain-tops, and there was no use trying to keep our feet dry. I got three shots at bull elk, two being very hurried snap-shots at animals running in thick timber, the other a running-shot in the open, at over two hundred yards; and I missed all three. On most days I saw no bull worth shooting; the two or three I did see or hear we failed to stalk, the light, shifty wind baffling us, or else an outlying cow which we had not seen giving the alarm. There were many blue, and a few ruffed, grouse in the woods, and I occasionally shot off the heads of a couple on my way homeward in the evening. In racing after one elk, I leaped across a gully and so bruised and twisted my heel on a rock that, for the remainder of my stay in the mountains, I had to walk on the fore part of that foot. This did not interfere much with my walking, however, except in going downhill.

    Our ill success was in part due to sheer bad luck; but the chief element therein was the presence of a great hunting-party of Shoshone Indians. Split into bands of eight or ten each, they scoured the whole country on their tough, sure-footed ponies. They always hunted on horseback, and followed the elk at full speed wherever they went. Their method of hunting was to organize great drives, the riders strung in lines far apart; they signaled to one another by means of willow whistles, with which they also imitated the calling of the bull elk, thus tolling the animals to them, or making them betray their whereabouts. As they slew whatever they could, but by preference cows and calves, and as they were very persevering, but also very excitable and generally poor shots, so that they wasted much powder, they not only wrought havoc among the elk, but also scared the survivors out of all the country over which they hunted.

    Day in and day out we plodded on. In a hunting-trip the days of long monotony in getting to the ground, and the days of unrequited toil after it has been reached, always far outnumber the red-letter days of success. But it is just these times of failure that really test the hunter. In the long run, common sense and dogged perseverance avail him more than any other qualities.

An Elk-Hunt at Two-Ocean Pass / 149

The man who does not give up, but hunts steadily and resolutely through the spells of bad luck until the luck turns, is the man who wins success in the end.

After a week at Two-Ocean Pass, we gathered our pack-animals one frosty morning, and again set off across the mountains. A two-days' jaunt took us to the summit of Wolverine Pass, near Piñon Peak, beside a little mountain tarn; each morning we found its surface skimmed with black ice, for the nights were cold. After three or four days, we shifted camp to the mouth of Wolverine Creek, to get off the hunting-grounds of the Indians. We had used up our last elk-meat that morning, and when we were within a couple of hours' journey of our intended halting-place, Woody and I struck off on foot for a hunt. Just before sunset we came on three or four elk. A spike-bull stood for a moment behind some thick evergreens a hundred yards off; guessing at his shoulder, I fired, and he fell dead after running a few rods. I had broken the luck after ten days of ill success.

Next morning Woody and I, with the packer, rode to where this elk lay. We loaded the meat on a pack-horse, and let the packer take both the loaded animal and our own saddle-horses back to camp, while we made a hunt on foot. We went up the steep, forest-clad mountain-side, and before we had walked an hour heard two elk whistling ahead of us. The woods were open, and quite free from undergrowth, and we were able to advance noiselessly; there was no wind, for the weather was still, clear, and cold. Both of the elk were evidently very much excited, answering each other continually; they had probably been master bulls, but had become so exhausted that their rivals had driven them from the herds, forcing them to remain in seclusion until they regained their lost strength. As we crept stealthily forward, the calling grew louder and louder, until we could hear the grunting sounds with which the challenge of the nearest ended. He was in a large wallow, which was also a lick. When we were still sixty yards off, he heard us, and rushed out, but wheeled and stood a moment to gaze, puzzled by my buckskin suit. I fired into his throat, breaking his neck, and down he went in a heap. Rushing in and turning, I called to Woody, "He 's a twelve-pointer, but the horns are small." As I spoke I heard the roar of the challenge of the other bull not two hundred yards ahead, as if in defiant answer to my shot.

Running quietly forward, I speedily caught a glimpse of his body. He was behind some fir-trees about seventy yards off, and I could not see which way he was standing, and so fired into the patch of flank which was visible, aiming high, to break the back. My aim was true, and the huge beast crashed downhill through the evergreens, pulling himself on his fore legs for fifteen or twenty rods, his hind quarters trailing. Racing forward, I broke his neck. His antlers were the finest I ever got. A couple of whisky-jacks appeared at the first crack of the rifle, with their customary astonishing familiarity and heedlessness of the hunter; they followed the wounded bull as he dragged his great carcass down the hill, and pounced with ghoulish bloodthirstiness on the clots of blood that were sprinkled over the green herbage.

These two bulls lay only a couple of hundred yards apart, on a broad game-trail, which was as well beaten as a good bridle-path. We began to skin out the heads; and as we were finishing we heard another bull challenging far up the mountain. He came nearer and nearer, and as soon as we had ended our work we grasped our rifles and trotted toward him along the game-trail. He was very noisy, uttering his loud, singing challenge every minute or two. The trail was so broad and firm that we walked in perfect silence. After going only five or six hundred yards, we got very close indeed, and stole forward on tiptoe, listening to the roaring music. The sound came from a steep, narrow ravine to one side of the trail, and I walked toward it with my rifle at the ready. A slight puff gave the elk my wind, and he dashed out of the ravine like a deer; but he was only thirty yards off, and my bullet went into his shoulder as he passed behind a clump of young spruce. I plunged into the ravine, scrambled out of it, and raced after him. In a minute I saw him standing with drooping head, and two more shots finished him. He also bore fine antlers. It was a great piece of luck to get three such fine bulls at the cost of half a day's light work; but we had fairly earned them, having worked hard for ten days, through rain, cold, hunger, and fatigue, to no purpose. That evening my home-coming to camp, with three elk-tongues and a brace of ruffed grouse hung at my belt, was most happy.

Next day it snowed, but we brought a pack-pony to where the three great bulls lay, and their heads to camp; the flesh was far too strong to be worth taking, for it was just at the height of the rut. This was the end of my hunt, and a day later Hofer and I, with two pack-ponies, made a rapid push for the Upper Geyser Basin. We traveled fast. The first day was gray and overcast, a cold wind blowing strong in our faces. Toward evening we came on a bull elk in a willow thicket; he was on his knees in a hollow, thrashing and beating the willows with his antlers. At dusk we halted and went into camp by some small pools on the summit of the pass north of Red Mountain. The elk were calling all around us. We pitched our cozy tent, dragged great stumps for the fire, cut evergreen boughs for our beds, watered the horses, tethered them to improvised picket-pins in a grassy glade, and then set about getting supper ready. The wind had gone down, and snow was falling thickly in large, soft flakes; we were evidently at the beginning of a heavy snowstorm. All night we slept soundly in our snug tent. When we arose at dawn there was a foot and a half of snow on the ground, and the flakes were falling as fast as ever. There is no more tedious work than striking camp in bad weather, and it was over two hours from the time we rose to the time we started. It is sheer misery to untangle picket-lines and to pack animals when the ropes are frozen, and by the time we had loaded the two shivering, wincing pack-ponies, and had bridled and saddled our own riding-animals, our hands and feet were numb and stiff with cold, though we were really hampered by our warm clothing. My horse was a wild, nervous roan, and as I swung carelessly into the saddle, he suddenly began to buck before I got my right leg over, and threw me off. My thumb was put out of joint. I pulled it in again, and speedily caught my horse in the dead timber. Then I treated him as what the cow-boys call a "mean horse," and mounted him carefully, so as not to let him either buck or go over backward. However, his preliminary success had inspired him, and a dozen times that day he began to buck, usually choosing a down grade, where the snow was deep and there was much fallen timber.

All day long we pushed steadily through the cold, blinding snow-storm. Neither squirrels nor rabbits were abroad, and a few Clarke's crows, whisky-jacks, and chickadees were the only living things we saw. At nightfall, chilled through, we reached the Upper Geyser Basin. Here I met a party of railroad surveyors and engineers coming in from their summer's field work. One of them lent me a saddle-horse and a pack-pony, and we went on together, breaking our way through the snow-choked roads to the Mammoth Hot Springs, while Hofer took my own horses back to Ferguson.

Liber Scriptorum
January, 1893

A Shot at a Bull Elk

A YEAR or two ago, while on a hunting trip in the Shoshones, I was camped near the Buffalo Fork of the Snake. My companion was an old hunter, Tazewell Woody, and I had with me also a cook and packer, and a "kid" to wrangle the horses. We were after elk, and had already met with good luck.

Our camp was pitched in a point of open pine forest which jutted into the marshy bottom of a singularly wild and beautiful valley. Our saddle- and pack-animals grazed in the glades nearby. High, steep mountains, their slopes covered with the unending evergreen forest, rose on either side of the valley; from their summits we looked out on a wilderness of peaks and ridges, the highest of the gray-rock mountains being capped with snow.

One evening Woody and I decided to cross the valley next day and make a hunt through a big basin lying to one side of the group of peaks immediately in front of us. Before nightfall, therefore, we brought in two of the saddle-animals and picketed them near by, where the grass was thick and luscious, so that we might have them ready to hand next morning. That night a bull elk came striding down the mountain close to our camp, uttering at short intervals his peculiar singing challenge; one of the wildest and most musical sounds to be heard by the hunter who roams over the timbered slopes of the Rockies. He did not pause, but crossed the valley, and plunged into the mountainous forests.

By daybreak we had eaten breakfast and were saddling our horses. It was not necessary to make a very early start, because in those lonely mountains the elk had been but little disturbed, and they fed and were on the move throughout the day. The air was clear and cold. Ice fringed the edges of the little brook whose loud, humming murmur had lulled us to sleep throughout the night, as we lay in our blankets on beds of odorous pine boughs. The morass in the bottom of the valley was frozen hard, and our horses crossed it with ease.

As the sun rose, we were riding in single file along an elk-trail which led through the dim archway of the pine forest on the side of the valley opposite our camp. We hailed its beams with joy, for they warmed the chilly air. Occasionally a Clark's crow flew by, its wings making a hollow flapping sound, and gray whisky-jacks, with multitudinous cries, fluttered boldly alongside of us. The hunter in these lonely forests is always struck by the comparative absence of small bird-life. Hawks, eagles, ravens, grouse—these large birds like the wilderness; but the small birds love farm-land. On the other hand, noisy chipmunks and chickarees abound, and enliven the gloomy woods as they scurry to and fro over the logs, chattering and scolding.

For two miles the trail led alongside the willow thickets and wet, open meadows of the valley bottom. Then we turned abruptly to the left, and struggled up through a steep, narrow gorge for a mile or two more, until we emerged into the big basin where we expected to find game. A rapid brook foamed down the bottom of the gorge, in a succession of little cataracts and rapids; there was no trail, and no animals less clear-headed and sure-footed than our veteran hunting-ponies could have picked their way over the timber-choked and boulder-strewn bottom of the pas.

In the basin itself the riding was easy, for it was all park-country, broad glades alternating with stretches of open woods. Here we began to see signs of game. In one place we came on a covey of blue grouse; they flew into the neighboring trees, and there sat motionless on the branches. If we had been on our way homeward, I should have been tempted to shoot off the heads of two or three, for they are very good eating, and offer a welcome change in the hunter's bill of fare; but it is never wise, when after big game, to run the risk of alarming it by firing at anything smaller. In another place two series of delicate, heart-shaped footprints betrayed where a blacktail doe and fawn had walked during the preceding night; and some vaguely defined marks proved on a close examination to be the week-old track of a bear. A number of fresh hoof-marks, looking much like those left by a herd of young cattle, and evidently made that morning, wrought us up to the highest point of attention; for they showed that a big band of elk had passed that way, probably heading toward their day beds on some spur of the mountains.

Our senses all on the alert, we rode silently forward, expecting every minute to hear afar off the roaring music of some bull elk's challenge. Suddenly Woody, who was ahead, pulled short up, and pointing downward to the dust of a game-trail, remarked with a disgusted expression, "Indians." Sure enough, there in the dust was the round footpring of an unshod horse, evidently not an hour old. We had known that a band of Shoshones was hunting to the southeast of our camp, and had come to this basin with the hope of forestalling them. It was very irritating; for the Indians hunt in parties, all going on horseback and scattering out in a widely spread line; they scour the whole country and shoot at anything they see, killing the cows or does and young by preference; and in consequence they not only work much havoc among the game, but drive all that they do not kill out of the country.

We soon saw the tracks of other Indian ponies; then we cam on the sharply indented footprints of flying elk; and half an hour later we heard two or three distant reports of rifles. It was evident that they were hunting straight across the basin, and that ll the game would be thoroughly alarmed and disturbed.

On one side of the big basin, however, lay another and smaller one—a tangle of wooded ravines which led into a different creek system; and we thought we might yet have a chance by hunting across these ravines. The forests were open and broken, the hillside steep. After picketing our horses near a little spring, where they could get fresh grass, Woody and I started on foot. Where possible, I like to use moccasins in woodland hunting; but this is not practicable in such rocky and mountainous ground as that in which we were. Moccasins are very hard upon the feet of those who are unaccustomed to wearing them, no matter how good as walkers and mountaineers they may be. Indians have soles as tough as leather, and therefore they are not subject to bruises which cripple a white man. The absence of heels makes going downhill in moccasins very tiresome; and leaping from rock to rock, with the feet protected by only one thickness of elk-hide or deer-hide, is sure to result in the laming of the unskilled adventurer. So on this occasion I was wearing stout shoes, well studded with nails. Even with these, if a man exercises reasonable caution, he can travel quite silently over the moss and pine-needles of the forest; but great care is necessary to avoid undue clatter on stones.

Woody and I had not gone more than half a mile before we found fresh elk signs; we moved slowly, both eyes and ears on the alert. We discovered our quarry, however, neither by sight nor sound, but through the exercise of another sense. Just as we were crossing a little steep gully, we both halted short, whispering simultaneously "I smell him." A band of elk have a strong, sweet smell, somewhat like that of a herd of Alderney cattle; in old bulls during the rutting season, it becomes very rank and pungent. If a man has a good nose, and is to leeward, he may smell a band of elk half a mile off.

As soon as the odor struck our nostrils, I moved forward with my rifle at the ready, and began to go along the ravine up wind. Now and then puffs of the scent were brought to me, and again I could smell nothing. In several places, where the ground was soft, I saw the elk's tracks; it was a bull, and evidently on the move.

Finally I came to an old burn, the dead trees standing erect and gray. Immediately afterward I caught a glimpse of the elk's antlers behind a mass of fallen logs, as he stood with head tossed aloft, suspecting danger. In a moment he wheeled and ran across me, some eighty yards off. I covered an opening between two trunks, waited until he appeared, and fired well forward; and again, as he ran quartering to me through the forests, I put in another shot. Both bullets told, inflicting mortal wounds, and a hundred yards on he failed in trying to leap a large dead log, and fell helplessly back into the big cavity left by the uprooted trunk. In a moment we were both standing over him, admiring the head, with its massive, shapely antlers; the neck, with its mane of brown hair; the huge yellow body, and the brown legs, strongly yet delicately molded, with polished, perfect hoofs.

Then we made back to camp, and next day returned with a pack-pony to carry in the meat and trophies.

Century Magazine
June, 1893

In Cowboy-Land

OUT on the frontier, and generally among those who spend their lives or on the borders of the wilderness, life is reduced to its elemental conditions. The passions and emotions of these grim hunters of the mountains and these wild rough-riders of the plains are simpler and stronger than those of people dwelling in more complicated states of society. As soon as communities become settled and begin to grow with any rapidity, the American instinct for law asserts itself; but in the earlier stages each individual is obliged to be a law to himself, and to guard his rights with a strong hand. Of course the transition stages are full of incongruities. Men have not yet adjusted their relations to morality and law with any niceness. They hold strongly by certain rude virtues, and, on the other hand, they quite fail to recognize even as shortcomings not a few traits that obtain scant mercy in older communities.

Many of the desperados, the man-killers, and road-agents have good sides to their characters. Often they are people who in certain stages of civilization do, or have done, good work, but who, when these stages have passed, find themselves surrounded by conditions which accentuate their worst qualities, and make their best qualities useless. The average desperado, for instance, has, after all, much the same standard of morals that the Norman nobles had in the days of the battle of Hastings, and ethically and morally he is decidedly in advance of the Vikings, who were the ancestors of these same nobles, and to whom, by the way, he himself could doubtless trace a portion of his blood. If the transition from the wild lawlessness of life in the wilderness or on the border to a higher civilization were stretched out over a term of centuries, he and his descendants would doubtless accommodate themselves by degrees to the changing circumstances. But, unfortunately, in the far West the transition takes place with marvelous abruptness, and at an altogether unheard-of speed, and many a man's nature is unable to change with sufficient rapidity to allow him to harmonize with his environment.

In consequence, unless he leaves for still wilder lands, he ends by getting hung, instead of founding a family which would revere his name as that of a very capable, although not in all respects a conventionally moral, ancestor.

Most of the men with whom I was intimately thrown during my life on the frontier and in the wilderness were good fellows, hard-working, brave, resolute, and truthful. At times, of course, they were forced of necessity to do deeds which would seem startling to dwellers in cities and in old settled places; and though they waged a very stern and relentless warfare upon evil-doers whose misdeeds had immediate and tangible bad results, they showed a wide toleration of all save the most extreme classes of wrong, and were not given to inquiring too curiously into a strong man's past, or to criticizing him too harshly for a failure to discriminate in finer ethical questions. Moreover, not a few of the men with whom I came in contact with, some of whom my relations were very close and friendly, had at different times led rather tough careers. This fact was accepted by them and by their companions as a fact, and nothing more. There were certain offenses, such as rape, the robbery of a friend, or murder under circumstances of cowardice and treachery, which were never forgiven; but the fact that when the country was wild a young fellow who had gone on the road, that is, become a highwayman, or had been chief of a gang of desperados, horse-thieves, and cattle-killers, it was scarcely held to weigh against him, it being treated as a regrettable, but certainly not shameful, trait of youth. He was regarded by his neighbors with the same kindly tolerance which respectable medieval Scotch borderers doubtless extended to their wilder young men, who would persist in raiding English cattle even in time of peace.

Of course, if these men were asked outright as to their stories, they would have refused to tell them, or else would have lied about them; but when they had grown to regard a man as a friend and companion, they would often recount various incidents of their past lives with perfect frankness; and as they combined in a very curious degree both a decided sense of humor, and a failure to appreciate that there was anything especially remarkable in what they related, their tales were always entertaining.

Early one spring, now nearly ten years ago, I was out hunting some lost horses. They had strayed from the ranch three months before, and we had in a roundabout way heard that they were ranging near some broken country where a man named Brophy had a ranch, nearly fifty miles from my own. When I started to go thither the weather was warm, but the second day out it grew colder, and a heavy snow-storm came on. Fortunately, I was able to reach the ranch all right, to find there one of the sons of a Little Beaver ranchman, and a young cow-puncher belonging to a Texas outfit, whom I knew very well. After putting my horse into the corral, and throwing him down some hay, I strode into the low hut, made partly of turf and partly of cottonwood logs, and speedily warmed myself before the fire. We had a good warm supper of bread, potatoes, fried venison, and tea. My two companions grew very sociable, and began to talk freely over their pipes. There were two bunks, one above the other. I climbed into the upper, leaving my friends, who were to occupy the lower, sitting together on a bench recounting different incidents in the careers of themselves and their cronies during the winter that had just passed. Soon one of them asked the other what had become of a certain horse, a noted cutting pony, which I myself had noticed the preceding fall. The question roused the other to the memory of a wrong which still rankled, and he began (I alter one or two of the proper names).

"Why, that was the pony that got stole. I had been workin' him on rough ground when I was out with the Three Bar outfit, and he went tender forward, so I turned him loose by the Lazy B ranch, and when I come back to get him there wasn't anybody at the ranch, and I couldn't find him. The sheep-man who lives about two miles west, under Red Clay Butte, told me he seen a fellow in a wolfskin coat, ridin' a pinto bronc' with white eyes, leadin' that pony of mine just two days before; and I hunted round till I hit his trail, and then I followed to where I'd reckoned he was headin' for the Short Pine Hills. When I got there a rancher told me he had seen the man pass on toward Cedartown; and, sure enough, when I struck Cedartown I found he lived there in a 'dobe house just outside the town. There was a boom on the town, and it looked pretty slick.

"There was two hotels, and I went into the first, and I says, 'Where's the justice of the peace?' says I to the bartender.

" 'There ain't no justice of the peace,' says he; 'ther justice of the peace got shot.'

" 'Well, where 's the constable?' says I.

" 'Why, it was him that shot the justice of the peace,' says he; 'he's skipped the country with a bunch of horses.'

" 'Well, ain't there no officer of the law left in this town?' says I.

" 'Why, of course,' says he, 'there 's a probate judge; he is over tendin' bar at the Last Chance Hotel.'

" So I went over to the Last Chance Hotel, and I walked in there.

" 'Mornin',' says I.

" 'Mornin',' says he.

" 'You 're the probate judge?' says I.

" 'That 's what I am,' says he. 'What do you want?' says he.

" 'I want justice,' says I.

" 'What kind of justice do you want?' says he. 'What's it for?'

" 'It 's for stealin' a horse,' says I.

" 'Then, by, you 'll get it,' says he.

" 'Who stole the horse?' says he.

" 'It is a man that lives in a 'dobe house just outside the town there,' says I.

" 'Well, where do you come from yourself?' says he.

" 'From Medory,' says I.

" 'With that he lost interest, and settled kind o' back; and says he, 'There won't no Cedartown jury hang a Cedartown man for stealin' a Medory man's horse,' says he.

" 'Well, what am I to do about my horse?' says I.

"'Do?' says he. 'Well, you know where the man lives, don't you?' says he. 'Then sit up outside his house to-night, and shoot him when he comes in,' says he, ' and skip out with the horse.'

" 'All right,' says I; 'that is what I'll do;' and I walked off. So I went off to his house, and I laid down behind some sage-brushes to wait for him. He was not at home, but I could see his wife movin' about inside now and then, and I waited and waited, and it growed darker, and I begun to say to myself, ' Now here you are lyin' out to shoot this man when he comes home; and it 's gettin' dark, and you don't know him, and if you do shoot the next man that comes into that house, like as not it won't be the fellow you 're after at all, but some perfectly innocent man a-comin' there after the other man's wife.'

"So I up and saddled the bronc', and lit out for home," concluded the narrator, with the air of one justly proud of his own self-abnegating virtue.

One of my valued friends in the mountains, and one of the best hunters with whom I ever traveled, was a man who had a peculiarly light-hearted way of looking at conventionally moral obligations. Though in some ways a true backwoods Donatello, he was a man of much shrewdness and of great courage and resolution. Moreover, he possessed what only a few men do possess, the capacity to tell the truth. He saw facts as they were, and could tell them as they were, and he never told an untruth unless for very weighty reasons. He was preeminently a philosopher, of a happy, skeptical turn of mind. He had no prejudices. He never looked down, as so many hard characters do, upon a person possessing a different code of ethics. His attitude was one of broad, genial tolerance. He saw nothing out of the way in the fact that he himself had been a road-agent, a professional gambler, and a desperado at different stages of his career. On the other hand, he did not in the least hold it against any one that he had always acted within the law. At the time that I knew him he had become a man of some substance, and naturally a stanch upholder of the existing order of things. But while he never boasted of his past deeds, he never apologized for them, and evidently would have been quite as incapable of understanding that they needed an apology as he would have been incapable of being guilty of mere vulgar boastfulness. He did not often refer to his past career at all. When he did, he recited its incidents perfectly naturally and simply as events, without any reference to, or regard for, their ethical significance. It was this quality which made him at times a specially pleasant companion, and always an agreeable narrator. The point of his story, or what seemed to him the point, was rarely that which struck me. It was the incidental side-lights the story threw upon his own nature, and the somewhat lurid surroundings in which he had moved.

On one occasion when we were out together we killed a bear, and, after skinning it, took a bath in a lake. I noticed that he had a scar on one side of his foot, and asked him how he got it. To my question he responded, with indifference:

"Oh, that? Why, a man shootin' at me to make me dance, that was all."

I expressed some curiosity in the matter, and he went on:

"Well, the way of it was this. It was when I was keepin' a saloon in New Mexico, and there was a man there by the name of Fowler, and there was a reward on him of three thousand dollars."

"Put on him by the State?" I interrupted.

"No; put on by his wife," said my friend; "and there was this—"

"Hold on," I interrupted; "put on by his wife, did you say?"

"Yes; by his wife. Him and her had been keepin' a faro bank, you see, and they quarreled about it, so she just put a reward on him, and so."

"Excuse me," I said, "but do you mean to say that this reward was put on publicly?" To which my friend answered, with an air of gentlemanly irritation at being interrupted to gratify my thirst for irrelevant detail:

"Oh, no ; not publicly. She had just mentioned it to six or eight intimate personal friends."

"Go on," I responded, somewhat overcome by this instance of the primitive simplicity with which New Mexican matrimonial disputes were managed; and he continued:

"Well, two men come ridin' in to see me, to borrow my guns. My guns was Colt's self-cockers. It was a new thing then, and they was the only ones in town. They come to me, and, 'Simpson,' says they, 'we want to borrow your guns; we are goin' to kill Fowler.'

" 'Hold on for a moment,' said I; 'I am willin' to lend you them guns, but I ain't goin' to know what you're goin' to do with them. No, sir; but of course you can have them guns.' " Here my friend's face brightened pleasantly, and he continued :

"Well, you may easily believe I felt surprised next day when Fowler come ridin' in, and, says he, 'Simpson, here 's your guns.' He had shot them two men! 'Well, Fowler,' says I, 'if I had known them men was after you, I 'd never have let them have them guns nohow,' says I. That wasn't true, for I did know it, but there was no cause to tell him that." I murmured my approval of such prudence, and Simpson continued, his eyes gradually brightening with the light of agreeable reminiscence:

"Well, they up and they took Fowler before the justice of the peace. The justice of the peace was a Turk."

"Now, Simpson, what do you mean by that?" I interrupted.

"Well, he come from Turkey," said Simpson; and I again sank back, wondering briefly what particular variety of Mediterranean outcast had drifted down to New Mexico to be made a justice of the peace. Simpson laughed, and continued:

"That Fowler was a funny fellow. The Turk he committed Fowler, and Fowler he riz up and knocked 'him down, and tromped all over him, and made him let him go."

"That was an appeal to a higher law," I observed. Simpson assented cheerily, and continued:

"Well, that Turk he got nervous for fear Fowler he was goin' to kill him, and so he comes to me and offers me twenty-five dollars a day to protect him from Fowler; and I went to Fowler, and, 'Fowler,' says I, 'that Turk 's offered me twenty-five dollars a day to protect him from you. Now, I ain't goin' to get shot for no twenty-five dollars a day, and if you are goin' to kill the Turk, just say so, and go and do it; but if you ain't goin' to kill the Turk, there 's no reason why I shouldn't earn that twenty-five dollars a day.' And Fowler, says he, 'I ain't goin' to touch the Turk; you just go right ahead and protect him.' "

So Simpson "protected" the Turk from the imaginary danger of Fowler for about a week, at twenty-five dollars a day. Then one evening he happened to go out, and met Fowler. "And," said he, "the moment I saw him I knowed he felt mean, for he begun to shoot at my feet"; which certainly did seem to offer presumptive evidence of meanness. Simpson continued:

"I didn't have no gun, so I just had to stand there and take it until something distracted his attention, and I went off home to get my gun and kill him; but I wanted to do it perfectly lawful, so I went up to the mayor (he was playin' poker with one of the judges), and says I to him, 'Mr. Mayor,' says I, 'I am goin' to shoot Fowler.' And the mayor he riz out of his chair, and he took me by the hand, and says he, 'Mr. Simpson, if you do, I will stand by you.' And the judge he says, 'I'll go on your bond.' "

Fortified by this cordial approval of the executive and judicial branches of the government, Mr. Simpson started on his quest. Meanwhile, however, Fowler had cut up another prominent citizen, and they already had him in jail. The friends of law and order, feeling some little distrust as to the permanency of their own zeal for righteousness, thought it best to settle the matter before there was time for cooling, and accordingly, headed by Simpson, the mayor, the judge, the Turk, and other prominent citizens of the town, they broke into the jail and hanged Fowler. The point in the hanging which especially tickled my friend's fancy as he lingered over the reminiscence was one that was rather too ghastly to appeal to our sense of humor. In the Turk's mind there still rankled the memory of Fowler's very unprofessional conduct while figuring before him as a criminal. Said Simpson, with a merry twinkle of the eye: "Do you know, that Turk he was a right funny fellow, too, after all. Just as the boys were going to string up Fowler, says he, 'Boys, stop; one moment, gentlemen Mr. Fowler, good-by,' and he blew a kiss to him!"

On the frontier there is not much attention paid to the nicer distinctions of ethnology and foreign geography. On one occasion, late in the fall, on returning from the last beef round-up, I found a little hunter staying at the ranch, a clean, honest, handy fellow, evidently a foreigner. After he had stayed two or three days, and it was evident that he regarded himself as domiciled with us for the winter, I asked one of my cowboys who he was, and received for an answer: "Well, he 's a kind of a Dutchman, but he hates the other Dutch mortal. He comes from an island Germany took from France in the last war." This seemed puzzling, and my curiosity was sufficiently aroused to prompt me to make inquiries of the hunter himself, although in the cow-country, as in the wilderness, one is not apt to cross-examine a stray guest too closely as to his antecedents. In this case, however, my inquiry developed nothing more startling than the fact that the "island" in question was Alsace.

Native Americans take the lead in every way in the far West, and give to the life its peculiar stamp. The sons of immigrants always lay especial stress upon their Americanism, and often dislike to be reminded of their kinship with the natives of their parents' country. On one occasion I was out with a very good hunter whose father had come from Germany, though his mother was a New England woman. He got into an altercation with a traveling party of Germans, and after peace was patched up one of them turned to him, with an idea of making himself agreeable, and said, "By your name, sir, you must be of German origin." To which my friend promptly answered "Y-e-s; my father was a Dutchman, but my mother was a white woman. I 'm white myself." Whereat the Germans glowered gloomily at him.

In the cow-country there is nothing more refreshing than the light-hearted belief entertained by the average man that any animal which by main force has been saddled and ridden, or harnessed and driven, a couple of times is a "broke horse." My present foreman is firmly wedded to this idea, as well as to its complement, the belief that any animals with hoofs, before any vehicle with wheels, can be driven across any country. One summer, on reaching the ranch, I was entertained with the usual accounts of the adventures and misadventures which had befallen my own men and my neighbors since I had been out last. In the course of the conversation my foreman remarked: "We had a great time out here about six weeks ago. There was a professor from Ann Arbor came out with his wife to see the Bad Lands, and they asked if we could rig them up a team, and we said we guessed we could, and Foley's boy and I did; but it run away with him, and broke his leg. He was here for a month. I guess he didn't mind it, though." Of this I was less certain, forlorn little Medora being a "busted" cow-town concerning which I once heard another of my men remark in reply to an inquisitive commercial traveler: "How many people lives here? Eleven, counting the chickens, when they 're all in town."

My foreman continued: "By George, there was something that professor said afterward that made me feel hot. I sent word up to him by Foley's boy that seein' as how it had come out, we wouldn't charge him nothing for the rig; and that professor he answered that he was glad we were showin' him some sign of consideration, for he'd begun to believe he'd fallen into a den of sharks, and that we 'd gave him a runaway team a-purpose. That made me hot, callin' that a runaway team. Why, there was one of them horses never could have run away before it hadn't never been druv but twice; and the other horse, maybe, had run away a few times, but there was lots of times he hadn't run away. I esteemed that team full as liable not to run away as it was to run away," concluded my foreman, evidently deeming this as good a warranty of gentleness as the most exacting could require.

The definition of good behavior in the cow country is even more elastic for a saddle-horse than for a team. Last spring one of the Three Seven riders, a magnificent horseman, was killed on the round-up near Belfield, his horse bucking and falling on him. "It was accounted a plumb gentle horse, too," said my informant; "only it sometimes sulked and acted a little mean when it was cinched up behind." The unfortunate rider did not know of this failing of the "plumb gentle horse," and as soon as he was in the saddle it threw itself over sidewise with a great bound, and he fell on his head, and never spoke again.

Such accidents are too common in the wild country to attract much attention; the men accept them, with grim quiet, as inevitable in such lives as theirs, lives that are harsh and narrow, in their toil and their pleasure alike, and that are ever bounded by an iron horizon of hazard and hardship. During the last year and a half three other men from the ranches in my immediate neighborhood have met their death in the course of their work. One, a trail boss of the O X, was drowned while swimming his herd across a swollen river. Another, one of the fancy ropers of the W Bar, was killed while roping cattle in a corral: his saddle turned, the rope twisted round him, he was pulled off, and was trampled to death by his own horse.

The fourth man, a cow-puncher named Hamilton, lost his life during the last week of October, 1891, in the first heavy snow-storm of the season. Yet he was a skilled plainsman, on ground he knew well, and, just before straying himself, had successfully instructed two men who did not know the country or how to get to camp. All three were with the round-up, and were making a circle through the Bad Lands. The wagons had camped on the eastern edge of the Bad Lands, where they merge into the prairie, at the head of an old, disused road which led almost due east from the Little Missouri. It was a gray, lowering day, and as darkness came on Hamilton's horse played out, and he told his two companions not to wait, as it had begun to snow, but to keep on toward the north, skirting some particularly rough buttes, and as soon as they struck the road to turn to the right and to follow it out to the prairie, where they would find camp. He particularly warned them to keep a sharp lookout, so as not to pass over the dim trail unawares, in the dusk and the falling snow. They followed his advice, and reached camp safely; but after they had left him nobody ever again saw him alive. Evidently he himself, plodding northward, passed over the road without seeing it, in the storm and the gathering gloom; probably he struck it at some point where the ground was bad and the dim trail in consequence disappeared entirely, as is the way with these prairie roads, making them landmarks to be used with caution.

He must then have walked on and on, over rugged hills and across deep ravines, until his horse came to a standstill; he took off its saddle and picketed it to a dwarfed ash; its frozen carcass was found, with the saddle near by, two months later. He now evidently recognized some landmark, and realized that he had passed the road, and was far to the north of the round-up wagons; but he was a resolute, self-confident man, and he determined to strike out for a line camp which he knew lay almost due east of him, two or three miles out on the prairie, on one of the head branches of Knife River. Night must have fallen by this time, and he missed the camp. He swerved slightly from his line, probably passing it within less than a mile; but he did pass it, and with it all hope of life, and walked wearily on to his doom through the thick darkness and the driving snow. At last his strength failed, and he lay down in the tall grass of a little hollow. Five months later, in the early spring, the riders from the line camp found his body, resting face downward, with the forehead on the folded arms.

Accidents of less degree are common. Men break their collar-bones, arms, or legs by falling when riding at speed over dangerous ground, when cutting cattle, or when trying to control a stampeded herd, or by being thrown or rolled on by bucking or rearing horses; or their horses, and on rare occasions even they themselves, are gored by fighting steers. Death by storm or in flood, death in striving to master a wild and vicious horse, or in handling maddened cattle, and too often death in brutal conflict with one of his own fellows, any one of these is the not unnatural end of the life of any dweller on the plains or in the mountains.

Only a few years ago other risks had to be run, from savage beasts and from the Indians. Since I have been ranching on the Little Missouri, two men have been killed by bears in the neighborhood of my range; and in the early years of my residence there, several men living or traveling in the county were slain by small war-parties of young braves. All the old-time trappers and hunters could tell stirring tales of their encounters with Indians.

My friend Tazewell Woody was among the chief actors in one of the most noteworthy adventures of this kind. He was a very quiet man, and it was exceedingly difficult to get him to talk over any of his past experiences; but one day, when he was in high good humor with me for having made three consecutive straight shots at elk, he became quite communicative, and I was able to get him to tell me one story which I had long wished to hear from his lips, having already heard of it through one of the other participants of the fight. When he found that I already knew a good deal of it, old Woody told me the rest.

It was in the spring of 1875, and Woody and two friends were trapping on the Yellowstone. The Sioux were very bad at the time, and had killed many prospectors, hunters, cowboys, and settlers; the whites retaliated whenever they got a chance, but, as always in Indian warfare, the sly, lurking, bloodthirsty savages usually inflicted much more loss than they suffered. The three men, having a dozen horses with them, were camped by the riverside in a triangular patch of brush shaped a good deal like a common flat-iron. On reaching camp they started to put out their traps, and when he came back in the evening Woody informed his companions that he had seen a great deal of Indian sign, and that he believed there were Sioux in the neighborhood. His companions both laughed at him, assuring him that they were not Sioux at all, but friendly Crows, and that they would be in camp next morning. "And, sure enough," said Woody, meditatively, "they were in camp next morning." By dawn one of the men went down the river to look at some of the traps, while Woody started out to where the horses were, the third man remaining in camp to get breakfast. Suddenly two shots were heard down the river, and in another moment a mounted Indian swept toward the horses. Woody fired, but missed him, and he drove off five horses, while Woody, running forward, succeeded in herding the other seven into camp. Hardly had this been accomplished before the man who had gone down the river appeared, out of breath from his desperate run, having been surprised by several Indians, and just succeeding in making his escape by dodging from bush to bush, threatening his pursuers with his rifle.

These proved to be the forerunners of a great war-party, for when the sun rose the hills around seemed black with Sioux. Had they chosen to dash right in on the camp, running the risk of losing several of their men in the charge, they could of course have eaten up the three hunters in a minute; but such a charge is rarely practiced by Indians, who, although they are admirable in defensive warfare, and even in certain kinds of offensive movements, and although from their skill in hiding they usually inflict much more loss than they suffer when matched against white troops, are yet very reluctant to make any movement where the advantage gained must be offset by considerable loss of life. The three men thought they were surely doomed; but being veteran frontiersmen, and long inured to every kind of hardship and danger, they instantly set to work with cool resolution to make as effective a defense as possible, to beat off their antagonists if they might, and, if this proved impracticable, to sell their lives as dearly as they could. Having tethered the horses in a slight hollow, the only one which offered any protection, each man crept out to a point of the triangular brush-patch, and lay down to await events.

In a very short while the Indians began closing in on them, taking every advantage of cover, and then, both from their side of the river and from the opposite bank, opened a perfect fusillade, wasting their cartridges with the recklessness which Indians are so apt to show when excited. The hunters could hear the hoarse commands of the chiefs, the war whoops, and the taunts in broken English which some of the warriors hurled at them. Very soon all of their horses were killed, and the brush was fairly riddled by the incessant volleys; but the three men themselves, lying flat on the ground and well concealed, were not harmed. The more daring young warriors then began to creep toward the hunters, going stealthily from one piece of cover to the next; and now the whites in turn opened fire. They did not shoot recklessly, as did their foes, but coolly and quietly, endeavoring to make each shot tell. Said Woody, "I only fired seven times all day; I reckoned on getting meat every time I pulled trigger." They had an immense advantage of their enemies in that they lay still and entirely concealed, whereas the Indians of course had to move from cover to cover in order to approach, and so had at times to expose themselves. When the whites fired at all, they fired at a man, whether moving or motionless, whom they could clearly see, while the Indians could shoot only at the smoke, which imperfectly marked the position of their unseen foes. In consequence, the assailants speedily found that it was a task of hopeless danger to try to close in such a manner with three plains veterans, men of iron nerves and skilled in the use of the rifle. Yet some of the more daring crept up very close to the patch of brush, and one actually got inside it, and was killed among the bedding that lay by the smoldering camp-fire. The wounded, and such of the dead as did not lie in too exposed positions, were promptly taken away by their comrades; but seven bodies fell into the hands of the three hunters. I asked Woody how many he himself had killed. He said he could be sure of only two that he got: one he shot in the head as he peeped over a bush, and the other as he attempted to rush in through the smoke. "My, how that Indian did yell!" said Woody, retrospectively. "He was no great of a stoic." After two or three hours of this deadly skirmishing, which resulted in nothing more serious to the whites than in two of them being slightly wounded, the Sioux became disheartened by the loss they were suffering, and withdrew, confining themselves thereafter to a long-range and harmless fusillade. When it was dark the three men crept out to the river-bed, and, taking advantage of the pitchy night, broke through the circle of their foes. They managed to reach the settlements without further molestation, having lost everything except their rifles.

For many years one of the most important dwellers of the wilderness was the West Point officer, and no man has played a greater part than he in the wild warfare which opened the regions beyond the Mississippi to white settlement. Since 1879 there has been but little regular Indian fighting in the North, though there have been one or two very tedious and wearisome campaigns waged against the Apaches in the South. Even in the North, however, there have been occasional difficulties which had to be quelled by the regular troops.

After an elk-hunt in September, 1891, I came out through the Yellowstone Park, riding in company with a surveyor of the Burlington and Quincy Railroad, who was just coming in from his summer's work. It was the first of October. There had been a heavy snow-storm, and the snow was still falling. Riding a stout pony each, and leading another packed with our bedding, etc., we broke our way down from the upper to the middle geyser basin. Here we found a troop of the First Cavalry camped, under the command of old friends of mine, Captain Frank Edwards and Lieutenant (now Captain) John Pitcher. They gave us hay for our horses, and, with the ready hospitality always shown by army officers, insisted upon our stopping to lunch. After lunch we began exchanging stories. My traveling companion, the surveyor, had that spring performed a feat of note, going through the Black Canyon of the Big Horn for the first time. He went with an old mining inspector, the two dragging a cottonwood sledge over the ice. The walls of the canyon are so sheer and the water is so rough that it can be descended only when the stream is frozen. However, after six days' labor and hardship the descent was accomplished, and the surveyor, in concluding, described his experience in going through the Crow Reservation.

This turned the conversation upon Indians, and it appeared that both of our hosts had been actors in Indian scrapes which had attracted my attention at the time they occurred, both taking place among tribes that I knew and in a country which I had sometimes visited, either when hunting or when purchasing horses for the ranch. One which occurred to Captain Edwards took place late in 1886, at the time when the Crow chief Sword-Bearer announced himself as the Messiah of the Indian race, during one of the usual epidemics of ghost-dancing. Sword-Bearer derived his name from always wearing a medicine sword that is, a saber painted red. He claimed to possess magic power, and, thanks to the performance of many dexterous feats of juggling, and the lucky outcome of certain prophecies, he deeply stirred the Indians, arousing the young warriors in particular to the highest pitch of excitement. They became sullen, and began to paint and arm themselves, the agent and the settlers near by growing so apprehensive that troops were ordered to the reservation. A body of cavalry, including Captain Edwards's troop, was accordingly marched thither, and found the Crow warriors, mounted on their war-ponies, and dressed in their striking battle-garb, waiting on a hill for them.

The position of troops at the beginning of such an affair is always peculiarly difficult. The settlers roundabout are sure bitterly to clamor against them, no matter what they do, on the ground that they are not thorough enough and are showing favor to the savages, while, on the other hand, even if they fight purely in self-defense, a large number of worthy but weak-minded sentimentalists in the East are sure to shriek about their having brutally attacked the Indians. The war authorities always insist that they must not fire the first shot under any circumstances, and such were the orders at this time. The Crows on the hilltop showed a sullen and threatening front, and the troops advanced slowly toward them, and then halted for a parley. Meanwhile a mass of black thunder-clouds, gathering on the horizon, threatened one of those cloudbursts of extreme severity and suddenness so characteristic of the plains country. While still trying to make arrangements for a parley, a horseman started out of the Crow ranks and galloped headlong down toward the troops. It was the medicine chief Sword-Bearer. He was painted and in his battle-dress, wearing his war-bonnet of floating, trailing eagle-feathers, and with the plumes of the same bird braided in the mane and tail of his fiery little horse. On he came at a gallop almost up to the troops, and then began to circle around them, calling and singing, and throwing his red sword into the air, catching it by the hilt as it fell. Twice he rode completely around the troops, who stood in uncertainty, not knowing what to make of his performance, and expressly forbidden to shoot at him. Then, paying no further heed to them, he rode back toward the Crows. It appears that he had told the latter that he would ride twice around the hostile force, and by his incantations would call down rain from heaven, which would make the hearts of the white men like water, so that they would go back to their homes. Sure enough, while the arrangements for the parley were still going forward, down came the cloudburst, drenching the command, and making the ground on the hills in front nearly impassable; and before it dried a courier arrived with orders to the troops to go back to camp.

  This fulfillment of Sword-Bearer's prophecy of course raised his reputation to the zenith, and the young men of the tribe prepared for war, while the older chiefs, who more fully realized the power of the whites, still hung back. When the troops next appeared they came upon the entire Crow force, the women and children with their tepees being off to one side, beyond a little stream, while almost all the warriors of the tribe were gathered in front. Sword-Bearer started to repeat his former ride, to the intense irritation of the soldiers. Luckily, however, this time some of his young men could not be restrained. They too began to ride near the troops, and one of them was unable to refrain from firing on Captain Edwards's troop, which was in the van. This gave the soldiers their chance. They instantly responded with a volley, and Edwards's troop charged. The fight lasted only a minute or two, for Sword-Bearer was struck by a bullet and fell; and as he had boasted himself invulnerable, and promised that his warriors should be invulnerable also if they would follow him, the hearts of the latter became as water, and they broke in every direction. One of the amusing, though irritating, incidents of the affair was to see the plumed and painted warriors race headlong for the camp, plunge into the stream, wash off their war-paint, and remove their feathers in an instant; in another moment they were stolidly sitting on the ground, with their blankets over their shoulders, rising to greet the pursuing cavalry with unmoved composure, and with calm assurances that they had always been friendly and had much disapproved the conduct of the young bucks who had just been scattered on the field outside. It was much to the credit of the discipline of the army that no bloodshed followed the fight proper. The loss to the whites was small.

Youth's Companion
June 22, 1893

Tales Told by a Ranch Fireside

I. - Wolfish Marauders

Around my ranch wolves molest full-grown animals but seldom, and never, so far as I know, attack or threaten human beings. They often kill calves and colts, and in one or two rare instances I have known of their hamstringing and tearing to pieces cows and steers. Westward of the Rockies, however, from the great main divide of the continent to the coastline of British Columbia, Washington and Oregon, the wolves are larger and fiercer.

Our plains wolf is usually called the buffalo wolf, and varies from gray to white in color. The great timber wolf which haunts the deep forests of the northern Rockies and the coast ranges resembles ours in color, but has better, and on the whole darker, fur; is a longer-legged, longer-toothed, more sinewy beast.

In winter the timber wolves become very bold, and then sometimes attack man. Whenever the snow is on the ground the become dangerous to the settlers' live stock. Sometimes singly, but more often in twos or threes, they will boldly assail the largest horse or horned animal. Unlike the panther they rarely make their main attack at the throat, preferring to hamstring their prey and then tear out the flanks and stomach.

A settler in northern Idaho once told me of the damage a small party of these great wolves inflicted on him, and the way in which he finally got rid of them.

His little outlying farm was situated in the heart of a great pine and spruce forest well up in the mountainns. There were some beaver meadows along the banks of the stream by which his olg house stood, and there were open glades in the valleys and on the hillsides, while a stump-dotted clearing surrounded his cabin.

He had put up a log barn and farm-yard corral; and his live stock consisted of a horse, a mare with her colt, a yoke of oxen for plowing his grain land, and a milch cow, together with four powerful dogs accustomed to battle with wild beasts.

Early one winter the wolves made their first descent upon him. The milch cow had been left out to pick up her living in the woods during the daytime, as it was certain that she would return at night to her calf in the yard. On the day in question, however, she did not come back; and early the next morning the settler started out to look for her, taking his dogs with him.

A mile from the house, in an open glade, the dogs suddenly struck the trail of some wild beast of a dangerous kind, as was indicated by the bristling of their hair and their low growling. This trail led up the mountain, but the settler called his dogs away from it and forced them to follow it back the other way until he came to a little glad, in which lay the remains of the cow.

There the ground was very much torn up, and in the soft soil were the footprints of several huge timber wolves. Following their tracks where they left the cow the settler soon discovered that there were three of them.

He came back that night and sat up in the clear, cold moonlight to get a shot at the marauders if they returned; but the cunning beasts circled around, got his wind and made off without giving him a chance at them. No animal is more difficult to outwit than one of these great wolves.

After this he carefully housed his stock at night and watched it during the day, keeping even the dogs from wandering off into the forest. One clear, cold day he took out his oxen to haul in some logs from a couple of miles up the mountain. On his second trip down some accident occurred which made it necessary for him to leave the yoke of steers hitched to a tree, and go back to the house for some tools.

He had no idea that there was any danger in thus leaving the animals, for it did not occur to him that the wolves would dare to make an assault in open daylight, where he had been passing and repassing along the road.

He went down to the cabin, got the axe and whatever tools were needed, and returned toward the oxen with one of his dogs frisking beside him. On nearing the place where the oxen had been left, the dog suddenly priced up its ears and raced off ahead of him. Stopping for a moment to listen, he heard up the mountain-side a crashing and struggling in the bushes and a savage growling and snarling, and instantly knew that his poor steers had been attacked by the wolves.

Shouting at the top of his voice, he ran up toward the place and soon heard the clamorous baying of the dog. On reaching a bend in the road he saw before him a scene of destruction.

The three wolves had come down the road and suddenly assailed the oxen, which, yoked as they were to a heavy sledge, and in addition tied to a tree, were unable either to escape or to make any resistance. The savage beasts had overthrown them and torn them terribly, although in their frantic dying struggles the oxen had overturned the sledge and smashed many of the neighboring saplings and small trees.

When the man came up, the three wolves were racening on the warm flesh, while the dog, at some distance off, was baying and afraid to come near them.

The wolves at first seemed inclined to resist the man's approach. His rifle had been left in the sledge, and was lying overturned in the snow some thirty feet from the wolves, slo that he had only his axe.

He advanced toward them, shouting and brandishing his weapon, and the dog, taking courage, went on slightly ahead of him. Two of the wolves slunk slowly off; the third, a huge gray beast, stood with its forepaws on one of the oxen, glaring at him and declining to leave.

The settler came on to within ten yards, and then skirted around to where his rifle lay in the snow, keeping a sharp lookout on the wolf for fear it might jump on him. On picking up the rifle he found that the snow had caked in the lock, and for a moment or two he was busy putting it in order.

During tthis time the great gray wolf wrenched the fore shoulder from the ox and trotted off with it into the forest. The two others then slouched along the edge of the clearing to join their comrade; but the settler was in time, bu a quick shot, to take partial vengeance by breaing the back of the rearmost of the three.

The dog rushed forward and shook the dying beast and then, excited by the blood, dashed into the forest after the two others. He had not gone a hundred yards before the man heard him yell in agony, and hurrying toward him through the snow, found him lying with his throat and flanks cut open.

Evidently as soon as the two wolves had got out of rifle-shot they had turned savagely on the unfortunate dog and killed him.

The settler, furious at his loss and misfortune, instantly went down to the nearest neighbor to borrow two large steel bear-traps, which he intended to set by some bait.

Three nights afterward one of his enemies bearded him on his very threshold; for as one of the dogs was walking from the barn over to the house just after nightfall a great wolf suddenly gallped out of the darkness, overthrew and throttled the dog in the twinling of an eye, though it was a large and strong beast, and started to drug the animal into the bushes.

The two remaining dogs, however, rushed forward to the rescue of their comrade, and as the man appeared at the same moment, the wolf sullenly drew off into the thicket. Immediately the man set one of the iron traps by the body of the dead dog, and went back into his house.

In an hour afterward the wolf returned. The carcass had been left not a hundred yards from the hut, and the spring of the trap and the savage growl of pain of the wolf were both distinctly audible.

Seizing a toch and his axe, the settler threw open the door and rushed out with his dogs, which raced ahead. As he ran up toward the trap a furious worrying and snarling told him that the trapped wolf was being throttled by the comrades of the dead dog.

On reaching the scene of conflict the torch showed the wolf held firmly by one forepaw, and yet holding his own fairly well against the two powerful dogs, both of which he had wounded. However, they had him fast, one by the side of the neck and the other by the flank, and the settler put an end to the conflict with his axe.

After this he believed he was safe, as he did not suppose that the third wolf would linger around the neighborhood where the other two had been killed. For six weeks, indeed, he saw no sign of it. Then one day he came across the huge footprints of the robber in the snow, where it had been walking around and around the house. Again it went off and did not come back until early in the spring.

The wolf was, as he saw by the tracks, the largest of the three--probably the one which had stood on the body of the ox and defied him as he approached. The game had been driven by the snow from the neighboring mountains, and evidently the brute was very hungry.

One morning early the settler decided to go down the mountain, and accordingly saddled his horse. In putting on the bridle the horse for some reason took fright at him, broke off and ran away up the wood road. He followed it at one.

After going half a mile he topped a slight rise and saw the horse in a beaver meadow, some six hundred yards ahead. As he saw it he also noticed a great gray figure come galloping out of the sprice woods through the snow toward the unfortunate animal.

The horse saw his foe at the same moment, and started down the road on a desperate run. But before he could get under way the wolf galloped alongside and seized it by the outstretched hock with such violence that the teeth met clean through the sinews, and the horse was brought down on his haunches.

It gave a piercing whinny of despair, and the wolf let go for a moment. But the instant the horse again attempted to start off it was seized by the other hock and completely hamstrung. Before the man could come up its flank was torn open and its life was extinct. Nevertheless the settler drove off the wolf before it had a chance to snatch more than a mouthful or two.

He brought out the mare and dragged the saddle horse down to his cabin, where he left it outside the door, intending to use it as bait the following day, That same evening, however, the wolf, evidently maddened with hunger, visited the farmhouse.

It was just dark, and the mare and her colt were in the corral, when the great gray beast crept up to the outside and leaped suddenly over the high stockade to get at the colt, which ran frantically toward the mare. As the wolf followed, the mare, wheeling around, lashed out with her hind legs and struck him squarely in the face, breaking his lower jaw.

The scuffle had called out the dogs, which rushed furiously to the rescue. The wolf turned and galloped toward the stockade, but stunned by the mare's blow, he missed his jump the first time and fell backward. As he rose one of the dogs seized him by the hamp.

He fought savagely, but with his broken under jaw he could do little damage. When the settler, roused by the tumult, rushed in with his rifle, it was to find the last one of the three beasts which had done himi so much damage dying under the fangs of the dogs.

Youth's Companion
July 13, 1893

Tales Told By a Ranch Fireside

II.- A Man-Killing Bear

The grizzly bear is without doubt the most formidable wild beast of North America, and the most dangerous antagonist to man. It must not be supposed, however, that the grizzly is likely to attack man unprovoked; though in the old days, at the beginning of the present century, the first trappers and hunters who crossed the great plains and the Rockies found these huge bears very fierce and aggressive.

But the advent of the white hunter, and later the introduction of the large-bored, breech-loading rifle, soon worked a radical change in bear nature. The grizzlies of today do not eagerly assail and molest travellers as their forefathers did in the days of Lewis and Clark, and of the hardy adventurers who followed in the footsteps of these first explorers.

Yet even now bears are occasionally found which will assail men in certain circumstances. A she-bear with cubs, if the cubs are menaced will often charge with reckless fury at any brute or human foe, although it is often the case that even a she-bear will flee with abject cowardice from an attack, leaving her cubs to their fate.

If a bear is suddenly surprised, where he sees no means of escape, he will often attack a man simply through dread or to get out of the way.

Finally there are a very few wicked and crafty old bears which will attack from sheer malice.

Almost every trapper past middle age who has spent his life in the wilderness has stories to tell about exceptionally savage bears of this kind. One of these stories was told in my ranch-house one winter evening by an old mountain hunter, clad in fur cap, buckskin hunting-shirt and leather trousers, who had come to the ranch at nightfall, when the cowboys were returning from their day's labor.

The old fellow, who was known by the nickname of "Buckskin," had camped for several months in the Bad Lands but a score of miles away from my ranch. Most of his previous life had been spent among the main chains of the Rockies. After supper the conversation drifted to bears, always a favorite subject of talk in frontier cabins, and some of my men began to recount their own adventures with these great, clumsy-looking beasts.

This at once aroused the trapper's interest. He soon had the conversation to himself, telling us story after story of the bears he had killed and the escapes he had met with in battling against them.

In particular he told us of one bear which, many years before, had killed the partner with whom at the time he was trapping.

The two men were camped in a high mountain valley in northwestern Wyoming, their camp being pitched at the edge of a "park country"--that is, a region where large glades and groves of tall evergreen-trees alternate.

They had been trapping beaver, the animal which, on account of its abundance and the value of the fur, was more eagerly followed than any other by the old-time plains and mountain trappers. They had with them four shaggy pack-ponies, such as most of these hunters use, and as these ponies were not needed at the moment, they had been turned loose to shift for themselves in the open glade country.

Late one evening three of the ponies surprised the trappers by galloping up to the campfire and there halting. The fourth did not make his appearance. The trappers knew that some wild beast must have assailed the animals and had probably caught one and caused the others to flee for protection toward the place which they had learned to associate with safety.

Before dawn the next morning the two men started off to look for the lost horse. They skirted several great glades, following the tracks off the ponies that had come to the fire the previous evening. Two miles away, at the edge of a tall pine wood, they found the body of the lost horse, already partially eaten.

The tracks round about showed that the assailant was a grizzly of uncommon size, which had evidently jumped at the horses just after dusk, as they fed up to the edge of the woods. The owner of the horse decided to wait by the carcass for the bear's return, while old Buckskin went off to do the day's work in looking after traps, and the like.

Buckskin was absent all day, and reached camp after nightfall. His friend had come in ahead of him, having waited in vain for the bear. As there was no moon he had not tought it worthwhile to stay by the bait during the night.

The next morning they returned to the carcass and found that the bear had returned and eaten his full, after which he had lumbered off up the hillside. They took up his tracks and followed him for some three hours; but the wary old brute was not to be surprised. When they at last reached the spot where he had made his bed, it was only to find that he must have heard them as they approached, for he had evidently left in a great hurry.

After following the roused animal for some distance they found they could not overtake him. He was in an ugly mood, and kept halting every mile or so to walk to and fro, bit and break down the saplings, and paw the earth and dead logs; but in spite of this bullying he would not absolutely await their approach, but always shambled off before they came in sight.

At last they decided to abandon the pursuit. They then separated, each to make an afternoon's hunt and return to camp by his own way.

Our friend reached camp at dusk, but his partner did not turn up that evening at all. However, it was nothing unusual for either one of the two to be off for a night, and Buckskin thought little of it.

Next morning he again hunted all day, and returned to camp fully expecting to see his friend there, but found no sign of him. The second night passed, still without his coming in.

The morning after, the old fellow became uneasy and started to hunt him up. All that day he searched in vain, and when, on coming back to camp, there was still no trace of him, he was sure that some accident had happened.

The next morning he went back to the pine grove in which they had separated on leaving the trail of the bear. His friend had worn hob-nailed boots instead of moccasins, and this made it much easier to follow his trackes. With some difficulty the old hunter traced him for some four miles, until he came to a rocky stretch of country where all sign of the footprints disappeared.

However, he was a little startled to observe footprints of a different sort. A great beast, without doubt the same one that had killed the horse, had been travelling in a course parallel to that of the man.

Apparently the beast had been lurking just in front of his two pursuers the day they followed him from the carcass; and from the character of the "sign" Buckskin judged that as soon as he separated from his friend, the bear had likewise turned and had begun to follow the trapper.

The bear had not followed the man into the rocky piece of ground, and when the old hunter failed in his efforts to trace up his friend, he took the trail of the bear instead.

Three-quarters of a mile on, the bear, which had so far been walking, had broken into a gallop, the claws making deep scratches here and there in the patches of soft earth. The trail then led into a very thick and dark wood, and here the footprints of the man suddenly reappeared.

For some little time the old hunter was unable to make up his mind with certainty as to which one was following the other; but finally, in the decayed mold by a rotten log, he found unmistakable sign where the print of the bear's foot overlaid that of the man. This put the matter beyond doubt. The bear was following the man.

For a couple of hours more the hunter slowly and with difficulty followed the dim trail.

The bear had apparently not cared to close in, but had slouched along some distance behind the man. Then in a marshy thicket where a mountain stream came down, the end had come.

Evidently at this place the man, still unconscious that he was followed, had turned and gone upward, and the bear, altering his course to an oblique angle, had intercepted him, making his rush just as he came through a patch of low willows. The body of the man lay under the willow branches beside the brook, terribly torn and disfigured.

Evidently the bear had rushed at him so quickly that he could not fire his gun, and had killed him with its powerful jaws. The unfortunate man's body was almost torn to pieces. The killing had evidently been done purely for malice, for the remains were uneaten, nor had the bear returned to them.

Angry and horrified at his friend's fate, old Buckskin spent the next two days in looking carefully through the neighboring groves for fresh tracks of the cunning and savage monster. At last he found an open spot of ground where the brute was evidently fond of sunning himself in the early morning; and to this spot the hunter returned before dawn the following day.

He did not have long to wait. By sunrise a slight crackling of the thick undergrowth told him that the bear was approaching. A few minutes afterward the brute appeared. It was a larg beast with a poor coat, its head scarred by teeth and claw marks gained in many a combat with others of its own kind.

It came boldly into the opening and lay down, but for some time kept turning its head from side to side so that no shot could be obtained.

At last, growing impatient, the hunter broke a stick., Instantly the bear swung his head around sidewise, and in another moment a bullet crashed into its skull at the base of the ear, and the huge body fell limply over on its side, lifeless.

Forum
August, 1893

Big Game Disappearing in the West

IT has been my good-luck to kill every kind of game properly belonging to the United States: though one beast which I never had a chance to slay, the jaguar, from the torrid South, sometimes comes just across the Rio Grande; nor have I ever hunted the musk-ox and polar bear in the boreal wastes where they dwell, surrounded by the frozen desolation of the uttermost North.

There are, in different parts of our country, chances to try so many various kinds of hunting, with rifle or with horse and hound, that it is nearly impossible for one man to have experience of them all. Then are many hunts I long hoped to take, but never did and never shall; they must be left for men with more time, or for those whose homes are nearer to the hunting grounds. I have never seen a grizzly roped by the riders of the plains, nor a black bear killed with the knife and hounds in the southern canebrakes; though at one time I had for many years a standing invitation to witness this last feat on a plantation in Arkansas. The friend who gave it, an old backwoods planter, at one time lost almost all his hogs by the numerous bears who infested his neighborhood. He took a grimly humorous revenge each fall by doing his winter killing among the bears instead of among the hogs they had slain; for as the cold weather approached he regularly proceeded to lay in a stock of bear-bacon, scouring the canebrakes in a series of systematic hunts, bringing the quarry to bay with the help of a big pack of hard-fighting mongrels, and then killing it with his long, broad-bladed bowie. Again, I should like to make a trial at killing peccaries with the spear, whether on foot or on horseback, and with or without dogs. I should like much to repeat the experience of a friend who cruised northward through the Bering Sea, shooting walrus and polar bear; and that of two other friends who travelled with dog-sleds to the Barren Grounds, in chase of the caribou, and of that last survivor of the Ice Age, the strange musk-ox. Once in a while it must be good sport to shoot alligators by torchlight in the everglades of Florida or the bayous of Louisiana.

Of American big game the bison, almost always known as the buffalo, was the largest and most important to man. When the first white settlers landed in Virginia the bison ranged east of the Alleghenies almost to the sea-coast, westward to the dry deserts lying beyond the Rocky Mountains, northward to the Great Slave Lake and southward to Chihuahua. It was a beast of the forests and mountains, in the Alleghenies no less than in the Rockies; but its true home was on the prairies, and the high plains. Across these it roamed, hither and thither, in herds of enormous, of incredible magnitude; herds so large that they covered the waving grass-land for hundreds of square leagues, and when on the march occupied days and days in passing a given point. But the seething myriads of shaggy-maned wild cattle vanished with remarkable and melancholy rapidity before the inroads of the white hunters, and the steady march of the oncoming settlers. Now they are on the point of extinction. Two or three hundred are left in that great national game-preserve, the Yellowstone Park; and it is said that others still remain in the wintry desolation of Athabasca. Elsewhere only a few individuals exist—probably considerably less than half a hundred all told—scattered in small parties in the wildest and most remote and inaccessible portions of the Rocky Mountains. A bison bull is the largest American animal. His huge bulk, his short, curved black horns, the shaggy mane clothing his great neck and shoulders, give him a look of ferocity which his conduct belies. Yet he is truly a grand and noble beast, and his loss from our prairies and forest is as keenly regretted by the lover of nature and of wildlife as by the hunter.

My friend, Gen. W. H. Walker, of Virginia, had an experience in the early fifties with buffaloes on the upper Arkansas River, which gives some idea of their enormous numbers at that time. He was camped with a scouting party on the banks of the river, and had gone out to try to shoot some meat. There were many buffaloes in sight, scattered, according to their custom, in large bands. When he was a mile or two away from the river a dull roaring sound in the distance attracted his attention, and he saw that a herd of buffalo far to the south, away from the river, had been stampeded and was running his way. He knew that if he was caught in the open by the stampeded herd his chance for life would be small, and at once ran for the river. By desperate efforts he reached the breaks in the sheer banks just as the buffaloes readied them, and got into a position of safety on the pinnacle of a little bluff. From this point of vantage lie could see the entire plain. To the very verge of the horizon the brown masses of the buffalo bands showed through the dust clouds, coming on with a thunderous roar like that of surf. Camp was a mile away, and the stampede luckily passed to one side of it. Watching his chance he finally dodged back to the tent, and all that afternoon watched the immense masses of buffalo, as band after band tore to the brink of the bluffs on one side, raced down them, rushed through the water, up the bluffs on the other side, and again off over the plain, churning the sandy, shallow stream into a ceaseless tumult. When darkness fell there was no apparent decrease in the numbers that were passing, and all through that night the continuous roar showed that the herds were still threshing across the river. Toward dawn the sound at last ceased, and General Walker arose somewhat irritated, as he had reckoned on killing au ample supply of meat, and he supposed that there would be now no bison left south of the river. To his astonishment, when he strolled up on the bluffs and looked over the plain, it was still covered far and wide with groups of buffalo, grazing quietly. Apparently there were as many on that side as ever, in spite of the many scores of thousands that must have crossed over the river during the stampede of the afternoon and night. The barren-ground caribou is the only American animal which is now ever seen in such enormous herds.

  In 1862 Mr. Clarence King, while riding along the overland trail through western Kansas, passed through a great buffalo herd, and was himself injured in an encounter with a bull. The great herd was then passing north, and Mr. King reckoned that it must have covered an area nearly seventy miles by thirty in extent; the figures representing his rough guess, made after travelling through the herd crosswise, and upon knowing how long it took to pass a given point going northward. This great herd of course was not a solid mass of buffaloes; it consisted of innumerable bands of every size, dotting the prairie within the limits given. Mr. King was mounted on a somewhat unmanageable horse. On one occasion in following a band he wounded a large bull, and became so wedged in by the maddened animals that he was unable to avoid the charge of the bull, which was at its last gasp. Coming straight toward him it leaped into the air and struck the afterpart of the saddle full with its massive forehead. The horse was hurled to the ground with a broken back, and King's leg was likewise broken, while the bull turned a complete somerset over them and never rose again.

In the recesses of the Rocky Mountains, from Colorado northward through Alberta, and in the depths of the sub-arctic forest beyond the Saskatchewan, there have always been found small numbers of the bison, locally called the mountain buffalo and wood buffalo; often indeed the old hunters term these animals "bison," although they never speak of the plains animals save as buffalo. They form a slight variety of what was formerly the ordinary plains bison, inter-grading with it; on the whole they are darker in color, with longer, thicker hair, and in consequence with the appearance of being heavier-bodied and shorter-legged. They have been sometimes spoken of as forming a separate species; but, judging from my own limited experience, and from a comparison of the many hides I have seen, 1 think they are really the same animal, many individuals of the two so-called varieties being quite indistinguishable. In fact the only moderate-sized herd of wild bison in existence to-day, the protected herd in the Yellowstone Park, is composed of animals intermediate in habits and coat between the mountain and plains varieties—as were all the herds of the Bighorn, Big Hole, Upper Madison, and Upper Yellowstone valleys.

Though it was always more difficult to kill the bison of the forests and mountains than the bison of the prairie, yet now that the species is, in its wild state, hovering on the brink of extinction, the difficulty is immeasurably increased. A merciless and terrible process of natural selection, in which the agents were rifle-bearing hunters, has left as the last survivors in a hopeless struggle for existence only the wariest of the bison and those gifted with the sharpest senses. That this was true of the last lingering individuals that survived the great slaughter on the plains is well shown by Mr. Hornaday in his graphic account of his campaign against the few scattered buffalo which still lived in 1886 between the Missouri and the Yellowstone, along the Big Dry. The bison of the plains and the prairies have now vanished; and so few of their brethren of the mountains and the northern forests are left, that they can just barely be reckoned among American game; but whoever is so fortunate as to find any of these animals must work his hardest, and show all his skill as a hunter if he wishes to get one.

The king of the game beasts of temperate North America, because the most dangerous to the hunter, is the grizzly bear; known to the few remaining old-time trappers of the Rookies and the Great Plains, sometimes as "Old Ephraim" and sometimes as "Moccasin Joe"—the last in allusion to his queer, half-human footprints, which look as if made by some misshapen giant, walking in moccasins. The grizzly is now chiefly a beast of the high hills and heavy timber; but this is merely because he has learned that he must rely on cover to guard him from man, and has forsaken the open ground accordingly. In old days, and in one or two very out-of-the-way places almost to the present time, he wandered at will over the plains. It is only the wariness born of fear which nowadays causes him to cling to the thick brush of the large river-bottoms throughout the plains country. When there were no rifle-bearing hunters in the land, to harass him and make him afraid, he roved hither and thither at will, in burly self-confidence. Then he cared little for cover, unless as a weather-break, or because it happened to contain food he liked. If the humor seized him he would roam for days over the rolling or broken prairie, searching for roots, digging up gophers, or perhaps following the great buffalo herds cither to prey on some unwary straggler which he was able to catch at a disadvantage in a washout, or else to feast on the carcasses of those which died by accident. Old hunters, survivors of the long-vanished ages when the vast herds thronged the high plains and were followed by the wild red tribes, and by bands of whites who were scarcely less savage, have told me that they often met bears under such circumstances; and these bears were accustomed to sleep in a patch of rank sage bush, in the niche of a washout, or under the lee of a boulder, seeking their food abroad even in full daylight. The bears of the Upper Missouri basin— which were so light in color that the early explorers often alluded to them as gray or even as "white"—were particularly given to this life in the open. To this day that close kinsman of the grisly known as the bear of the barren grounds continues to lead this same kind of life, in the far north. My friend Mr. Rockhill, of Maryland, who was the first white man to explore eastern Tibet, describes the large, grizzly-like bear of those desolate uplands as having similar habits.

However, the grizzly is a shrewd beast and shows the usual bearlike capacity for adapting himself to changed conditions. He has in most places become a cover-haunting animal, sly in his ways, wary to a degree, and clinging to the shelter of the deepest forests in the mountains and of the most tangled thickets in the plains. Hence he has held his own far better than such game as the bison and elk. He is much less common than formerly, but he is still to be found throughout most of his former range; save of course in the immediate neighborhood of the large towns.

Next to the bison in size, and much superior in height to it and to all other American game—for it is taller than the tallest horse—comes the moose, or broad-horned elk. It is a strange, uncouth-looking beast, with very long legs, short thick neck, a big, ungainly head, a swollen nose, and huge shovel horns. Its home is in the cold, wet pine and spruce forests, which stretch from the sub-arctic region of Canada southward in certain places across our frontier. Two centuries ago it was found as far south as Massachusetts. It has now been exterminated from its former haunts in northern New York and Vermont, and is on the point of vanishing from northern Michigan. It is still found in northern Maine and northeastern Minnesota and in portions of northern Idaho and Washington; while along the Rockies it extends its range southward through western Montana to northwestern Wyoming, south of the Tetons. In 1884 I saw the fresh hide of one that was killed in the Bighorn Mountains.

The wapiti, or round-horned elk, like the bison, and unlike the moose, had its centre of abundance in the United States, though extending northward into Canada. Originally its range reached from ocean to ocean and it went in herds of thousands of individuals; but it has suffered more from the persecution of hunters than any other game except the bison. By the beginning of this century it had been exterminated in most localities east of the Mississippi; but a few lingered on for many years in the Alleghenies. Colonel Cecil Clay informs me that an Indian whom he knew killed one in Pennsylvania in 1869. A very few still exist here and there in northern Michigan and Minnesota, and in one or two spots on the western boundary of Nebraska and the Dakotas; but it is now properly a beast of the wooded western mountains. It is still plentiful in western Colorado, Wyoming, and Montana, and in parts of Idaho, Washington, and Oregon. Though not so large as the moose it is the most beautiful and stately of all animals of the deer kind, and its antlers are marvels of symmetrical grandeur.

The woodland caribou is inferior to the wapiti both in size and symmetry. The tips of the many branches of its long, irregular antlers are slightly palmated. Its range is the same as that of the moose, save that it does not go so far southward. Its hoofs are long and round; even larger than the long, oval hoofs of the moose, and much larger than those of the wapiti. The tracks of all three can be told apart at a glance, and cannot be mistaken for the footprints of other game. Wapiti tracks, however, look much like those of yearling and two-year-old cattle, unless the ground is steep or muddy, in which case the marks of the false hoofs appear, the joints of wapiti being more flexible than those of domestic stock.

The whitetail deer is now, as it always has been, the best known and most abundant of American big game, and though its numbers have been greatly thinned it is still found in almost every state of the union. The common blacktail or mule deer, which has likewise been sadly thinned in numbers, though once extraordinarily abundant, extends from the great plains to the Pacific; but is supplanted on the Puget Sound coast by the Columbian blacktail. The delicate, heart-shaped footprints of all three are nearly indistinguishable; when the animal is running the hoof points are of course separated. The track of the antelope is more oval, growing squarer with age. Mountain sheep leave footmarks of a squarer shape, the points of the hoof making little indentations in the soil, well apart, even when the animal is only walking; and a yearling's track is not unlike that made by a big prong-buck when striding rapidly with the toes well apart. White-goat tracks are also square, and as large as those of the sheep; but there is less indentation of the hoof points, which come nearer together.

The antelope, or prong-buck, was once found in abundance from the eastern edge of the great plains to the Pacific, but it has everywhere diminished in numbers, and has been exterminated along the eastern and western borders of its former range. The bighorn, or mountain sheep, is found in the Rooky Mountains from northern Mexico to Alaska; and in the United States from the Coast and Cascade ranges to the Bad Lands of the western edges of the Dakotas, wherever there are mountain chains or tracts of rugged hills. It was never very abundant, and, though it has become less so, it has held its own better than most game. The white goat, however, alone among our game animals, has positively increased in numbers since the advent of settlers; because white hunters rarely follow it, and the Indians who once sought its skin for robes now use blankets instead. Its true home is in Alaska and Canada, but it crosses our borders along the lines of the Rockies and Cascades, and a few small isolated colonies are found here and there southward to California and New Mexico. The cougar and wolf, once common throughout the United States, have now completely disappeared from all save the wildest regions. The black bear holds its own better; it was never found on the great plains. The little peccary or Mexican wild hog merely crosses our Southern bonier.

The finest hunting-ground in America was, and indeed is, the mountainous region of western Montana and northwestern Wyoming. In this high, cold land, of lofty mountains, deep forests, and open prairies, with its beautiful lakes and rapid rivers, all the species of big game mentioned above, except the peccary and Columbian black-tail, arc to be found. Until 1880 they were very abundant, and they are still, with the exception of the bison, fairly plentiful. On most of the long hunting expeditions which I made away from my ranch, I went into this region. The bulk of my hunting has been done in the cattle country, near my ranch on the Little Missouri, and in the adjoining lands round the lower Powder and Yellowstone. Until 1881 the valley of the Little Missouri was fairly thronged with game, and was absolutely unchanged in any respect from its original condition of primeval wildness. With the incoming of the stockmen all this changed, and the game was woefully slaughtered; but plenty of deer and antelope, a few sheep and bear, and an occasional elk are still left.

    I have never sought to make large bags, for a hunter should not be a gamebutcher. It is always lawful to kill dangerous or noxious animals, like the bear, cougar, and wolf; but other game should only be shot when there is need of the meat, or for the sake of an unusually fine trophy. Killing a reasonable number of bulls, bucks, or rams does no harm whatever to the species; to slay half the males of any kind of game would not stop the natural increase, and they yield the best sport, and are the legitimate objects of the chase. From its very nature, the life of the hunter is in most places evanescent; and when it has vanished there can be no real substitute in old settled countries. Shooting in a private game-preserve is but a dismal parody; the manliest and healthiest features of the sport are lost with the change of the conditions. We need, in the interest of the community at large, a rigid system of game-laws rigidly enforced, and it is not only admissible, but one may almost say necessary, to establish, under the control of the State, great national forest reserves, which shall also be breeding-grounds and nurseries for wild game; though I should much regret to see grow up in this country a system of large private game-preserves kept for the enjoyment of the very rich.

Youth's Companion
August, 1893

Tales Told By a Ranch Fireside

A Mysterious Enemy

Frontiersman are not as a rule apt to be very superstitious. They lead lives too hard and practical, and have too little imagination in things spiritual. I have heard but few ghost stories while living on the frontier, and these few were of a perfectly commonplace and conventional type.

But I once listened to a sort of goblin story which impressed me. It was told by a grizzled, weather-beaten old mountain hunter named Bauman, whose father was a German immigrant, but who himself was born and had passed all his life on the frontier. He evidently believed what he said, for he could hardly repress a shudder at certain points of the tale; but of course it was impossible to tell exactly how accurate was his recollection of the details.

When the event occurred he was still a young man, and was trapping with a partner among the mountains which divided the forks of the Salmon from the head of Wisdom river. Not having had much luck, he and his partner determined to go up into a particularly wild and lonely pass through which ran a small stream said to contain many beaver.

The pass had an evil reputation because the year before a solitary hunter who had wandered into it was there slain, seemingly by a wild beast; the half-eaten remains were found by some mining prospectors who had passed his camp only the night before.

But this event weighed very lightly with the two trappers, who were as adventurous and hardy as others of their kind. They took their two lean mountain ponies to the foot of the pass, where they left them in an open beaver meadow, the rocky-timber-clad ground being from thence onward impracticable for horses.

Then they struck out on foot through the vast, gloomy forest, and in about four hours reached a little open glade where they concluded to camp, as there signs of game were plenty.

There was still an hour or two of daylight left, and after building a brush lean-to and throwing down and opening their packs, they started up stream. The country was very dense and hard to traverse, for much timber was down, although here and there the somber forest was broken by small glades of mountain grass.

At dusk they again reached their camp. The glade in which it was pitched was not many yards across. Tall, close-set pines and firs rose around it like a wall. On one side was a little stream, beyond which rose the steep mountain slopes, covered with evergreen forest.

The men were surprised to find that during their short absence something, apparently a bear, had visited camp, and had rummaged about among their things, scattering the contents of their packs, and in sheer wantonness destroying their lean-to.

While Bauman got supper, his companion began to examine the tracks, and soon took a brand from the fire to follow them up, where the intruder had walked along a game trail after leaving the camp. When the brand flickered out, he returned and took another, repeating his inspection of the footprints very closely.

He then came back to the fire, stood by it a minute or two peering out into the darkness, and suddenly remarked with a queer lauch, "Bauman, that bear has been walking on two legs."

Bauman laughed at this, but his partner insisted he was right, and when they again examined the tracks with a torch they certainl seemed made by two paws or feet. However, it was too dark to make sure.

After expressing a conjecture that the tracks might be those of a human being, and coming to the conclusion that they could not be, the two men rolled up in their blankets and went to sleep under the lean-to.

At midnight Bauman was awakened by some noise, and sat up in his blankets. As he did so his nostrils were struck by a strong-wild-beast odor, and he caught the loom of a great body in the darkness at the mouth of the lean-to.

Grasping his rifle, he fired it at the vague, formless, shadow; but he must have missed, for immediately afterwards he heard the smashing of the underwood as the thing, whatever it was, rushed off into the impenetrable blackness of the forest and the night. After this the two men slept but little, sitting up by the rekindled fire. But they heard nothing more, and in the morning they started out to look at the few traps they had set, and to put out new ones.

By an unspoken agreement they kept together all day, and returned to camp towards evening. On nearing it they saw, to their astonishment, that the lean-to had again been torn down. The visitor of the preceding day had returned, and in wanton malice had tossed about their camp kit and bedding, and destroyed the shanty. The ground was marked up by the creature's tracks, and on leaving the camp it had gone along the soft earth by the brook, where its trail was as plain as on snow.

A glance at this trail made one thing evident. Whatever the creature was which had made it, it had certainly walked on but two legs.

The men, thoroughly uneasy, gathered a great heap of dead logs, and kept up a roaring fire throughout the night, one or the other sitting up on guard most of the time. About midnight the thing came down through the forest opposite, across the brook, and stayed there on the hillside for nearly an hour.

In the morning the two trappers, after discussing the strange events of the last thirty-six hours, decided that they would shoulder their packs and leave the valley that afternoon. They were the more ready to do this because, in spite of seeing a good deal of game-sign, they had caught very little fur. However, it was necessary first to gather their traps.

All the morning they kept together, picking up trap after trap, each one empty. On first leaving camp they had the disagreeable sensation of being followed. In the dense spruce thickets they heard a branch snap occasionally after they had passed; or there would be slight rustling noises among the small pines to one side of them.

Finally, oppressed and made angry by this extraordinary pursuit, they turned suddenly and ran back on their trail.

In a minute, in a mossy open space they came on fresh footprints, of great size, of the same kind as those they had seen in camp. But the creature itself had vanished, nor did they hear it again during their walk.

At noon they were back within a couple of miles of camp. In the high, bright sunlight their fears seemed absurd to the two armed men. accustomed as they were through long years of lonely wandering in the wilderness, to face every kind of danger from man, brute, or element.

Tere were still three beaver traps to collect from a little pond in a wide racing near by. Bauman volunteered to gather these and bring them in, while his companion went ahead to camp, and made ready the packs.

On reaching the pond Bauman found three beaver in the traps; and one of the traps had been pulled loose and carried into a beaver-house. He took several hours in securing and preparing the beaver, and when he started homeward he marked with some uneasiness how low the sun was getting.

As he hurried towards camp, under the tall trees, the silence and desolation of the forest weighed on him. His feet made no sound on the pine needles; and the slanting sun rays, striking through among the straight trunks, made a gray twilight in which objects at a distance glimmered indistinctly. There was nothing to break the ghostly stillness which, when there is no breeze, always brookds over these sombre primeval forests.

At last he came to the edge of the little glade where the camp lay, and shouted as he approached it but got no answer. The camp-fire had one out, though the thin, blue smoke was still curling upwards. The packs all arranged were by it.

At first Bauman could not see his friend; nor did he receive and answer to his call. Stepping forward he shouted again, and as he did so his eye fell on the body of his friend, stretched out dead beside the trunk of a great fallen spruce.

The footprints of the unknown beast-creature, printed deep in the soft soil, told the whole story.

The unfortunate man, having finished his packing, had

sat down on the spruce log with his face to the fire, and his back to the dense woods, to wait for his friend. While thus waiting, his monstrous assailant, which had evidently been lurking near by in the woods waiting for a chance to catch one of the adventurers unprepared, came silently up from behind, walking with long, noiseless steps, and as the tracks showed, still on two legs.

Evidently unheard, it reached the man, and must have broken his neck by wrenching his head back with its forepaws, while it buried its teeth in his throat. It had not eaten the body, but apparently had gambolled round it in uncouth and ferocious glee; had rolled it savagely over and over and had then fled back into the soundless depths of the woods.

Bauman, utterly unnerved, and believing that the creature with which he had to deal was something either half-human or half-devilish, some great goblin-beast, abandoned everything but his rifle and struck off at speed down the pass, not halting until he reached the beaver meadows where the hobbled ponies were still grazing.

Mounting, he rode onwards through the night, until far beyond the reach of pursuit.

Such was his story. Bauman was of German ancestry, and in his childhood had doubtless been saturated with the ghost and goblin lore of the German peasantry, so all kinds of gruesome superstitions were latent in his mind. As for the tracks being seemingly those of an animal walking on two feet, it is perfectly possible that the bear may have been injured, by a trap or otherwise, in one of its forelegs, and that in consequence it was apt to move about on its hind legs even more commonly than its brethren, who all walk quite freely in an erect position.

In recnnoitring the camp it may have frequently assumed this upright posture from mere desire of keeping a better lookout; and it may be that by chance those places where its tracks were clearest were precisely those where it had happened to rise for a few paces on its hind legs.

Travel
January, 1895

Hunting in the Cattle Country

For the last two or three years whatever hunting I have done has been from my ranch house, or while out on the range among the cattle. It is still possible in the cattle country to kill an occasional mountain sheep, bear, or elk; but nowadays deer and antelope are the only big game upon which the ranchman of the great plains can safely count.

In September of this year I made a ten-days' trip out on the great plains some fifty miles from my ranch, part of the time riding among the cattle, part of the time hunting antelope. My foreman was with me, and we took the ranch wagon, driven by a cowboy who had just come over the trail with cattle from Colorado.

After inspecting a lot of Maltese-cross "dogies" which had been put on in the spring, and which were still hanging around the river bottoms, as stock generally do until the winter weather gets them back into the hills, we headed for the prairies. The first night we passed by a stagnant pool in a creek bottom, and late on the second day reached the hunting-grounds; we struck a region where I had found antelope very abundant in 1893. At that time they had been so plentiful that it was an easy matter to get as many fine heads as one wished, and our party had spent but one or two days on the ground before killing all that we felt we had any right to; but as we left we encountered several bands of Sioux Indians from the Standing Rock and Cheyenne River reservations, coming in to hunt, and I at once felt that the chances for any future sport were small. Indians are not good shots, but they hunt in great numbers, killing everything, does, fawns, and bucks alike, and they follow the wounded animals with the utmost perseverance, so that they cause great destruction to game.

On reaching the ground, in this year, I found my fears sadly verified; and there was one unforeseen drawback to our sport. Not only had the Indians made a great killing of antelope the season before, but in the spring one or two sheep-men had come into the country. The big flocks had been moving from one spring pool to another, eating the pasturage bare, while the shepherds, wild-looking men on rough horses, each accompanied by a pair of furtive sheep-dogs, had taken every opportunity to get a shot at antelope so as to provide themselves with meat. Two days of fruitless hunting in this sheep-ridden region was sufficient to show that the pronghorns were too scarce and shy to give us hope for sport, and we shifted quarters. As so often on such a trip, when we started to have bad luck we had plenty. One night two of the three saddle-horses stampeded, and went back straight as the crow flies to their home range, so that we did not get them until on our return. On another occasion the team succeeded in breaking the wagon pole, and as there was an entire absence of wood we had to make a splice for it with the two tent-poles and the picket ropes.

Nevertheless it was very enjoyable, out on the great grassy plains. Although we had a tent with us, I always slept in the open, in my buffalo bag, with the tarpaulin to pull over me if it rained. On each night before going to sleep I lay for many minutes gazing at the extraordinary multitude of stars above, or watching the rising of the red moon. We had plenty of fresh meat; prairie fowl and young sage fowl for the first forty-eight hours, and antelope venison afterwards. We camped by little pools, generally getting fair water; and from the camps where there was plenty of wood we took enough to build the fires at those where there was none. The nights were frosty and the days cool and pleasant, and from sunrise to sunset we were off riding or walking among the low hills and over the level uplands ; so that we slept well and ate well, and felt the beat of hardy life in our veins.

Much of the time we were on a high divide between two creek systems, from which we could see the great landmarks of all the region round about, Sentinel Butte, Square Butte, and Middle Butte, far to the north and east of us. Nothing could be more lonely and nothing more beautiful than the view at nightfall across the prairies to these huge hill masses. The lengthening shadows at last merged into one; the faint after-glow of the red sunset filled the west; the rolling prairie, sweeping in long waves to the feet of the great hills, turned violet and purple in the dim dusk; while the buttes themselves grew into vague, mysterious beauty as their sharp outlines softened in the twilight.

Even when we got out of reach of the sheep-men we never found antelope very plentiful, and they were shy; yet I had pretty good sport. There is no kind of hunting in which one spends so many cartridges as with antelope, and though, if anything, I spent rather less for each head of game killed than usual this trip, I still used up a good many. The first animal I killed was a doe, slain for meat, because I had missed two long shots at bucks already, and we were all feeling hungry for venison. After that I killed nothing but bucks.

The reason that, in antelope shooting, more cartridges are expended in proportion to the amount of game killed than with any other game is because the shots are generally taken at long range, and yet, being taken in the open, there is usually a chance to use four or five cartridges before the animal gets out of sight. These extra shots do not generally kill, but every now and then they do; and so the hunter is encouraged to try them, especially as, after the first shot, the game has been scared anyway, and no harm results from firing the others.

In 1893, on this same ground, I had a friend from the East with me, to whom I gave the shots, and I only fired myself at two antelope, both of which he had already missed. In each case a hard run and much firing at long ranges, together with, in one case, some skilful maneuvering, got me my game; yet one buck cost ten cartridges and the other nine. This year I had exactly the reverse experience. I killed five antelope for thirty-six shots, but each one that I killed was killed with the first bullet, and in not one case where I missed the first time did I hit with any subsequent one. These five antelope were shot at an average distance of about one hundred and fifty yards. Those that I missed were much farther off, on the average. The number of cartridges spent would seem extraordinary to a tyro; and an unusually good shot, or else a very timid shot, who fears to take risks, will, of course, make a better showing per head killed; but

I doubt if men with much experience in antelope hunting, who keep an accurate account of the cartridges they expend, and who are game shots of only ordinary excellence, will see anything out of the way in the performance.

During the twelve years I have hunted in the West, I have always, where possible, kept a record of the number of cartridges expended for every head of game killed, and of the distances at which it was shot. I have found that with bison, bear, moose, elk, caribou, big-horn, and white goat, where the animals shot at were mostly of good size and usually stationary, and where the mountainous or wooded country gave a chance for close approach, the average distance at which I have killed game has been eighty yards, and the average number of cartridges per head three—one of these representing the death shot, and the two others standing either for misses outright, of which there were not very many, or else for wounding game which escaped or which I afterwards overtook, or for stopping cripples and charging beasts. Black-tail deer I have generally shot at about ninety yards, at an expenditure of about four bullets for every deer bagged. White-tail I have usually killed at shorter range; but the shots were generally running, and often taken under difficult circumstances, so that my average expenditure of bullets was rather larger. Antelope, on the other hand, I have on the average shot at a little short of one hundred and fifty yards, and they have cost me about nine cartridges apiece. This, of course, as I have explained above, does not mean that I have missed eight out of nine antelope; for often the entire nine cartridges would be spent at one antelope which I eventually got. It merely means that, counting all the shots fired at antelope of every description, I had one head to show for each nine cartridges expended.

On this trip the prongbuck were shy, and they were for the most part out in the flat country. Of the five I killed, one I got by a headlong gallop to cut off his line of flight. As sometimes happens with this queer, erratic animal, when the buck saw that I was trying to cut him off, instead of turning he simply raced ahead just as hard as he knew how; and as my pony was not fast the buck got to the little pass for which he was pointed two hundred yards ahead of me. I then jumped off, and his curiosity made him commit the fatal mistake of halting for a moment to look round at me. He was standing end on, and offered a very small mark at two hundred yards, but I made a good line shot, and though I held a trifle too high, I hit him in the head and down he came. Another buck, a young one, I shot from under the wagon early one morning, as he was passing just beyond the picketed horses.

  The other three I got after much maneuvering and long, tedious stalks. I made several such stalks that were failures. Sometimes, after infinite labor, and perhaps after crawling on all-fours for an hour, or pulling myself flat on my face among small sagebrush for ten or fifteen minutes, the game took alarm and went off. Sometimes, when I finally did get a shot, it was under such circumstances that I missed. Once or twice the buck was too far for accurate shooting; once or twice he had taken alarm and was already in motion. One afternoon I had to spend so much time waiting for the antelope to get into a favorable place, that when I at last got within range I found the light so bad that my front sight glimmered indistinctly, and the bullet went wild. Another time I met with one of those misadventures which are especially irritating. It was at midday, and I made out at a long distance a band of antelope lying for their noon rest in a slight hollow. A careful stalk brought me up within fifty yards of them. I was crawling flat on my face, for the crest of the hillock sloped so gently that this was the only way to get near them. At last, peering through the grass, I saw the head of a doe. In a moment she saw me and jumped to her feet, and up stood the whole band, including the buck. I immediately tried to draw a bead on the latter, and to my horror found that, lying flat as I was, and leaning on my elbows, I could not bring the rifle above the tall, wind-shaken grass, and was utterly unable to get a sight. In another second away tore the antelope. I jumped to my feet, took a snap shot at the buck as he raced round a low-cut bank, missed, and then walked drearily home, chewing the cud of my failure, and trying to convince myself that it was due to ill luck rather than to my own shortcomings. Yet again, in more than one instance, after making a good stalk upon a baud seen at some distance, I found it contained only does and fawns, and would not shoot at them.

Three times, however, my stalk was successful Twice I was out alone; on the third occasion my foreman was with me and held my horse while I maneuvered hither and thither, and finally succeeded in getting into range. In both the first instances I got a long standing shot; but on this last occasion, after half an hour's running and crawling on my part, two of the watchful does which were in the band saw me, before I was within rifle-shot of the master buck. I was creeping up a low washout, and by ducking hastily down again and running back and up a side coulee, I managed to get within rather long range of the band as they cantered off, not yet thoroughly alarmed. The buck was behind, and I held just ahead of him. He plunged to the shot, but went off over the hill, and when I had panted up to the crest I found him dead just beyond; a fine old fellow, with the best head I got.

After killing the antelope, if I was on foot, I would take the head, saddle, and hams, and bring them in on my shoulders. If on horseback, I would take the whole antelope, packing it behind the saddle—of course, after it was dressed, and the legs cut off below the knees. I cut slashes between the sinews of the legs just above the joints; then I lifted the buck behind the saddle; then I ran the picket rope of my horse from the horn of the saddle, under the belly of the horse, to the antelope's legs on the other side, and through the slashes, bringing the end back, swaying well down on it, and fastening it again to the horn; after which I repeated the operation for the other side. Packed in this way the carcass always rides perfectly steady, and cannot by any possibility shake loose. Of course, a horse has to have some little training before it will submit to being packed.

After coming in from the antelope hunt I did but little shooting. Yet on the last day I spent at the ranch, and with the last bullet I fired from my rifle, I killed a fine white-tail buck. The sharp fall weather had just begun, and the river bottoms were very beautiful, for the clusters of wild plum-trees had turned dull red, and the young cottonwoods bright yellow, while the old trees, gnarled and storm-splintered, still kept their dark green foliage. On the day in question I left the ranch house early in the afternoon, on my favorite pony, Muley, my foreman going with me; and, after riding a couple of miles, by sheer good luck we stumbled on three white-tail, a buck, a doe, and a fawn. They were in a long winding coulee, with a belt of brush and timber running down its bottom. When we saw them they were trying to sneak off quietly through the brush; and immediately my foreman loped to the upper end of the coulee and started to ride down through it, while I ran Muley to the other end, to cut off the deer. They were, of course, quite likely to break off to one side, but this happened to be one of the occasions when everything went right, and they came straight on. When I reached a place from which I covered the exits from the timber I leaped off, and immediately afterwards heard a shout from my foreman, to tell me the deer were on foot. Muley is a pet horse, and he always enjoys immensely the gallop after game; but his nerves invariably fail him at the shot. He stood snorting beside me, and finally, as the deer came in sight, away he tore; only to go about two hundred yards, however, and stand on a hillside to watch us, with his ears pricked forward, until, when I needed him, I went for him. At the moment, however, I paid no heed to Muley, for a cracking and snapping in the brush told me the game was close; and in another second I caught the shadowy outlines of the doe and fawn as they sped through the low, thick growth. By good luck the buck, evidently a little flurried, came along on the edge of the woods next me, and as he passed, running like a quarter horse, I held well ahead of him and pulled trigger. The bullet broke his neck, and down he went in a heap—a fine fellow, with a handsome ten-point head and beautiful coat. He was very fat, for it was just before the rut.

Then we rode home; and I sat in a rocking-chair on the ranch house veranda, looking across the river at the strangely shaped and colored buttes, and at the groves of shimmering cottonwoods, until the sun went down, and the frosty air bade me go within.

Century Magazine
February, 1895

A Plan to Save the Forests

It is almost needless to say that this country needs a thoroughly scientific and permanent system of forest management in the interests of the people of today, and, above all, in the interests of their children and grandchildren. There is need of this in the East, but the need is greatest in the Rocky Mountain regions, and it is precisely in these regions that the destruction of the forest is most reckless. Many of the people in these imperiled legions are not permanent inhabitants at all; they are mere nomads, with no intention of remaining for any great length of time in the locality where they happen to be for the moment, and with still less idea of seeing their children grow op there. They, of course, care nothing whatever for the future of the country; they destroy the trees and render the land barren, often from sheer brutal carelessness, often for a pecuniary reward which is absolutely trivial in comparison with the damage done; yet their selfish clamor is allowed to stand in the way of a great measure intended to benefit the whole community.

The damage from deforestation is often very severely felt in land remote from the deforested region. Because of this fact alone the whole matter should be in the hands of the National Government. Professor Sargent's scheme seems to me in its general outlines to be good, and West Point would seem to be the propel place in which to establish the chair of instruction of which be speaks. Without more information I cannot express an opinion as to whether it would be well to try to instruct all the officers in forestry, or merely to have a special corps trained in forestry in addition to other subjects, with the idea or producing a specialized permanent body of foresters. The duties of the ordinary West Point graduate ought always to be mainly military. The specially educated men who intend to enter the profession of forestry would be entrusted with the supervision of the forest reservations. Of course a body of local foresters would have to he enlisted to work under these officers. There should be more than one forest reservation. In the East this might have to be purchased, but in the West there is no such need: Yellowstone National Park, for instance, and the other timber-land reserves, stand ready to hand.

The question of forest preservation is one of utmost moment to the American people, and no effort should be spared to awaken them to a sense of its importance; for at present they are steeped in a profound ignorance of the matter, and of how it affects the interests of themselves and their children.

The Outlook
June 3, 1899

Among the High Hills

No man living better exemplifies the truth that healthful out-of-door activity gives strength and nerve for moral and intellectual courage than does Governor Theodore Roosevelt. The following story of his hunting days, before war and politics laid their claims upon him, aptly preaches the "recreation gospel" upon which The Outlook's Recreation Number is founded. We reprint it from Mr. Roosevelt's book, "The Wilderness Hunter," by special permission of the publishers, Messrs. G. P. Putnam's Sons, of New York City —THE EDITORS.

DURING the summer of 1886 I hunted chiefly to keep the ranch in meat. It was a very pleasant summer; although it was followed by the worst winter we ever witnessed on the plains. I was much at the ranch, where I had a good deal of writing to do; but every week or two I left, to ride among the line camps, or spend a few days on any round-up which happened to be in the neighborhood.

These days of vigorous work among the cattle were themselves full of pleasure. At dawn we were in the saddle, the morning air cool in our faces; the red sunrise saw us loping across the grassy reaches of prairie land, or climbing in single file among the rugged buttes. All the forenoon we spent riding the long circle with the cow-punchers of the round-up; in the afternoon we worked the herd, cutting the cattle, with much breakneck galloping and dextrous halting and vigorous range calves; in a corral, if one was handy, otherwise in a ring of horsemen. Soon after nightfall we lay down, in a log hut or tent, if at a line camp; under the open sky, if with the round-up wagon.

After ten days or so of such work, in which every man had to do his full share—for laggards and idlers, no matter who, get no mercy in the real and healthy democracy of the round up—I would go back to the ranch to turn to my books with added zest for a fortnight Yet even during these weeks at the ranch there was some outdoor work; for I was breaking two or three colts. I took my time, breaking them gradually and gently, not, after the usual cowboy fashion, in a hurry, by sheer main strength and rough riding, with the attendant danger to the limbs of the man and very probable ruin to the manners of the horse. We rose early; each morning I stood on the low-roofed veranda, looking out under the line of murmuring, glossy-leaved cottonwoods, across the shallow river, to see the sun flame above the line of bluffs opposite. In the evening I strolled off for an hour or two's walk, rifle in hand. The roomy, homelike ranch house, with its long walls, shingled roof, and big chimneys and fireplaces, stands in a glade, in the midst of the thick forest, which covers half the bottom; behind rises, bare and steep, the wall of peaks, ridges, and table-lands.

During the summer in question I once or twice shot a whitetail buck right on this large bottom; once or twice I killed a blacktail in the hills behind, not a mile from the ranch house. Several times I killed and brought in prong-bucks, rising before dawn and riding off on a good horse for an all day's hunt in the rolling prairie country twelve or fifteen miles away. Occasionally I took the wagon and one of the men, driving to some good hunting-ground and spending a night or two; usually returning with two or three prong-bucks, and once with an elk—but this was later in the fall. Not infrequently I went away by myself on horseback for a couple of days, when all the men were on the round-up, and when I wished to hunt thoroughly some country quite a distance from the ranch. I made one such hunt in late August, because I happened to hear that a small bunch of mountain sheep were haunting a tract of very broken ground, with high hills, about fifteen miles away.

I left the ranch early in the morning, riding my favorite hunting-horse, old Manitou. The blanket and oilskin slicker were rolled and strapped behind the saddle; for provisions I carried salt, a small bag of hardtack, and a little tea and sugar, with a metal cup in which to boil my water. The rifle and a score of cartridges in my woven belt completed my outfit. On my journey I shot two prairie chickens from a covey in the bottom of a brush coulee.

I rode more than six hours before reaching a good spot to camp. At first my route lay across grassy plateaus and along smooth, wooded coulies; but after a few miles the ground became very rugged and difficult At last I got into the heart of the Bad Lands proper, where the hard, wrinkled earth was torn into shapes as sullen and grotesque as those of dreamland. The hills rose high, their barren flanks carved and channeled, their tops mere needles and knife-crests. Bands of black, red, and purple varied the gray and yellow-brown of their sides; the tufts of scanty vegetation were dull green. Sometimes I rode my horse at the bottom of narrow washouts, between straight walls of clay, but a few feet apart; sometimes I had to lead him as he scrambled up, down, and across the sheer faces of the buttes. The glare from the bare clay walls dazzled the eye; the air was burning under the hot August sun. I saw nothing living except the rattlesnakes, of which there were very many.

At last, in the midst of this devil's wilderness, I came on a lovely valley. A spring trickled out of a cedar canyon, and below this spring the narrow, deep ravine was green with luscious grass and was smooth for some hundreds of yards. Here I unsaddled, and turned old Manitou loose to drink and feed at his leisure. At the edge of the dark cedar wood I cleared a spot for my bed, and drew a few dead sticks for the fire. Then I lay down and watched drowsily until the afternoon shadows filled the wild and beautiful gorge in which I was camped. This happened early, for the valley was very narrow and the hills on either hand were steep and high.

Springing to my feet, I climbed the nearest ridge, and then made my way, by hard clambering, from peak to peak and from crest to crest, sometimes crossing and sometimes skirting the deep washouts and canons. When possible I avoided appearing on the sky line, and I moved with the utmost caution, walking in a wide sweep so as to hunt across and up wind. There was much sheep sign, some of it fresh, though I saw none of the animals themselves; the square slots, with the indented marks of the toe points wide apart, contrasting strongly with the heart-shaped and delicate footprints of deer. The animals had, according to their habit, beaten trails along the summits of the higher crests; little side trails leading to any spur, peak or other vantage-point from which there was a wide outlook over the country roundabout.

The bighorns of the Bad Lands, unlike those of the mountains, shift their range but little, winter or summer. Save in the breeding season when each master ram gets together his own herd, the ewes, lambs and yearlings are apt to go in bands by themselves, while the males wander in small parties; now and then a very morose old fellow lives by himself, in some precipitous, out-of-the-way retreat. The rut begins with them much later than with deer; the exact time varies with the locality, but it is always after the bitter winter weather has set in. Then the old rams fight fiercely together, and on rare occasions utter a long grunting bleat or call. They are marvelous climbers, and dwell by choice always among cliffs and jagged, broken ground, whether wooded or not. An old bighorn ram is heavier than the largest buck; his huge curved horns, massive yet supple build, and proud bearing mark him as one of the noblest beasts of the chase. He is wary; great skill and caution must be shown in approaching him; and no one but a good climber, with a steady head, sound lungs, and trained muscles, can successfully hunt him in his own rugged fastnesses. The chase of no other kind of American big game ranks higher, or more thoroughly tests the manliest qualities of the hunter.

I walked back to camp in the gloaming, taking care to reach it before it grew really dark; for in the Bad Lands it is entirely impossible to travel, or to find any given locality, after nightfall. Old Manitou had eaten his fill, and looked up at me with pricked ears and wise, friendly face as I climbed down the side of the cedar canyon; then he came slowly towards me to see if I had not something for him. I rubbed his soft nose and gave him a cracker; then I picketed him to a solitary cedar, where the feed was good. Afterwards I kindled a small fire, roasted both prairie fowl, ate one, and put the other by for breakfast; and soon rolled myself in my blanket, with a saddle for a pillow, and the oilskin beneath. Manitou was munching the grass near by. I lay just outside the line of stiff black cedars; the night air was soft in my face; I gazed at the shining and brilliant multitude of stars until my eyelids closed.

The chill breath which comes before dawn awakened me. It was still and dark. Through the gloom I could indistinctly make out the loom of the old horse, lying down. I was speedily ready, and groped and stumbled slowly up the hill, and then along its crest to a peak. Here I sat down and waited a quarter of an hour or so, until gray appeared in the east, and the dim light-streaks enabled me to walk farther. Before sunrise I was two miles from camp; then I crawled cautiously to a high ridge, and, crouching behind it, scanned all the landscape eagerly. In a few minutes a movement about a third of a mile to the right, midway down a hill, caught my eye. Another glance showed me three white specks moving along the hillside. They were the white rumps of three fine mountain sheep, on their way to drink at a little alkaline pool in the bottom of a deep, narrow valley. In a moment they went out of sight round a bend of the valley; and I rose and trotted briskly towards them, along the ridge. There were two or three deep gullies to cross, and a high shoulder over which to clamber; so I was out of breath when I reached the bend beyond which they had disappeared. Taking advantage of a scrawny sagebrush as cover, I peeped over the edge, and at once saw the sheep, three big young rams. They had finished drinking and were standing beside the little miry pool, about three hundred yards distant. Slipping back, I dropped down into the bottom of the valley, where a narrow washout zigzagged from side to side, between straight walls of clay.

An indistinct game trail, evidently sometimes used by both bighorn and blacktail, ran up this washout; the bottom was of clay, so that I walked noiselessly; and the crookedness of the washout's course afforded ample security against discovery by the sharp eyes of the quarry. In a couple of minutes I stalked stealthily round the last bend, my rifle cocked and at the ready, expecting to see the rams by the pool. However, they had gone, and the muddy water was settling in their deep hoof-marks. Running on, I looked over the edge of the cut' bank, and saw them slowly quartering up the hillside, cropping the sparse tufts of coarse grass. I whistled, and as they stood at gaze I put a bullet into the biggest, a little too far aft of the shoulder, but ranging forward. He raced after the others, but soon fell behind, and turned off on his own line, at a walk, with drooping head. I followed his tracks, found him in a washout a quarter of a mile beyond, and finished him with another shot. I walked back to camp, breakfasted, and rode Manitou to where the sheep lay. Packing it securely behind the saddle, and shifting the blanket-roll to in front of the saddle-horn, I led the horse until we were clear of the Bad Lands; then mounted him, and was back at the ranch soon after midday. The mutton of a fat young mountain ram, at this season of the year, is delicious.

Such quick success is rare in hunting sheep. Generally each head has cost me several days of hard, faithful work; and more than once I have hunted over a week without any reward whatsoever. But the quarry is so noble that the ultimate triumph—sure to come, if the hunter will but persevere long enough—atones for all previous toil and failure.

Scribner's
October, 1901

With the Cougar Hounds

First Paper

IN January, 1901, I started on a five weeks' cougar hunt from Meeker in Northwest Colorado. My companions were Mr. Philip K. Stewart and Dr. Gerald Webb, of Colorado Springs; Stewart was the captain of the victorious Yale nine of '86. We reached Meeker on January 11th, after a forty-mile drive from the railroad, through the bitter winter weather; it was eighteen degrees below zero when we started. At Meeker we met John B. Goff, the hunter, and left town the next morning on horseback for his ranch, our hunting beginning that same afternoon, when after a brisk run our dogs treed a bobcat. After a fortnight Stewart and Webb returned, Goff and I staying out three weeks longer. We did not have to camp out, thanks to the warm-hearted hospitality of the proprietor and manager of the Keystone Ranch, and of the Mathes Brothers and Judge Foreman, both of whose ranches I also visited. The five weeks were spent hunting north of the White River, most of the time in the neighborhood of Coyote Basin and Colorow Mountain. In midwinter, hunting on horseback in the Rockies is apt to be cold work, but we were too warmly clad to mind the weather. We wore heavy flannels, jackets lined with sheepskin, caps which drew down entirely over our ears, and on our feet heavy ordinary socks, German socks, and overshoes. Galloping through the brush and among the spikes of the dead cedars, meant that now and then one got snagged; I found tough overalls better than trousers; and most of the time I did not need the jacket, wearing my old buckskin shirt, which is to my mind a particularly useful and comfortable garment.

It is a high, dry country, where the winters are usually very cold, but the snow not under ordinary circumstances very deep. It is wild and broken in character, the hills and low mountains rising in sheer slopes, broken by cliffs and riven by deeply cut and gloomy gorges and ravines. The sagebrush grows everywhere upon the flats and hillsides. Large open groves of pinyon and cedar are scattered over the peaks, ridges, and table-lands. Tall spruces cluster in the cold ravines. Cottonwoods grow along the stream courses, and there are occasional patches of scrub-oak and quaking asp. The entire country is taken up with cattle ranges wherever it is possible to get a sufficient water-supply, natural or artificial.

Some thirty miles to the east and north the mountains rise higher, the evergreen forest becomes continuous, the snow lies deep all through the winter, and such Northern animals as the wolverine and snow-shoe rabbit are found. This high country is the summer home of the Colorado elk, which are now rapidly becoming extinct, and of the Colorado blacktail deer, which are still very plentiful, but which, unless better protected, will follow the elk in the next decade or so. In winter both elk and deer come down to the lower country, through a part of which I made my hunting trip. We did not come across any elk, but I have never, even in the old days, seen blacktail more abundant than they were in this region. There was hardly a day that we did not see scores, and there were some days that we saw hundreds. The bucks had not lost their antlers, and were generally, but not always, found in small troops by themselves; 418 the does, yearlings, and fawns — now almost yearlings themselves — went in bands. They seemed tame, and we often passed close to them before they took alarm. Of course at that season it was against the law to kill them; and even had this not been so none of our party would have dreamed of molesting them. It was very interesting to see the way the deer got under — never over or through — the wire fences; they did not slide, but crouched, so that it was almost like crawling; yet they hardly checked their speed. The midwinter mountain landscape was very beautiful, whether under the brilliant blue sky of the day, or the starlight or glorious moonlight of the night, or when under the dying sun the snowy peaks, and the light clouds above, kindled into flame, and sank again to gold and amber and somber purple. After the snow storms trees, almost hidden beneath the light, feathery masses, gave a new and strange look to the mountains, as if they were giant masses of frosted silver. Even the storms had a beauty of their own. The keen, cold air, the wonderful scenery, and the interest and excitement of the sport, made our veins thrill and beat with buoyant life.

In cougar hunting the success of the hunter depends absolutely upon his hounds. As hounds that are not perfectly trained are worse than useless, this means that success depends absolutely upon the man who trains and hunts the hounds. Goff was one of the best hunters with whom I have ever been out, and he had trained his pack to a point of perfection for its special work which I have never known another such pack to reach. With the exception of one new hound, which he has just purchased, and of a puppy, which was being trained, not one of the pack would look at a deer even when they were all as keen as mustard, were not on a trail, and when the deer got up but fifty yards or so from them. By the end of the hunt both the new hound and the puppy were entirely trustworthy; of course, Goff can only keep up his pack by continually including new or young dogs with the veterans. As cougar are only plentiful where deer are infinitely more plentiful, the first requisite for a good cougar hound is that it shall leave its natural prey, the deer, entirely alone. Goff's pack ran only bear, cougar, and bobcat. Under no circumstances were they ever permitted to follow elk, deer, antelope or, of course, rabbit. Nor were they allowed to follow a wolf unless it was wounded; for in such a rough country they would at once run out of sight and hearing, and moreover if they did overtake the wolf they would be so scattered as to come up singly and probably be overcome one after another. Being bold dogs they were always especially eager after wolf and coyote, and when they came across the trail of either, though they would not follow it, they would usually challenge loudly. If the circumstances were such that they could overtake the wolf in a body, it could make no effective fight against them, no matter how large and powerful. On the one or two occasions when this had occurred, the pack had throttled "Isegrim" without getting a scratch.

As the dogs did all the work, we naturally became extremely interested in them, and rapidly grew to know the voice, peculiarities, and special abilities of each. There were eight hounds and four fighting-dogs. The hounds were of the ordinary Eastern type, used from the Adirondacks to the Mississippi in the chase of deer and fox. Six of them were black and tan and two were mottled. They differed widely in size and voice. The biggest, and, on the whole, the most useful, was Jim, a very fast, powerful, and true dog with a great voice. When the animal was treed or bayed, Jim was especially useful because he never stopped barking; and we could only find the hounds, when at bay, by listening for the sound of their voices. Among the cliffs and precipices the pack usually ran out of sight and hearing if the chase lasted any length of time. Their business was to bring the quarry to bay, or put it up a tree, and then to stay with it and make a noise until the hunters came up. During this hunt there were two or three occasions when they had a cougar up a tree for at least three hours before we arrived, and on several occasions Goff had known them to keep a cougar up a tree overnight and to be still barking around the tree when the hunters at last found them the following morning. Jim always did his share of the killing, being a formidable fighter, though too wary to take hold until one of the professional fighting-dogs had seized. He was a great bully with the other dogs, robbing them of their food, and yielding only to Turk. He possessed great endurance, and very stout feet.

On the whole the most useful dog next to Jim was old Boxer. Age had made Boxer slow, and in addition to this, the first cougar we tackled bit him through one hind leg, so that for the remainder of the trip he went on three legs, or, as Goff put it, "packed one leg"; but this seemed not to interfere with his appetite, his endurance, or his desire for the chase. Of all the dogs he was the best to puzzle out a cold trail on a bare hillside, or in any difficult place. He hardly paid any heed to the others, always insisting upon working out the trail for himself, and he never gave up. Of course, the dogs were much more apt to come upon the cold than upon the fresh trail of a cougar, and it was often necessary for them to spend several hours in working out a track which was at least two days old. Both Boxer and Jim had enormous appetites. Boxer was a small dog and Jim a very large one, and as the relations of the pack among themselves were those of brutal wild-beast selfishness, Boxer had to eat very quickly if he expected to get anything when Jim was around. He never ventured to fight Jim, but in deep-toned voice appealed to heaven against the unrighteousness with which he was treated; and time and again such appeal caused me to sally out and rescue his dinner from Jim's highway robbery. Once, when Boxer was given a biscuit, which he tried to bolt whole, Jim simply took his entire head in his jaws, and convinced him that he had his choice of surrendering the biscuit, or sharing its passage down Jim's capacious throat. Boxer promptly gave up the biscuit, then lay on his back and wailed a protest to fate—his voice being deep rather than loud, so that on the trail, when heard at a distance, it sounded a little as if he was croaking. After killing a cougar we usually cut up the carcass and fed it to the dogs, if we did not expect another chase that day. They devoured it eagerly, Boxer, after his meal, always looking as if he had swallowed a mattress.

Next in size to Jim was Tree'em. Tree'em was a good dog, but I never considered him remarkable until his feat on the last day of our hunt, to be afterward related. He was not a very noisy dog, and when "barking treed" he had a meditative way of giving single barks separated by intervals of several seconds, all the time gazing stolidly up at the big, sinister cat which he was baying. Early in the hunt, in the course of a fight with one of the cougars, he received some injury to his tail, which made it hang down like a piece of old rope. Apparently it hurt him a good deal and we let him rest for a fortnight. This put him in great spirits and made him fat and strong, but only enabled him to recover power over the root of the tail, while the tip hung down as before; it looked like a curved pump-handle when he tried to carry it erect.

Lil and Nel were two very staunch and fast bitches, the only two dogs that could keep up to Jim in a quick burst. They had shrill voices. Their only failing was a tendency to let the other members of the pack cow them so that they did not get their full share of the food. It was not a pack in which a slow or timid dog had much chance for existence. They would all unite in the chase and the fierce struggle which usually closed it; but the instant the quarry was killed each dog resumed his normal attitude of greedy anger or greedy fear toward the others.

Another bitch rejoiced in the not very appropriate name of Pete. She was a most ardent huntress. In the middle of our trip she gave birth to a litter of puppies, but before they were two weeks old she would slip away after us and join with the utmost ardor in the hunting and fighting. Her brother Jimmie, although of the same age (both were young), was not nearly as far advanced. He would run well on a fresh trail, but a cold trail or a long check always discouraged him and made him come back to Goff. He was rapidly learning; a single beating taught him to let deer alone. The remaining hound, Bruno, had just been added to the pack. He showed tendencies both to muteness and babbling, and at times, if he thought himself unobserved, could not resist making a sprint after a deer; but he occasionally rendered good service. If Jim or Boxer gave tongue every member of the pack ran to the sound; but not a dog paid any heed to Jimmie or Bruno. Yet Jimmie certainly, and Bruno very probably, will be first-class hounds in a year.

The fighting-dogs always trotted at the heels of the horses, which had become entirely accustomed to them, and made no objection when they literally rubbed against their heels. The fighters never left us until we came to where we could hear the hounds "barking treed," or with their quarry at bay. Then they tore in a straight line to the sound. They were the ones who were expected to do the seizing and take the punishment, though the minute they actually had hold of the cougar, the hounds all piled on too, and did their share of the killing; but the seizers fought the head while the hounds generally took hold behind. All of them, fighters and hounds alike, were exceedingly good-natured and affectionate with their human friends, though short-tempered to a degree with one another. The best of the fighters was old Turk, who was by blood half hound and half " "Siberian blood-hound." Both his father and his mother were half-breeds of the same strains, and both were famous fighters. Once, when Goff had wounded an enormous gray wolf in the hind leg, the father had overtaken it and fought it to a standstill. The two dogs there were an overmatch for any wolf. Turk had had a sister who was as good as he was; but she had been killed the year before by a cougar which bit her through the skull; accidents being, of course, frequent in the pack, for a big cougar is a much more formidable opponent to dogs than a wolf. Turk's head and body were seamed with scars. He had lost his lower fangs; but he was still a most formidable dog. While we were at the Keystone Ranch a big steer which had been driven in, got on the fight, and the foreman, William Wilson, took Turk out to aid him. At first Turk did not grasp what was expected of him, because all the dogs were trained never to touch anything domestic—at the different ranches where we stopped the cats and kittens wandered about, perfectly safe, in the midst of this hard-biting crew of bear and cougar fighters. But when Turk at last realized that he was expected to seize the steer, he did the business with speed and thoroughness; he not only threw the steer, but would have killed it then and there had he not been, with much difficulty, taken away. Three dogs like Turk, in their prime and with their teeth intact, could, I believe, kill an ordinary female cougar, and could hold even a big male so as to allow it to be killed with the knife.

Next to Turk were two half-breeds between bull and shepherd, named Tony and Baldy. They were exceedingly game, knowing-looking little dogs, with a certain alert swagger that reminded one of the walk of some light-weight prize-fighters. In fights with cougars, bears, and lynx, they too had been badly mauled and had lost a good many of their teeth. Neither of the gallant little fellows survived the trip. Their place was taken by a white bulldog bitch, Queen, which we picked up at the Keystone Ranch; a very affectionate and good-humored dog, but, when her blood was aroused, a dauntless though rather stupid fighter. Unfortunately she did not seize by the head, taking hold of any part that was nearest.

The pack had many interesting peculiarities, but none more so than the fact that four of them climbed trees. Only one of the hounds, little Jimmie, ever tried the feat; but of the fighters, not only Tony and Baldy but big Turk climbed every tree that gave them any chance. The pinyons and cedars were low, multi-forked, and usually sent off branches from near the ground.

In consequence the dogs could, by industrious effort, work their way almost to the top. The photograph of Turk and the bobcat in the pinyon shows them at an altitude of about thirty feet above the ground. Now and then a dog would lose his footing and come down with a whack which sounded as if he must be disabled, but after a growl and a shake he would start up the tree again. They could not fight well while in a tree, and were often scratched or knocked to the ground by a cougar; and when the quarry was shot out of its perch and seized by the expectant throng below, the dogs in the tree, yelping with eager excitement, dived headlong down through the branches, regardless of consequences.

 The horses were stout, hardy, surefooted beasts, not very fast, but able to climb like goats, and to endure an immense amount of work. Goff and I each used two for the trip.

 The bear were all holed up for the winter, and so our game was limited to cougars and bobcats. In the books the bobcat is always called a lynx, which it of course is; but whenever a hunter or trapper speaks of a lynx (which he usually calls "link," feeling dimly that the other pronunciation is a plural), he means a lucivee. Bobcat is a good distinctive name, and it is one which I think the book people might with advantage adopt; for wildcat, which is the name given to the small lynx in the East, is already pre-empted by the true wild-cat of Europe. Like all people of European descent who have gone into strange lands, we Americans have christened our wild beasts with a fine disregard for their specific and generic relations. We called the bison "buffalo" as long as it existed, and we still call the big stag an "elk," instead of using for it the excellent term wapiti; on the other hand, to the true elk and the reindeer we gave the new names of moose and caribou—excellent names, too, by the way. The prong buck is always called antelope, though it is not an antelope at all; and the white goat is not a goat; while the distinctive name of "big-horn" is rarely used for the mountain sheep. In most cases, however, it is mere pedantry to try to upset popular custom in such matters; and where, as with the bobcat, a perfectly good name is taken, it would be better for scientific men to adopt it. I may add that in this particular of nomenclature we are no worse sinners than other people. The English in Ceylon, the English and Dutch in

South Africa, and the Spanish in South America, have all shown the same genius for misnaming beasts and birds.

Bobcats were very numerous where we were hunting. They fed chiefly upon the rabbits, which fairly swarmed; mostly cotton-tails, but a few jacks. Contrary to the popular belief, the winter is in many places a time of plenty for carnivorous wild beasts. In this place, for instance, the abundance of deer and rabbits made good hunting for both cougar and bobcat, and all those we killed were as fat as possible, and in consequence weighed more than their inches promised. The bobcats are very fond of prairie dogs, and haunt the dog towns as soon as spring comes and the inhabitants emerge from their hibernation. They sometimes pounce on higher game. We came upon an eight months' fawn — very nearly a yearling — which had been killed by a big male bobcat; and Judge Foreman informed me that near his ranch, a few years previously, an exceptionally large bobcat had killed a yearling doe. Bobcats will also take lambs and young pigs, and if the chance occurs will readily seize their small kinsman, the house cat.

We found that the bobcats sometimes made their lairs along the rocky ledges or in holes in the cut banks, and sometimes in thickets, prowling about during the night, and now and then even during the day. We never chased them unless the dogs happened to run across them by accident when questing for cougar, or when we were returning home after a day when we had failed to find cougar. Usually the cat gave a good run, occasionally throwing out the dogs by doubling or jack-knifing. Two or three times one of them gave us an hour's sharp trotting, cantering, and galloping through the open cedar and pinyon groves on the table lands; and the runs sometimes lasted for a much longer period when the dogs had to go across ledges and through deep ravines.

On one of our runs a party of ravens fluttered along from tree to tree beside us, making queer gurgling noises and evidently perfectly aware that they might expect to reap a reward from our hunting. Ravens, multitudes of magpies, and golden and bald eagles were seen continually, and all four flocked to any carcass which was left in the open. The eagle and the raven are true birds of the wilderness, and in a way their presence both heightened and relieved the iron desolation of the wintry mountains.

Over half the cats we started escaped, getting into caves or deep holes in washouts. In the other instances they went up trees and were of course easily shot. Tony and Baldy would bring them out of any hole into which they themselves could get. After their loss, Lil, who is a small hound, once went into a hole in a washout after a cat. After awhile she stopped barking, though we could still hear the cat growling. What had happened to her we did not know. We spent a couple of hours calling to her and trying to get her to come out, but she neither came out nor answered, and, as sunset was approaching and the ranch was some miles off, we rode back there, intending to return with spades in the morning. However, by breakfast we found that Lil had come back. We supposed that she had got on the other side of the cat and had been afraid or unable to attack it; so that as Collins the cow-puncher, who was a Southerner, phrased it, "she just naturally stayed in the hole" until some time during the night the cat went out and she followed. When once hunters and hounds have come into the land, it is evident that the bobcats which take refuge in caves have a far better chance of surviving than those which make their lairs in the open and go up trees. But trees are sure havens against their wilderness foes. Goff informed me that he once came in the snow to a place where the tracks showed that some coyotes had put a bobcat up a tree, and had finally abandoned the effort to get at it. A single coyote will rarely meddle with a bobcat. Any good fighting dog will kill one; but an untrained dog, even of large size, will probably fail, as the bobcat makes good use of both teeth and claws; they frequently left marks on some of the pack. We found them very variable in size. My two largest—both of course males—weighed respectively thirty-one and thirty-nine pounds. The latter, Goff said, was of exceptional size, and as large as any he had ever killed. The full-grown females went down as low as eighteen pounds, or even lower.

When the bobcats were in the treetops we could get up very close. They looked like large malevolent pussies. I once heard one of them squawl defiance when the dogs tried to get it out of a hole. Ordinarily they confined themselves to a low growling. Stewart and Goff went up the trees with their cameras whenever we got a bobcat in a favorable position, and endeavored to take its photograph. Sometimes they were very successful. Although they were frequently within six feet of a cat, and occasionally even poked it in order to make it change its position, I never saw one make a motion to jump on them. Two or three times on our approach the cat jumped from the tree almost into the midst of the pack, but it was so quick that it got off before they could seize it. They invariably put it up another tree before it had gone any distance.

Hunting the bobcat was only an incident. Our true quarry was the cougar. I had long been anxious to make a regular hunt after cougar in a country where the beasts were plentiful and where we could follow them with a good pack of hounds. Astonishingly little of a satisfactory nature has been left on record about the cougar by hunters, and in most places the chances for observation of the big cats steadily grow less. They have been thinned out almost to the point of extermination throughout the Eastern States. In the Rocky Mountain region they are still plentiful in places, but are growing less so; while on the contrary the wolf, which was exterminated even more quickly in the East, is in the West at present increasing in numbers. In northwestern Colorado a dozen years ago, cougars were far more plentiful than wolves; whereas at the present day the wolf is probably the more numerous. Nevertheless, there are large areas, here and there among the Rockies, in which cougars will be plentiful for many years.

No American beast has been the subject of so much loose writing or of such wild fables as the cougar. Even its name is unsettled. In the Eastern States it is usually called panther or painter; in the Western States, mountain lion, or, toward the South, Mexican lion. The Spanish-speaking people usually call it simply lion. It is, however, sometimes called cougar in the West and Southwest of our country, and in South America, puma. As it is desirable where possible not to use a name that is misleading and is already appropriated to some entirely different animal, it is best to call it cougar.

The cougar is a very singular beast, shy and elusive to an extraordinary degree, very cowardly and yet bloodthirsty and ferocious, varying wonderfully in size, and subject, like many other beasts, to queer freaks of character in occasional individuals. This fact of individual variation in size and temper is almost always ignored in treating of the animal; whereas it ought never to be left out of sight.

The average writer, and for the matter of that, the average hunter, where cougars are scarce, knows little or nothing of them, and in describing them merely draws upon the stock of well-worn myths which portray them as terrible foes of man, as dropping on their prey from trees where they have been lying in wait, etc., etc. Very occasionally there appears an absolutely trustworthy account like that by Dr. Hart Merriam in his "Adirondack Mammals." But many otherwise excellent writers are wholly at sea in reference to the cougar. Thus one of the best books on hunting in the far West in the old days is by Colonel Dodge. Yet when Colonel Dodge came to describe the cougar he actually treated of it as two species, one of which, the mountain lion, is painted as a most ferocious and dangerous opponent of man; while the other, the panther, is described as an abject coward, which will not even in the last resort defend itself against man—the two of course being the same animal.

However, the wildest of all fables about the cougar has been reserved not for hunter or popular writer, but for a professed naturalist. In his otherwise most charming and interesting book, "The Naturalist in La Plata," Mr. Hudson actually describes the cougar as being friendly to man, disinterestedly adverse to harming him, and at the same time an enemy of other large carnivores. Mr. Hudson bases his opinion chiefly upon the assertions of the Guachos. The Guachos, however, go one degree beyond Mr. Hudson, calling the puma the "friend of Christians"; whereas Mr. Hudson only ventures to attribute to the beast humanitarian, not theological, preferences. As a matter of fact, Mr. Hudson's belief in the cougar's peculiar friendship for man, and peculiar enmity to other large beasts of prey, has not one particle of foundation in fact as regards at any rate the North American form—and it is hardly to be supposed that the South American form would alone develop such extraordinary traits. For instance, Mr. Hudson says that the South American puma when hunted will attack the dogs in preference to the man. In North America he will fight the dog if the dog is nearest, and if the man comes to close quarters at the same time as the dog he will attack the man if anything more readily, evidently recognizing in him his chief opponent. He will often go up a tree for a single dog. On Mr. Hudson's theory he must do this because of his altruistic feeling toward the dog. In fact, Mr. Hudson could make out a better case of philo-humanity for the North American wolf than for the North American cougar. Equally absurd is it to talk, as Mr. Hudson does, of the cougar as the especial enemy of other ferocious beasts. Mr. Hudson speaks of it as attacking and conquering the jaguar. Of this I know nothing, but such an extraordinary statement should be well fortified with proofs; and if true it must mean that the jaguar is an infinitely less formidable creature than it has been painted. In support of his position Mr. Hudson alludes to the stories about the cougar attacking the grizzly bear. Here I am on ground that I do know. It is true that an occasional old hunter asserts that the cougar does this, but the old hunter who makes such an assertion also invariably insists that the cougar is a ferocious and habitual man-killer, and the two statements rest upon equally slender foundations of fact. I have never yet heard of a single authentic instance of a cougar interfering with a full-grown bear. It will kill bear cubs if it gets a chance; but then so will the fox and the fisher, not to speak of the wolf. In 1894, a cougar killed a colt on a brushy river bottom a dozen miles below my ranch on the Little Missouri. I went down to visit the carcass and found that it had been taken possession of by a large grizzly. Both I and the hunter who was with me were very much interested in what had occurred, and after a careful examination of the tracks we concluded that the bear had arrived on the second night after the kill. He had feasted heartily on the remains, while the cougar, whose tracks were evident here and there at a little distance from the carcass, had seemingly circled around it, and had certainly not interfered with the bear, or even ventured to approach him. Now, if a cougar would ever have meddled with a large bear it would surely have been on such an occasion as this. If very much pressed by hunger, a large cougar will, if it gets the chance, kill a wolf; but this is only when other game has failed, and under all ordinary circumstances neither meddles with the other. When I was down in Texas, hunting peccaries on the Nueces, I was in a country where both cougar and jaguar were to be found; but no hunter had ever heard of either molesting the other, though they were all of the opinion that when the two met the cougar gave the path to his spotted brother. Of course, it is never safe to dogmatize about the unknown in zoology, or to generalize on insufficient evidence; but as regards the North American cougar there is not a particle of truth of any kind, sort, or description in the statement that he is the enemy of the larger carnivores, or the friend of man; and if the South American cougar, which so strongly resembles its Northern brother in its other habits, has developed on these two points the extraordinary peculiarities of which Mr. Hudson speaks, full and adequate proof should be forthcoming; and this proof is now wholly wanting.

Fables aside, the cougar is a very interesting creature. It is found from the cold, desolate plains of Patagonia to north of the Canadian line, and lives alike among the snow-clad peaks of the Andes and in the steaming forests of the Amazon. Doubtless careful investigation will disclose several varying forms in an animal found over such immense tracts of country and living under such utterly diverse conditions. But in its essential habits and traits, the big, slinking, nearly uni-colored cat seems to be much the same everywhere, whether living in mountain, open plain, or forest, under arctic cold or tropic heat. When the settlements become thick, it retires to dense forest, dark swamp or inaccessible mountain gorge, and moves about only at night. In wilder regions it not infrequently roams during the day and ventures freely into the open. Deer are its customary prey where they are plentiful, bucks, does, and fawns being killed indifferently. Usually the deer is killed almost instantaneously, but occasionally there is quite a scuffle, in which the cougar may get bruised, though, as far as I know, never seriously. It is also a dreaded enemy of sheep, pigs, calves, and especially colts, and when pressed by hunger a big male cougar will kill a full-grown horse or cow, moose or wapiti. It is the special enemy of mountain sheep. In 1886, while hunting white goats north of Clarke's fork of the Columbia, in a region where cougar were common, I found them preying as freely on the goats as on the deer. It rarely catches antelope, but is quick to seize rabbits, other small beasts, and even porcupines.

No animal, not even the wolf, is so rarely seen or so difficult to get without dogs. On the other hand, no other wild beast of its size and power is so easy to kill by the aid of dogs. There are many contradictions in its character. Like the American wolf, it is certainly very much afraid of man; yet it habitually follows the trail of the hunter or solitary traveler, dogging his footsteps, itself always unseen. I have had this happen to me personally. When hungry it will seize and carry off any dog; yet it will sometimes go up a tree when pursued even by a single small dog wholly unable to do it the least harm. It is small wonder that the average frontier settler should grow to regard almost with superstition the great furtive cat which he never sees, but of whose presence he is ever aware, and of whose prowess sinister proof is sometimes afforded by the deaths not alone of his lesser stock, but even of his milch cow or saddle horse.

The cougar is as large, as powerful, and as formidably armed as the Indian panther, and quite as well able to attack man; yet the instances of its having done so are exceedingly rare. The vast majority of the tales to this effect are undoubtedly inventions. But it is foolish to deny that such attacks on human beings ever occur. There are a number of authentic instances, the latest that has come to my knowledge being related in the following letter, of May 15, 1893, written to Dr. Merriam by Professor W. H. Brewer, of Yale: "In 1880 I visited the base of Mount Shasta, and stopped a day to review the memories of 1862, when I had climbed and measured this mountain. Panthers were numerous and were so destructive to sheep that poisoning by strychnine was common. A man living near who had (as a young hunter) gone up Mount Shasta with us in '62, now married (1880) and on a ranch, came to visit me, with a little son five or six years old. This boy when younger, but two or three years old, if I recollect rightly, had been attacked by a panther. He was playing in the yard by the house when a lean two-thirds grown panther came into the yard and seized the child by the throat. The child screamed, and alarmed the mother (who told me the story). She seized a broom and rushed out, while an old man at the house seized the gun. The panther let go the child and was shot. I saw the boy. He had the scars of the panther's teeth in the cheek, and below on the under side of the lower jaw, and just at the throat. This was the only case that came to my knowledge at first hand of a panther attacking a human being in that State, except one or two cases where panthers, exasperated by wounds, had fought with the hunters who had wounded them." This was a young cougar, bold, stupid, and very hungry. Goff told me of one similar case where a cougar stalked a young girl, but was shot just before it was close enough to make the final rush. As I have elsewhere related, I know of two undoubted cases, one in Mississippi, one in Florida, where a negro was attacked and killed by a cougar, while alone in a swamp at night. But these occurred many years ago. The instance related by Professor Brewer is the only one I have come across happening in recent years, in which the cougar actually seized a human being with the purpose of making prey of it; though doubtless others have occurred. I have never known the American wolf actually to attack a human being from hunger or to make prey of him; whereas the Old World wolf, like the Old-World leopard, undoubtedly sometimes turns man-eater.

Even when hunted the cougar shows itself, as a rule, an abject coward, not to be compared in courage and prowess with the grizzly bear, and but little more dangerous to man than is the wolf under similar circumstances. Without dogs it is usually a mere chance that one is killed. Goff has killed some 300 cougars during the sixteen years he has been hunting in northwestern Colorado, yet all but two of them were encountered while he was with his pack; although this is in a region where they are plentiful. When hunted with good dogs their attention is so taken up with the pack that they have little time to devote to men. When hunted without dogs they never charge unless actually cornered, and, as a general rule, not even then, unless the man chooses to come right up to them. I knew of one Indian being killed in 1887, and near my ranch a cowboy was mauled; but in the first instance the cougar had been knocked down and the Indian was bending over it when it revived; and in the next instance, the cowboy literally came right on top of the animal. Now, under such circumstances either a bull elk or a blacktail buck will occasionally fight; twice I have known of wounded wapiti regularly charging, and one of my own cowboys, George Myer, was very roughly handled by a blacktail buck which he had wounded. In all his experience Goff says that he never but once had a cougar start to charge him, and on that occasion it was promptly killed by a bullet. Usually the cougar does not even charge at the dogs beyond a few feet, confining itself to seizing or striking any member of the pack which comes close up; although it will occasionally, when much irritated, make a rapid dash and seize some bold assailant. While I was on my hunt, one of Goff's brothers lost a hound in hunting a cougar; there were but two hounds, and the cougar would not tree for them, finally seizing and killing one that came too near. At the same time a ranchman not far off set his cattle dog on a cougar, which after a short run turned and killed the dog. But time and again cougars are brought to bay or treed by dogs powerless to do them the slightest damage; and they usually meet their death tamely when the hunter comes up. I have had no personal experience either with the South American jaguar or the Old World leopard or panther; but these great spotted cats must be far more dangerous adversaries than the cougar.

It is true, as I have said, that a cougar will follow a man; but then a weasel will sometimes do the same thing. Whatever the cougar's motive, it is certain that in the immense majority of cases there is not the slightest danger of his attacking the man he follows. Dr. Hart Merriam informs me, however, that he is satisfied that he came across one genuine instance of a cougar killing a man whose tracks he had dogged. It cannot be too often repeated, that we must never lose sight of the individual variation in character and conduct among wild beasts. A thousand times a cougar might follow a man either not intending or not daring to attack him, while in the thousandth and first case it might be that the temper of the beast and the conditions were such that the attack would be made.

Other beasts show almost the same wide variation in temper. Wolves, for instance, are normally exceedingly wary of man. In this Colorado hunt I often came across their tracks, and often heard their mournful, but to my ears rather attractive, baying at night, but I never caught a glimpse of one of them; nor during the years when I spent much of my time on my ranch did I ever know of a wolf venturing to approach anywhere near a man in the daytime, though I have had them accompany me after nightfall. But on the Keystone Ranch, where I spent three weeks on this particular trip, an incident which occurred before my arrival showed that wolves occasionally act with extraordinary boldness. The former owner of the ranch, Colonel Price, and one of the cowhands, Sabey (both of whom told me the story), were driving out in a buggy from Meeker to the ranch accompanied by a setter dog. They had no weapon with them. Two wolves joined them and made every effort to get at the dog. They accompanied the wagon for nearly a mile, venturing to within twenty yards of it. They paid no heed whatever to the shouts and gestures of the men, but did not quite dare to come to close quarters, and finally abandoned their effort. Now, this action on their part was, as far as my experience goes, quite as exceptional among American wolves as it is exceptional for a cougar to attack a man. Of course, these wolves were not after the men. They were simply after the dog; but I have never within my own experience come upon another instance of wolves venturing to attack a domestic animal in the immediate presence of and protected by a man. Exactly as these two wolves suddenly chose to behave with an absolutely unexpected daring, so a cougar will occasionally lose the fear of man which is inherent in its race.

    Normally, then, the cougar is not in any way a formidable foe to man, and it is certainly by no means as dangerous to dogs as it could be if its courage and intelligence equalled its power to do mischief. It strikes with its forepaw like a cat, lacerating the foe with its sharp claws; or else it holds the animal with them, while the muscular forearm draws it in until the fatal bite may be inflicted. Whenever possible it strives to bite an assailant in the head. Occasionally, when fighting with a large dog, a cougar will throw itself on its back and try to rip open its antagonist with its hind feet. Male cougars often fight desperately among themselves.

Although a silent beast, yet at times, especially during the breeding season, the males utter a wild scream, and the females also cry or call. I once heard one cry while prowling for game. On an evening in the summer of 1897 Dr. Merriam had a rather singular experience with a cougar. His party was camped in the forest by Tannum Lake, on the east slope of the Cascades, near the headwaters of a branch of the Yakima. The horses were feeding near by. Shortly after dark a cougar cried loudly in the gloom, and the frightened horses whinnied and stampeded. The cougar cried a number of times afterward, but the horses did not again answer. None of them was killed, however; and next morning, after some labor, all were again gathered together. In 1884 I had a somewhat similar experience with a bear, in the Bighorn Mountains.

Occasionally, but not often, the cougars I shot snarled or uttered a low, thunderous growl as we approached the tree, or as the dogs came upon them in the cave. In the death-grapple they were silent, excepting that one young cougar snarled and squawled as it battled with the dogs.

The cougar is sometimes tamed. A friend of mine had one which was as good-natured as possible until it was a year old, when it died. But one kept by another friend, while still quite young, became treacherous and dangerous. I doubt if they would ever become as trustworthy as a tame wolf, which, if taken when a very young puppy, will often grow up exactly like a dog. At the present time there is such a tame wolf with the Colorado Springs greyhounds. It is safer and more friendly than many collies, and is on excellent terms with the great greyhounds; though these are themselves solely used to hunt wolves and coyotes, and tackle them with headlong ferocity, having, unaided, killed a score or two of the large wolves and hundreds of coyotes.

Hunting in the snow we were able to tell very clearly what the cougars whose trails we were following had been doing. Goff's eye for a trail was unerring, and he read at a glance the lesson it taught. All the cougars which we came across were living exclusively upon deer, and their stomachs were filled with nothing else; much hair being mixed with the meat. In each case the deer was caught by stalking and not by lying in wait, and the cougar never went up a tree except to get rid of the dogs. In the daytime it retires to a ledge, or ravine, or dense thicket, starting to prowl as the dark comes on. So far as I could see the deer in each case was killed by a bite in the throat or neck. The cougar simply rambled around in likely ground until it saw or smelled its quarry, and then crept up stealthily until with one or two tremendous bounds it was able to seize its prey. If, as frequently happened, the deer took alarm in time to avoid the first few bounds, it always got away, for though the cougar is very fast for a short distance, it has no wind whatever. It cannot pursue a deer for any length of time, nor run before a dog for more than a few hundred yards, if the dog is close up at the start. I was informed by the ranchmen that when in May the deer leave the country, the cougars turn their attention to the stock, and are very destructive. They have a special fondness for horseflesh and kill almost every colt where they are plentiful, while the big males work havoc with the saddle bands on the ranches, as well as among the brood mares. Except in the case of a female with young they are roving, wandering beasts, and roam great distances. After leaving their day lairs, on a ledge, or in a gorge or thicket, they spend the night travelling across the flats, along the ridges, over the spurs. When they kill a deer they usually lie not very far away, and do not again wander until they are hungry. The males travel very long distances in the mating season. Their breeding time is evidently irregular. We found kittens with their eyes not yet open in the middle of January. Two of the female cougars we killed were pregnant — in one case the young would have been born almost immediately, that is, in February; and in the other case in March. One, which had a partially grown young one of over fifty pounds with it, still had milk in its teats. At the end of January we found a male and female together, evidently mating. Goff has also found the young just dropped in May, and even June. The females outnumber the males. Of the fourteen we killed, but three were males.

    When a cougar kills a deer in the open it invariably drags it under some tree or shelter before beginning to eat. All the carcasses we came across had been thus dragged, the trail showing distinctly in the snow. Goff, however, asserted that in occasional instances he had known a cougar to carry a deer so that only its legs trailed on the ground.

The fourteen cougars we killed showed the widest variation not only in size but in color, as shown by the following table. Some were as slatey-gray as deer when in the so-called "blue"; others, rufous, almost as bright as deer in the "red." I use these two terms to describe the color phases; though in some instances the tint was very undecided. The color phase evidently has nothing to do with age, sex, season, or locality. In this table the first cougar is the one killed by Stewart, the sixth by Webb. The length is measured in a straight line, "between uprights," from the nose to the extreme tip of the tail, when the beast was stretched out. The animals were weighed with the steelyard and also spring scales. Before measuring, we pulled the beast out as straight as we possibly could; and as the biggest male represents about, or very nearly, the maximum for the species, it is easy to see that there can be no basis for the talk one sometimes hears about ten and eleven foot cougars. No cougar, measured at all fairly, has ever come anywhere near reaching the length of nine feet. The fresh hide can easily be stretched a couple of feet extra.

Sex	Color	Length		Weight	Date.
		Feet.	Inches.	Pounds	1901
*Female	Blue	4	11	47	January 19
*Female	Red	4	11-1/2	51	February 12
Female	Blue	6		80	January 14
Female	Red.	6	4	102	January 28
Female	Blue	6	5	105	February 12
Female	Blue	6	5	107	January 18
Female	Red	6	9	108	January 24
Female	Blue	6	7	118	January 15
Female	Blue	6	7	120	January 31
Female	Red	6	9	124	February 5
Female	Blue	7		133	February 8
Male	Red.	7	6	163	February 13
Male	Blue	7	8	164	January 27
Male	Red	8		227	February 14

* Young.

Except the first two, all were full grown; the biggest male was nearly three times the size of the smallest female.

I shot five bobcats; two old males weighing 39 and 31 pounds respectively; and three females, weighing, respectively, 25, 21, and 18 pounds. Webb killed two, a male of 29 pounds and a female of 20; and Stewart two females, one of 22 pounds, and the other a young one of 11 pounds.

I sent the cougar and bobcat skulls to Dr. Merriam, at the Biological Survey, Department of Agriculture, Washington. He wrote me as follows: "The big [cougar] skull is certainly a giant. I have compared it with the largest in our collection from British Columbia and Wyoming, and find it larger than either. It is in fact the largest skull of any member of the Felis concolor group I have seen. A hasty preliminary examination indicates that the animal is quite different from the northwest coast form, but that it is the same as my horse-killer from Wyoming — Felis hippolestes. In typical Felis concolor from Brazil the skull is lighter, the braincase thinner and more smoothly rounded, devoid of the strongly developed sagittal crest; the under jaw straighter and lighter.

"Your series of skulls from Colorado is incomparably the largest, most complete and most valuable series ever brought together from any single locality, and will be of inestimable value in determining the amount of individual variation."

Scribner's
November, 1901

With the Cougar Hounds

Second Paper

WE rode in to the Keystone Ranch late on the evening of the second day after leaving Meeker. We had picked up a couple of bobcats on the way, and had found a cougar's kill (or bait, as Goff called it) — a doe, almost completely eaten. The dogs puzzled for several hours over the cold trail of the cougar; but it was old, and ran hither and thither over bare ground, so that they finally lost it. The ranch was delightfully situated at the foot of high wooded hills broken by cliffs, and it was pleasant to reach the warm, comfortable log buildings, with their clean rooms, and to revel in the abundant, smoking-hot dinner, after the long, cold hours in the saddle. As everywhere else in the cattle country nowadays, a successful effort had been made to store water on the Keystone, and there were great stretches of wire fencing — two improvements entirely unknown in former days. But the foreman, William Wilson, and the two punchers or cow-hands, Sabey and Collins, were of the old familiar type — skilled, fearless, hardy, hard-working, with all the intelligence and self-respect that we like to claim as typical of the American character at its best. All three carried short saddle guns when they went abroad, and killed a good many coyotes, and now and then a gray wolf. The cattle were for the most part grade Herefords, very different from the wild, slab-sided, long-horned creatures which covered the cattle country a score of years ago.

The next day, January 14th, we got our first cougar. This kind of hunting was totally different from that to which I had been accustomed. In the first place, there was no need of always being on the alert for a shot, as it was the dogs who did the work. In the next place, instead of continually scanning the landscape, what we had to do was to look down so as to be sure not to pass over any tracks; for frequently a cold trail would be indicated so faintly that the dogs themselves might pass it by, if unassisted by Goff's keen eyes and thorough knowledge of the habits of the quarry. Finally, there was no object in making an early start, as what we expected to find was not the cougar, but the cougar's trail; moreover, the horses and dogs, tough though they were, could not stand more than a certain amount, and to ride from sunrise to sunset, day in and day out, for five weeks, just about tested the limits of their endurance.

  We made our way slowly up the snow-covered, pinyon-clad side of the mountain back of the house, and found a very old cougar trail which it was useless to try to run, and a couple of fresh bobcat trails which it was difficult to prevent the dogs from following. After criss-crossing over the shoulders of this mountain for two or three hours, and scrambling in and out of the ravines, we finally struck another cougar trail, much more recent, probably made thirty-six hours before. The hounds had been hunting free to one side or the other of our path. They were now summoned by a blast of the horn, and with a wave of Goff's hand away they went on the trail. Had it been fresh they would have run out of hearing at once, for it was fearfully rough country. But they were able to work but slowly along the loops and zigzags of the trail, where it led across bare spaces, and we could keep well in sight and hearing of them. Finally they came to where it descended the sheer side of the mountain and crossed the snow-covered valley beneath. They were still all together, the pace having been so slow, and in the snow of the valley the scent was fresh. It was a fine sight to see them as they rushed across from one side to the other, the cliffs echoing their chiming. Jim and the three bitches were in the lead, while Boxer fell behind, as he always did when the pace was fast.

  Leading our horses, we slid and scrambled after the hounds; but when we reached the valley they had passed out of sight and sound, and we did not hear them again until we had toiled up the mountain opposite. They were then evidently scattered, having come upon many bare places; but while we were listening, and working our way over to the other side of the divide, the sudden increase in the baying told Goff that they had struck the fresh trail of the beast they were after; and in two or three minutes we heard Jim's deep voice "barking treed." The three fighters, who had been trotting at our heels, recognized the difference in the sound quite as quickly as we did, and plunged at full speed toward it down the steep hill-side, throwing up the snow like so many snow-ploughs. In a minute or two the chorus told us that all the dogs were around the tree, and we picked our way down toward them.

While we were still some distance off we could see the cougar in a low pinyon moving about as the dogs tried to get up, and finally knocking one clean out of the top. It was the first time I had ever seen dogs with a cougar, and I was immensely interested; but Stewart's whole concern was with his camera. When we were within fifty yards of the tree, and I was preparing to take the rifle out of the scabbard, Stewart suddenly called "halt," with the first symptoms of excitement he had shown, and added, in an eager undertone: "Wait, there is a rabbit right here, and I want to take his picture." Accordingly we waited, the cougar not fifty yards off and the dogs yelling and trying to get up the tree after it, while Stewart crept up to the rabbit and got a kodak some six feet distant. Then we resumed our march toward the tree, and the cougar, not liking the sight of the reinforcements, jumped out. She came down just outside the pack and ran up hill. So quick was she that the dogs failed to seize her, and for the first fifty yards she went a great deal faster than they did. Both in the jump and in the run she held her tail straight out behind her; I found out afterward that sometimes one will throw its tail straight in the air, and when walking along, when first roused by the pack, before they are close, will, if angry, lash the tail from side to side, at the same time grinning and snarling.

In a minute the cougar went up another tree, but, as we approached, again jumped down, and on this occasion, after running a couple of hundred yards, the dogs seized it. The worry was terrific; the growling, snarling, and yelling rang among the rocks; and leaving our horses we plunged at full speed through the snow down the rugged ravine in which the fight was going on. It was a small though old female, only a few pounds heavier than either Turk or Jim, and the dogs had the upper hand when we arrived. They would certainly have killed it unassisted, but as it was doing some damage to the pack, and might at any moment kill a dog, I ended the struggle by a knife-thrust behind the shoulder. To shoot would have been quite as dangerous for the dogs as for their quarry. Three of the dogs were badly scratched, and Turk had been bitten through one foreleg, and Boxer through one hind leg.

As will be seen by the measurements given before, this was much the smallest full-grown cougar we got. It was also one of the oldest, as its teeth showed, and it gave me a false idea of the size of cougars; although I knew they varied in size I was not prepared for the wide variation we actually found.

The fighting dogs were the ones that enabled me to use the knife. All three went straight for the head, and when they got hold they kept their jaws shut, worrying and pulling, and completely absorbing the attention of the cougar, so as to give an easy chance for the death-blow. The hounds meanwhile had seized the cougar behind, and Jim, with his alligator jaws, probably did as much damage as Turk. However, neither in this nor in any other instance, did any one of the dogs manage to get its teeth through the thick skin. When cougars fight among themselves their claws and fangs leave great scars, but their hides are too thick for the dogs to get their teeth through. On the other hand, a cougar's jaws have great power, and dogs are frequently killed by a single bite, the fangs being driven through the brain or spine; or they break a dog's leg or cut the big blood-vessels of the throat.

I had been anxious to get a set of measurements and weights of cougars to give to Dr. Hart Merriam. Accordingly I was carrying a tape, while Goff, instead of a rifle, had a steelyard in his gun scabbard. We weighed and measured the cougar, and then took lunch, making as impartial a distribution of it as was possible among ourselves and the different members of the pack; for, of course, we were already growing to have a hearty fellow-feeling for each individual dog.

The next day we were again in luck. After about two hours' ride we came upon an old trail. It led among low hills, covered with pinyon and cedar, and broken by gullies or washouts, in whose sharp sides of clay the water had made holes and caves. Soon the hounds left it to follow a bobcat, and we had a lively gallop through the timber, dodging the sharp snags of the dead branches as best we might. The cat got into a hole in a side washout; Baldy went in after it, and the rest of us, men and dogs, clustered about to look in. After a considerable time he put the cat out of the other end of the hole, nearly a hundred yards off, close to the main washout. The first we knew of it we saw it coming straight toward us, its tail held erect like that of a white-tail deer. Before either we or the dogs quite grasped the situation it bolted into another hole almost at our feet, and this time Baldy could not find it, or else could not get at it. Then we took up the cougar trail again. It criss-crossed in every direction. We finally found an old "bait," a buck. It was interesting to see the way in which the cougar had prowled from point to point, and the efforts it had made to approach the deer which it saw or smelled. Once we came to where it had sat down on the edge of a cliff, sitting on its haunches with its long tail straight behind it and looking out across the valley. After it had killed, according to the invariable custom of its kind, it had dragged the deer from the open, where it had overtaken it, to the shelter of a group of trees.

We finally struck the fresh trail; but it, also, led hither and thither, and we got into such a maze of tracks that the dogs were completely puzzled. After a couple of hours of vain travelling to and fro, we gave up the effort, called the dogs off, and started back beside a large washout which led along between two ridges. Goff, as usual, was leading, the dogs following and continually skirting to one side or the other. Suddenly they all began to show great excitement, and then one gave furious tongue at the mouth of a hole in some sunken and broken ground not thirty yards to our right. The whole pack rushed toward the challenge, the fighters leaped into the hole, and in another moment the row inside told us that they had found a cougar at home. We jumped off and ran down to see if we could be of assistance. To get into the hole was impossible, for two or three hounds had jumped down to join the fighters, and we could see nothing but their sterns. Then we saw Turk backing out with a dead kitten in his mouth. I had supposed that a cougar would defend her young to the last, but such was not the case in this instance. For some minutes she kept the dogs at bay, but then gradually gave ground, leaving her three kittens. Of course, the dogs killed them instantly, much to our regret, as we would have given a good deal to have kept them alive. As soon as she had abandoned them, away she went completely through the low cave or hole, leaped out of the other end, which was some thirty or forty yards off, scaled the bank, and galloped into the woods, the pack getting after her at once. She did not run more than a couple of hundred yards, and as we tore up on our horses we saw her standing in the lower branches of a pinyon only six or eight feet from the ground. She was not snarling or grinning, and looked at us as quietly as if nothing had happened. As we leaped out of the saddles she jumped down from the tree and ran off through the pack. They were after her at once, however, and a few yards farther on she started up another tree. Either Tony or Baldy grabbed her by the tip of the tail, she lost her footing for a moment, and the whole pack seized her. She was a powerful female of about the average size, being half as heavy again as the one we first got, and made a tremendous fight; and savage enough she looked, her ears tight back against her head, her yellow eyes flashing, and her great teeth showing as she grinned. For a moment the dogs had her down, but biting and striking she freed her head and forequarters from the fighters, and faced us as we ran up, the hounds still having her from behind. This was another chance for the knife, and I cheered on the fighters. Again they seized her by the head, but though absolutely stanch dogs, their teeth, as I have said, had begun to suffer, and they were no longer always able to make their holds good. Just as I was about to strike her she knocked Turk loose with a blow, bit Baldy, and then, her head being free, turned upon me. Fortunately, Tony caught her free paw on that side, while I jammed the gun-butt into her jaws with my left hand and struck home with the right, the knife going straight to the heart. The deep fang marks she left in the stock, biting the corner of the shoulder clean off, gave an idea of the power of her jaws. If it had been the very big male cougar which I afterward killed, the stock would doubtless have been bitten completely in two.

The dogs were pretty well damaged, and all retired and lay down under the trees, where they licked their wounds, and went to sleep; growling savagely at one another when they waked, but greeting us with demonstrative affection, and trotting eagerly out to share our lunch as soon as we began to eat it. Unaided, they would ultimately have killed the cougar, but the chance of one or two of them being killed or crippled was too great for us to allow this to be done; and in the mix-up of the struggle it was not possible to end it with the rifle. The writhing, yelling tangle offered too shifting a mark; one would have been as apt to hit a dog as the cougar. Goff told me that the pack had often killed cougars unassisted; but in the performance of such feats the best dogs were frequently killed, and this not a risk to be taken lightly.

In some books the writers speak as if the male and female cougar live together and jointly seek food for the young. We never found a male cougar anywhere near either a female with young or a pregnant female. According to my observation the male only remains with the female for a short time, during the mating season, at which period he travels great distances in search of his temporary mates — for the females far outnumber the males. The cougar is normally a very solitary beast. The young — two to four in number, though more than one or two rarely grow up — follow the mother until over half grown. The mother lives entirely alone with the kittens while they are small. As the males fight so fiercely among themselves, it may be that the old he-cougars kill the young of their own sex; a ranchman whom I knew once found the body of a young male cougar which had evidently been killed by an old one; but I cannot say whether or not this was an exceptional case.

During the next ten days Stewart and Webb each shot a cougar. Webb's was got by as pretty an exhibition of trailing on the part of Goff and his hounds as one could wish to see. We ran across its old tracks while coming home on Wednesday, January 16th. The next day, Thursday, we took up the trail, but the animal had travelled a long distance; and, as cougars so often do, had spent much of its time walking along ledges, or at the foot of the cliffs, where the sun had melted the snow off the ground. In consequence, the dogs were often at fault. Moreover, bobcats were numerous, and twice the pack got after one, running a couple of hours before, in one instance, the cat went into a cave, and, in the other, took to a tree, where it was killed by Webb. At last, when darkness came on, we were forced to leave the cougar trail and ride home; a very attractive ride, too, loping rapidly over the snow-covered flats, while above us the great stars fairly blazed in the splendor of the winter night.

Early next morning we again took up the trail, and after a little while found where it was less than thirty-six hours old. The dogs now ran it well, but were thrown out again on a large bare hillside, until Boxer succeeded in recovering the scent. They went up a high mountain and we toiled after them. Again they lost the trail, and while at fault jumped a big bobcat which they ran up a tree. After shooting him we took lunch, and started to circle for the trail. Most of the dogs kept with Goff, but Jim got off to one side on his own account; and suddenly his baying told us that he had jumped the cougar. The rest of the pack tore toward him and after a quarter of a mile run they had the quarry treed. The ground was too rough for riding, and we had to do some stiff climbing to get to it on foot.

Stewart's cougar was a young-of-the-year, and, according to his custom, he took several photographs of it. Then he tried to poke it so that it would get into a better position for the camera; whereupon it jumped out of the tree and ran headlong down hill, the yelling dogs but a few feet behind. Our horses had been left a hundred yards or so below, where they all stood, moping, with their heads drooped and their eyes half shut, in regular cow-pony style. The chase streamed by not a yard from their noses, but evidently failed to arouse even an emotion of interest in their minds, for they barely looked up, and made not a movement of any kind when the cougar treed again just below them.

We killed several bobcats; and we also got another cougar, this time in rather ignominious fashion. We had been running a bobcat, having an excellent gallop, during the course of which Stewart's horse turned a somersault. Without our knowledge the dogs changed to the fresh trail of a cougar, which they ran into its den in another cut bank. When we reached the place they had gone in after it, Baldy dropping into a hole at the top of the bank, while the others crawled into the main entrance, some twenty-five yards off at the bottom. It was evidently a very rough house inside, and above the baying, yelping, and snarling of the dogs we could hear the rumbling overtone of the cougar's growl. On this day we had taken along Queen, the white bull bitch, to "enter" her at cougar. It was certainly a lively experience for a first entry. We reached the place in time to keep Jim and the hound bitches out of the hole. It was evident that the dogs could do nothing with the cougar inside. They could only come at it in front, and under such circumstances its claws and teeth made the odds against them hopeless. Every now and then it would charge, driving them all back, and we would then reach in, seize a dog and haul him out. At intervals there would be an awful yelling and a hound would come out bleeding badly, quite satisfied, and without the slightest desire to go in again. Poor Baldy was evidently killed inside. Queen, Turk, and Tony were badly clawed and bitten, and we finally got them out too; Queen went in three times, and came out on each occasion with a fresh gash or bite; Turk was, at the last, the only one really anxious to go in again. Then we tried to smoke out the cougar, for as one of the dogs had gotten into the cave through an upper entrance, we supposed the cougar could get out by the same route. However, it either could not or would not bolt; coming down close to the entrance where we had built the sagebrush fire, there it stayed until it was smothered. We returned to the ranch carrying its skin, but not over-pleased, and the pack much the worse for wear. Dr. Webb had to sew up the wounds of three of the dogs. One, Tony, was sent back to the home ranch, where he died. In such rough hunting as this, it is of course impossible to prevent occasional injuries to the dogs when they get the cougar in a cave, or overtake him on the ground. All that can be done is to try to end the contest as speedily as possible, which we always did.

    Judging from the experience of certain friends of mine in the Argentine, I think it would be safe to crawl into a cave to shoot a cougar under normal circumstances; but in this instance the cave was a long, winding hole, so low that we could not get in on hands and knees, having to work our way on our elbows.

It was pitch dark inside, so that the rifle sights could not be seen, and the cougar was evidently very angry and had on two or three occasions charged the dogs, driving them out of the entrance of the hole. In the dark, the chances were strongly against killing it with a single shot; while if only wounded, and if it had happened to charge, the man, in his cramped position, would have been utterly helpless.

The day after the death of the smoked cougar Stewart and Webb started home. Then it snowed for two days, keeping us in the ranch. While the snow was falling, there was no possibility of finding or following tracks; and as a rule wild creatures lie close during a storm. We were glad to have fresh snow, for the multitude of tracks in the old snow had become confusing; and not only the southern hillsides but the larger valleys had begun to grow bare, so that trailing was difficult.

The third day dawned in brilliant splendor, and when the sun arose all the land glittered dazzling white under his rays. The hounds were rested, we had fresh horses, and after an early breakfast we started to make a long circle. All the forenoon and early afternoon we plodded through the snowdrifts, up and down the valleys, and along the ridge crests, without striking a trail. The dogs trotted behind us or circled from one side to the other. It was no small test of their stanchness, eager and fresh as they were, for time after time we aroused bands of deer, to which they paid no heed whatever. At last, in mid-afternoon, we suddenly struck the tracks of two cougars, one a very large one, evidently an old male. They had been playing and frolicking together, for they were evidently mating, and the snow in the tracks showed that they had started abroad before the storm was entirely over. For three hours the pack followed the cold trail, through an exceedingly rugged and difficult country, in which Goff helped them out again and again.

Just at sunset the cougars were jumped, and ran straight into and through a tangle of spurs and foothills, broken by precipices, and riven by long deep ravines. The two at first separated and then came together, with the result that Tree'em, Bruno, and Jimmie got on the back trail and so were left far behind; while old Boxer also fell to the rear, as he always did when the scent was hot, and Jim and the bitches were left to do the running by themselves. In the gathering gloom we galloped along the main divide, my horse once falling on a slippery sidehill, as I followed headlong after Goff — whose riding was like the driving of the son of Nimshi. The last vestige of sunlight disappeared, but the full moon was well up in the heavens when we came to a long spur, leading off to the right for two or three miles, beyond which we did not think the chase could have gone. It had long run out of hearing. Making our way down the rough and broken crest of this spur, we finally heard far off the clamorous baying which told us that the hounds had their quarry at bay. We did not have the fighters with us, as they were still under the weather from the results of their encounter in the cave.

  As it afterward appeared, the cougars had run three miles before the dogs ovetook them, making their way up, down and along such difficult cliffs that the pack had to keep going round. The female then went up a tree, while the pack followed the male. He would not climb a tree and came to bay on the edge of a cliff. A couple of hundred yards from the spot, we left the horses and scrambled along on foot, guided by the furious clamor of the pack. When we reached them, the cougar had gone along the face of the cliff, most of the dogs could not see him, and it was some time before we could make him out ourselves. Then I got up quite close. Although the moonlight was bright I could not see the sights of my rifle, and fired a little too far back. The bullet, however, inflicted a bad wound, and the cougar ran along the edge, disappearing around the cliff shoulder. The conduct of the dogs showed that he had not left the cliff, but it was impossible to see him either from the sides or from below. The cliff was about fifty feet high and the top overhung the bottom, while from above the ground sloped down to the brink at a rather steep angle, so that we had to be cautious about our footing. There was a large projecting rock on the brink; to this I clambered down, and, holding it with one hand, peeped over the edge. After a minute or two I made out first the tail and then the head of the cougar, who was lying on a narrow ledge only some eight feet below me, his body hidden by the overhang of the cliff. Thanks to the steepness of the incline, I could not let go of the rock with my left hand, because I should have rolled over; so I got Goff to come down, brace his feet against the projection, and grasp me by my legs. He then lowered me gently down until my head and shoulders were over the edge and my arms free; and I shot the cougar right between the ears, he being in a straight line underneath me. The dogs were evidently confident that he was going to be shot, for they had all gathered below the cliff to wait for him to fall; and sure enough, down he came with a crash, luckily not hitting any of them. We could hear them seize him, and they all, dead cougar and worrying dogs, rolled at least a hundred yards down the steep slope before they were stopped by a gully. It was a very interesting experience, and one which I shall not soon forget. We clambered down to where the dogs were, admired our victim, and made up our minds not to try to skin him until the morning. Then we led down our horses, with some difficulty, into the snow-covered valley, mounted them, and cantered home to the ranch, under the cold and brilliant moon, through a white wonderland of shimmering light and beauty.

Next morning we came back as early as possible, intending first to skin the male and then to hunt up the female. A quarter of a mile before we reached the carcass we struck her fresh trail in the snow of the valley. Calling all the dogs together and hustling them forward, we got them across the trail without their paying any attention to it; for we wanted to finish the job of skinning before taking up the hunt. However, when we got off our horses and pulled the cougar down to a flat place to skin it, Nellie, who evidently remembered that there had been another cougar besides the one we had accounted for, started away on her own account while we were not looking. The first thing we knew we heard her giving tongue on the mountains above us, in such rough country that there was no use in trying to head her off. Accordingly we jumped on the horses again, rode down to where we had crossed the trail and put the whole pack on it. After crossing the valley the cougar had moved along the ledges of a great spur or chain of foothills, and as this prevented the dogs going too fast we were able to canter alongside them up the valley, watching them and listening to their chiming. We finally came to a large hillside bare of snow, much broken with rocks, among which grew patches of brush and scattered pinyons. Here the dogs were at fault for over an hour. It had evidently been a favorite haunt of the cougars; they had moved to and fro across it, and had lain sunning themselves in the dust under the ledges. Owing to the character of the ground we could give the hounds no assistance, but they finally puzzled out the trail for themselves. We were now given a good illustration of the impossibility of jumping a cougar without dogs, even when in a general way its haunt is known. We rode along the hillside, and quartered it to and fro, on the last occasion coming down a spur where we passed within two or three rods of the brush in which the cougar was actually lying; but she never moved and it was impossible to see her. When we finally reached the bottom, the dogs had disentangled the trail; and they passed behind us at a good rate, going up almost where we had come down. Even as we looked we saw the cougar rise from her lair, only fifty yards or so ahead of them, her red hide showing bright in the sun. It was a very pretty run to watch while it lasted. She left them behind at first, but after a quarter of a mile they put her up a pinyon. Approaching cautiously — for the climbing was hard work and I did not wish to frighten her out of the tree if it could be avoided, lest she might make such a run as that of the preceding evening — I was able to shoot her through the heart. She died in the branches, and I climbed the tree to throw her down. The only skill needed in such shooting is in killing the cougar outright so as to save the dogs. Six times on the hunt I shot the cougar through the heart. Twice the animal died in the branches. In the other four cases it sprang out of the tree, head and tail erect, eyes blazing, and the mouth open in a grin of savage hate and anger; but it was practically dead when it touched the ground. Although these cougars were mates, they were not of the same color, the female being reddish, while the male was slate-colored. In weighing this male we had to take off the hide and weigh it separately (with the head and paws attached), for our steelyard only went up to 150 pounds. When we came to weigh the biggest male we had to take off the quarters as well as the hide.

    Thinking that we had probably exhausted the cougars around the Keystone Ranch, we spent the next fortnight off on a trip. We carried only what we could put in the small saddle-pockets — our baggage being as strictly limited as it ought to be with efficient cavalry who are on an active campaign. We worked hard, but, as so often happens, our luck was not in proportion to our labor.

The first day we rode to the Mathes brothers' ranch. On the high divides it was very cold, the thermometer standing at nearly twenty degrees below zero. But we were clad for just such weather, and were not uncomfortable. The three Mathes brothers lived together, with the wives and children of the two married ones. Their ranch was in a very beautiful and wild valley, the pinyon-crowned cliffs rising in walls on either hand. Deer were abundant and often in sight from the ranch doors. At night the gray wolves came down close to the buildings and howled for hours among the precipices, under the light of the full moon. The still cold was intense; but I could not resist going out for half an hour at a time to listen to them. To me their baying, though a very eerie and lonesome sound, full of vaguely sinister associations, has, nevertheless, a certain wild music of its own which is far from being without charm.

We did not hear the cougars calling, for they are certainly nothing like as noisy as wolves; yet the Mathes brothers had heard them several times, and once one of them had crept up and seen the cougar, which remained in the same place for many minutes, repeating its cry continually. The Mathes had killed but two cougars, not having any dogs trained to hunt them. One of these was killed under circumstances which well illustrate the queer nature of the animal. The three men, with one of their two cattle dogs, were walking up the valley not half a mile above the ranch house, when they saw a cougar crossing in front of them, a couple of hundred yards off. As soon as she saw them she crouched flat down with her head toward them, remaining motionless. Two, with the dog, stayed where they were, while the other ran back to the ranch house for a rifle and for the other dog. No sooner had he gone than the cougar began deliberately to crawl toward the men who were left. She came on slowly but steadily, crouched almost flat to the ground. The two unarmed men were by no means pleased with her approach. They waved their hands and jumped about and shouted; but she kept approaching, although slowly, and was well within a hundred yards when the other brother arrived, out of breath, accompanied by the other dog. At sight of him she jumped up, ran off a couple of hundred yards, went up a tree, and was killed. I do not suppose she would have attacked the men; but as there was an unpleasant possibility that she might, they both felt distinctly more comfortable when their brother rejoined them with the rifle.

There was a good deal of snowy weather while we were at the Mathes ranch, but we had fair luck, killing two cougars. It was most comfortable, for the ranch was clean and warm, and the cooking delicious. It does not seem to me that I ever tasted better milk and butter, hot biscuits, rice, potatoes, pork and bulberry and wildplum jam; and of course the long days on horseback in the cold weather gave an edge to our appetites. One stormy day we lost the hounds; and we spent most of the next day in finding such of them as did not come straggling in of their own accord. The country was very rough, and it was astounding to see some of the places up and down which we led the horses. Sometimes I found that my horse climbed rather better than I did, for he would come up some awkward-looking slope with such a rush that I literally had to scramble on all fours to get out of his way.

There was no special incident connected with killing either of these two cougars. In one case Goff himself took the lead in working out the trail and preventing the hounds getting off after bobcats. In the other case the trail was fresher and the dogs ran it by themselves, getting into a country where we could not follow; it was very rough, and the cliffs and gorges rang with their baying. In both cases they had the cougar treed for about three hours before we were able to place them and walk up to them. It was hard work, toiling through the snow over the cliffs toward the baying; and on each occasion the cougar leaped from the tree at our approach, and ran a quarter of a mile or so before going up another, where it was shot. As I came up to shoot most of the dogs paid no attention, but Boxer and Nellie always kept looking at me until I actually raised the rifle, when they began to spring about the spot where they thought the cougar would come down. The cougar itself always seemed to recognize the man as the dangerous opponent; and as I strode around to find a place where I could deliver an instantaneously fatal shot, it would follow me steadily with its evil yellow eyes. I came up very close, but the beasts never attempted to jump at me. Judging from what one reads in books about Indian and African game, a leopard under such circumstances would certainly sometimes charge.

Three days of our trip were spent on a ride to Colorow Mountain; we went down to Judge Foreman's ranch on White River to pass the night. We got another cougar on the way. She must really be credited to Jim. The other dogs were following in our footsteps through the snow, after having made various futile excursions of their own. When we found that Jim was missing, we tried in vain to recall him with the horn, and at last started to hunt him up. After an hour's ride we heard him off on the mountain, evidently following a trail, but equally evidently not yet having jumped the animal. The hounds heard him quite as quickly as we did, and started toward him. Soon we heard the music of the whole pack, which grew fainter and fainter, was lost entirely as they disappeared around a spur, and then began to grow loud again, showing that they were coming toward us. Suddenly a change in the note convinced us that they had jumped the quarry. We stood motionless; nearer and nearer they came; and then a sudden burst of clamor proclaimed that they were barking treed. We had to ride only a couple of hundred yards; I shot the cougar from across a little ravine. She was the largest female we got.

The dogs were a source of unceasing amusement, not merely while hunting, but because of their relations to one another when off duty. Queen's temper was of the shortest toward the rest of the pack, although, like Turk, she was fond of literally crawling into my lap, when we sat down to rest after the worry which closed the chase. As soon as I began to eat my lunch, all the dogs clustered close around and I distributed small morsels to each in turn. Once Jimmie, Queen, and Boxer were sitting side by side, tightly wedged together. I treated them with entire impartiality; and soon Queen's feelings overcame her, and she unostentatiously but firmly bit Jimmie in the jaw. Jimmie howled tremendously and Boxer literally turned a back somersault, evidently fearing lest his turn should come next.

On February 11th we rode back to the Keystone Ranch, carrying the three cougar skins behind our saddles. It was again very cold, and the snow on the divides was so deep that our horses wallowed through it up to their saddle-girths. I supposed that my hunt was practically at an end, for I had but three days left; but as it turned out these were the three most lucky days of the whole trip.

The weather was beautiful, the snow lying deep enough to give the dogs easy trailing even on the southern slopes. Under the clear skies the landscape was dazzling, and I had to wear snow-glasses. On the first of the three days, February 12th, we had not ridden half an hour from the ranch before we came across the trail of a very big bobcat. It was so heavy that it had broken through the crust here and there, and we decided that it was worth following. The trail went up a steep mountain to the top, and we followed on foot after the dogs. Among the cliffs on the top they were completely at fault, hunting every which way. After awhile Goff suddenly spied the cat, which had jumped off the top of a cliff into a pinyon. I killed it before any of the dogs saw it, and at the shot they all ran in the wrong direction. When they did find us skinning it, they were evidently not at all satisfied that it was really their bobcat — the one which they had been trailing. Usually as soon as the animal was killed they all lay down and dozed off; but on this occasion they kept hurrying about and then in a body started on the back trail. It was some time before we could get them together again.

After we had brought them in we rode across one or two ridges, and up and down the spurs without finding anything, until about noon we struck up a long winding valley where we came across one or two old cougar trails. The pack were following in our footsteps behind the horses, except Jim, who took off to one side by himself. Suddenly he began to show signs that he had come across traces of game; and in another moment he gave tongue and all the hounds started toward him. They quartered around in the neighborhood of a little gulch for a short while, and then streamed off up the mountain-side; and before they had run more than a couple of minutes we heard them barking treed. By making a slight turn we rode almost up to the tree, and saw that their quarry was a young cougar. As we came up it knocked Jimmie right out of the tree. On seeing us it jumped down and started to run, but it was not quite quick enough. Turk seized it and in a minute the dogs had it stretched out. It squawled, hissed, and made such a good fight that I put an end to the struggle with the knife, fearing lest it might maim one of the hounds.

While Goff was skinning it I wandered down to the kill near which it had been lying. This was a deer, almost completely devoured. It had been killed in the valley and dragged up perhaps a hundred yards to some cedar. I soon saw from the tracks around the carcass that there was an older cougar with the younger one — doubtless its mother — and walked back to Goff with the information. Before I got there, however, some of the pack had made the discovery for themselves. Jim, evidently feeling that he had done his duty, had curled up and gone to sleep, with most of the others; but old Boxer and the three bitches (Pete had left her pups and joined us about the time we roused the big bobcat), hunted about until they struck the fresh trail of the old female. They went off at a great rate, and the sleeping dogs heard them and scampered away to the sound. The trail led them across a spur, into a valley, and out of it up the precipitous side of another mountain. When we got to the edge of the valley we could hear them barking treed nearly at the summit of the mountain opposite. It was over an hour's stiff climbing before we made our way around to them, although we managed to get the horses up to within a quarter of a mile of the spot. On approaching we found the cougar in a leaning pinyon on a ledge at the foot of a cliff. Jimmie was in the lower branches of the pinyon, and Turk up within a couple of feet of the cougar. Evidently he had been trying to tackle her and had been knocked out of the tree at least once, for he was bleeding a good deal and there was much blood on the snow beneath. Yet he had come back into the tree, and was barking violently not more than three feet beyond her stroke. She kept up a low savage growling, and as soon as I appeared, fixed her yellow eyes on me, glaring and snarling as I worked around into a place from which I could kill her outright. Meanwhile Goff took up his position on the other side, hoping to get a photograph when I shot. My bullet went right through her heart. She bit her paw, stretched up her head and bit a branch, and then died where she was, while Turk leaped forward at the crack of the rifle and seized her in the branches. I had some difficulty in bundling him and Jimmie out of the tree as I climbed up to throw down the cougar.

Next morning we started early, intending to go to Juniper Mountain, where we had heard that cougars were plentiful; but we had only ridden about half an hour from the ranch when we came across a trail which by the size we knew must belong to an old male. It was about thirty-six hours old and led into a tangle of badlands where there was great difficulty in working it out. Finally, however, we found where it left these badlands and went straight up a mountain-side, too steep for the horses to follow. From the plains below we watched the hounds working to and fro until they entered a patch of pinyons in which we were certain the cougar had killed a deer, as ravens and magpies were sitting around in the trees. In these pinyons the hounds were again at fault for a little while, but at last evidently found the right trail, and followed it up over the hill-crest and out of sight. We then galloped hard along the plain to the left, going around the end of the ridge and turning to our right on the other side. Here we entered a deep narrow valley or gorge which led up to a high plateau at the farther end. On our right, as we rode up the valley, lay the high and steep ridge over which the hounds had followed the trail. On the left it was still steeper, the slope being broken by ledges and precipices. Near the mouth of the gorge we encountered the hounds, who had worked the trail down and across the gorge, and were now hunting up the steep cliff-shoulder on our left. Evidently the cougar had wandered to and fro over this shoulder, and the dogs were much puzzled and worked in zigzags and circles around it, gradually getting clear to the top. Then old Boxer suddenly gave tongue with renewed zest and started off on a run almost on top of the ridge, the other dogs following. Immediately afterward they jumped the cougar.

We had been waiting below to see which direction the chase would take and now put spurs to our horses and galloped up the ravine, climbing the hillside on our right so as to get a better view of what was happening. A few hundred yards of this galloping and climbing brought us again in sight of the hounds. They were now barking treed and were clustered around a pinyon below the ridge crest on the side hill opposite us. The two fighters, Turk and Queen, who had been following at our horses' heels, appreciated what had happened as soon as we did, and, leaving us, ran down into the valley and began to work their way through the deep snow up the hillside opposite, toward where the hounds were. Ours was an ideal position for seeing the whole chase. In a minute the cougar jumped out of the tree down among the hounds, who made no attempt to seize him, but followed him as soon as he had cleared their circle. He came down hill at a great rate and jumped over a cliff, bringing after him such an avalanche of snow that it was a moment before I caught sight of him again, this time crouched on a narrow ledge of a cliff some fifteen or twenty feet below the brink from which he had jumped, and about as far above the foot of the cliff, where the steep hill-slope again began. The hounds soon found him again and came along the ledge barking loudly, but not venturing near where he lay facing them, with his back arched like a great cat. Turk and Queen were meanwhile working their way up hill. Turk got directly under the ledge and could not find a way up. Queen went to the left and in a minute we saw her white form as she made her way through the dark-colored hounds straight for the cougar. "That's the end of Queen," said Goff; "he'll kill her now, sure." In another moment she had made her rush and the cougar, bounding forward, had seized her, and as we afterward discovered had driven his great fangs right through the side of her head, fortunately missing the brain. In the struggle he lost his footing and rolled off the ledge, and when they struck the ground below he let go of the bitch. Turk, who was near where they struck, was not able to spring for the hold he desired, and in another moment the cougar was coming down hill like a quarterhorse. We stayed perfectly still, as he was travelling in our direction. Queen was on her feet almost as quick as the cougar, and she and Turk tore after him, the hounds following in a few seconds, being delayed in getting off the ledge. It was astonishing to see the speed of the cougar. He ran considerably more than a quarter of a mile down hill, and at the end of it had left the dogs more than a hundred yards behind. But his bolt was shot, and after going perhaps a hundred yards or so up the hill on our side and below us, he climbed a tree, under which the dogs began to bay frantically, while we scrambled toward them. When I got down I found him standing half upright on a big branch, his forepaws hung over another higher branch, his sides puffing like bellows, and evidently completely winded. In scrambling up the pinyon he must have struck a patch of resin, for it had torn a handful of hair off from behind his right forearm. I shot him through the heart. At the shot he sprang clean into the top of the tree, head and tail up, and his face fairly demoniac with rage; but before he touched the ground he was dead. Turk jumped up, seized him as he fell, and the two rolled over a low ledge, falling about eight feet into the snow, Turk never losing his hold.

No one could have wished to see a prettier chase under better circumstances. It was exceedingly interesting. The only dog hurt was Queen, and very miserable indeed she looked. She stood in the trail, refusing to lie down or to join the other dogs, as, with prodigious snarls at one another, they ate the pieces of the carcass we cut out for them. Dogs hunting every day, as these were doing, and going through such terrific exertion, need enormous quantities of meat, and as old horses and crippled steers were not always easy to get, we usually fed them the cougar carcasses. On this occasion, when they had eaten until they could eat no longer, I gave most of my lunch to Queen — Boxer, who after his feast could hardly move, nevertheless waddling up with his ears forward to beg a share. Queen evidently felt that the lunch was a delicacy, for she ate it, and then trotted home behind us with the rest of the dogs. Rather to my astonishment, next day she was all right, and as eager to go with us as ever. Though one side of her head was much swollen, in her work she showed no signs of her injuries.

Early the following morning, February 14th, the last day of my actual hunting, we again started for Juniper Mountain, following the same course on which we had started the previous day. Before we had gone a mile, that is, only about half way to where we had come across the cougar track the preceding day, we crossed another, and as we deemed a fresher, trail, which Goff pronounced to belong to a cougar even larger than the one we had just killed. The hounds were getting both weary and footsore, but the scent put heart into them and away they streamed. They followed it across a sagebrush flat, and then worked along under the base of a line of cliffs — cougar being particularly apt thus to travel at the foot of cliffs. The pack kept well together, and it was pleasant, as we cantered over the snowy plain beside them, to listen to their baying, echoed back from the cliffs above. Then they worked over the hill and we spurred ahead and turned to the left, up the same gorge or valley in which we had killed the cougar the day before. The hounds followed the trail straight to the cliff shoulder where the day before the pack had been puzzled until Boxer struck the fresh scent. Here they seemed to be completely at fault, circling everywhere, and at one time following their track of yesterday over to the pinyon-tree up which the cougar had first gone.

We made our way up the ravine to the head of the plateau, and then, turning, came back along the ridge until we reached the top of the shoulder where the dogs had been; but when we got there they had disappeared. It did not seem likely that the cougar had crossed the ravine behind us — although as a matter of fact this was exactly what had happened — and we did not know what to make of the affair.

We could barely hear the hounds; they had followed their back trail of the preceding day, toward the place where we had first come across the tracks of the cougar we had already killed. We were utterly puzzled, even Goff being completely at fault, and we finally became afraid that the track which the pack had been running was one which, instead of having been made during the night, had been there the previous morning, and had been made by the dead cougar. This meant, of course, that we had passed it without noticing it, both going and coming, on the previous day, and knowing Goff's eye for a track I could not believe this. He, however, thought we might have confused it with some of the big wolf tracks, of which a number had crossed our path. After some hesitation, he said that at any rate we could find out the truth by getting back into the flat and galloping around to where we had begun our hunt the day before; because if the dogs really had a fresh cougar before them he must have so short a start that they were certain to tree him by the time they got across the ridge-crest. Accordingly we scrambled down the precipitous mountain-side, galloped along the flat around the end of the ridge and drew rein at about the place where we had first come across the cougar trail on the previous day. Not a dog was to be heard anywhere, and Goff's belief that the pack was simply running a back track became a certainty both in his mind and mine, when Jim suddenly joined us, evidently having given up the chase. We came to the conclusion that Jim, being wiser than the other dogs, had discovered his mistake while they had not; "he just naturally quit," said Goff.

After some little work we found where the pack had crossed the broad flat valley into a mass of very rough broken country, the same in which I had shot my first big male by moonlight. Cantering and scrambling through this stretch of cliffs and valleys, we began to hear the dogs, and at first were puzzled because once or twice it seemed as though they were barking treed or had something at bay; always, however, as we came nearer we could again hear them running a trail, and when we finally got up tolerably close we found that they were all scattered out. Boxer was far behind, and Nellie, whose feet had become sore, was soberly accompanying him, no longer giving tongue. The others were separated one from the other, and we finally made out Tree'em all by himself, and not very far away. In vain Goff called and blew his horn; Tree'em disappeared up a high hillside, and with muttered comments on his stupidity we galloped our horses along the valley around the foot of the hill, hoping to intercept him. No sooner had we come to the other side, however, than we heard Tree'em evidently barking treed. We both looked at one another, wondering whether he had come across a bobcat, or whether it had really been a fresh cougar trail after all.

Leaving our horses we scrambled up the canon until we got in sight of a large pinyon on the hillside, underneath which Tree'em was standing, with his preposterous tail arched like a pump-handle, as he gazed solemnly up in the tree, now and then uttering a bark at a huge cougar, which by this time we could distinctly make out standing in the branches. Turk and Queen had already left us and were running hard to join Tree'em, and in another minute or two all of the hounds, except the belated Boxer and Nellie, had also come up. The cougar having now recovered his wind, jumped down and cantered off. He had been running for three hours before the dogs and evidently had been overtaken again and again, but had either refused to tree, or if he did tree had soon come down and continued his flight, the hounds not venturing to meddle with him, and he paying little heed to them. It was a different matter, however, with Turk and Queen along. He went up the hill and came to bay on the top of the cliffs, where we could see him against the skyline. The hounds surrounded him, but neither they nor Turk came to close quarters. Queen, however, as soon as she arrived rushed straight in, and the cougar knocked her a dozen feet off. Turk tried to seize him as soon as Queen had made her rush; the cougar broke bay, and they all disappeared over the hilltop, while we hurried after them. A quarter of a mile beyond, on the steep hill-side, they again had him up a pinyon-tree. I approached as cautiously as possible so as not to alarm him. He stood in such an awkward position that I could not get a fair shot at the heart, but the bullet broke his back well forward, and the dogs seized him as he struck the ground. There was still any amount of right in him, and I ran in as fast as possible, jumping and slipping over the rocks and the bushes as the cougar and dogs rolled and slid down the steep mountain-side — for, of course, every minute's delay meant the chance of a dog being killed or crippled. It was a day of misfortunes for Jim, who was knocked completely out of the fight by a single blow. The cougar was too big for the dogs to master, even crippled as he was; but when I came up close Turk ran in and got the great beast by one ear, stretching out the cougar's head, while he kept his own forelegs tucked way back so that the cougar could not get hold of them. This gave me my chance and I drove the knife home, leaping back before the creature could get round at me. Boxer did not come up for half an hour, working out every inch of the trail for himself, and croaking away at short intervals, while Nellie trotted calmly beside him. Even when he saw us skinning the cougar he would not hurry nor take a short cut, but followed the scent to where the cougar had gone up the tree, and from the tree down to where we were; then he meditatively bit the carcass, strolled off, and lay down, satisfied.

It was a very large cougar, fat and heavy, and the men at the ranch believed it was the same one which had at intervals haunted the place for two or three years, killing on one occasion a milch cow, on another a steer, and on yet another a big work horse. Goff stated that he had on two or three occasions killed cougars that were quite as long, and .he believed even an inch or two longer, but that he had never seen one as large or as heavy. Its weight was 227 pounds, and as it lay stretched out it looked like a small African lioness. It would be impossible to wish a better ending to a hunt.

The next day Goff and I cantered thirty miles into Meeker, and my holiday was over.

from The Archive

Richard Harding Davis: Journalism
ISBN: 978-0-9907137-4-6
With "The Death of Adolfo Rodriguez," Richard Harding Davis created a sensation -- and public outrage that helped bring about the Spanish-American War. This collection of 25 original newspaper and magazine stories, complete and unabridged, offers the reader a front page seat to compelling events all over the globe, and newspaper reporting as done with literary skill, social conscience and a flair for the dramatic.

Nellie Bly: Undercover: Reporting for *The New York World*
ISBN: 978-0-9907137-2-2
Nellie Bly's convincing disguises gained her admission to oppressive sweatshops, underground gambling parlors, illicit adoption agencies and creepy mesmerists' parlors, all in the service of sensational headlines and the steadily rising circulation numbers boasted by the New York World. This fascinating collection of original, unabridged articles—compiled for the first time since their original publication--traces Bly's brief yet astounding career as an undercover journalist.

Lincoln Steffens: The System
ISBN: 978-0-9907137-3-9
The muckraker Lincoln Steffens dug deep into business criminality and political corruption in a powerful series of articles written for McClure's magazine. Establishment newspapers and "System" politicians dismissed his work as just another example of the decrepit modern journalism that could never pass for genuine writing. But Steffens' dogged quest for truth and justice set the bar high for investigative journalists in print, television and the Internet who follow in his footsteps. This new collection from The Archive includes the author's detailed and dramatic pieces on the civic troubles in Chicago, Minneapolis, St. Louis, Philadelphia, Rhode Island, Wisconsin, New Jersey, Ohio, and New York.

Sources

Almanac of Theodore Roosevelt
http://www.theodore-roosevelt.com/treditorials.html

History Matters: The U.S. Survey Course on the Web
http://historymatters.gmu.edu/d/5733/

Carnegie Liibrary of Pittsburgh
http://www.clpgh.org/exhibit/steffens.html

Unz.org
http://www.unz.org/

Internet Archive
https://archive.org/

Hathitrust Digital Library
http://www.hathitrust.org/

Further Reading

Cooper, Jr., Milton J. *Pivotal Decades: The United States, 1900 - 1920.* W. W. Norton, 1990.

Goodwin, Doris Kearns. *The Bully Pulpit: Theodore Roosevelt, William Howard Taft, And The Golden Age of Journalism.* Simon & Schuster, 2014.

Hofstadter, Richard. *The Age of Reform.* Vintage Books, 1960.

Link, William A. (ed.) and Susannah J. Link (ed.). *The Gilded Age and Progressive Era: A Documentary Reader.* Wiley-Blackwell, 2012.

Thomas, Evan. *The War Lovers: Roosevelt, Lodge, Hearts, and the Rush to Empire, 1898.* Little, Brown 2010.

Traxel, David. *1898: The Birth of the American Century.* Alfred A. Knopf, 1998.

Wiinfield, Betty Hochin, ed. *Journalism 1908: Borth of a Profession.* University of Missouri Press, 2008.

Wolraich, Michael. *Unreasonable Men: Theodore Roosevelt and the Republican Rebels Who Created Progressive Politics.* Palgrave Macmillan, 2014.

Online Collections

Chronicling America: Historic American Newspapers
http://chroniclingamerica.loc.gov/

HathiTrust Digital Library
http://www.hathitrust.org/

Internet Archive
https://archive.org/

Project Gutenberg
http://www.gutenberg.org/

Unz.org
http://www.unz.org/Home/Introduction

www.ingramcontent.com/pod-product-compliance
Lightning Source LLC
Chambersburg PA
CBHW031410290426
44110CB00011B/330